GANDHI

GANDHI

The True Man Behind Modern India

JAD ADAMS

PEGASUS BOOKS
NEW YORK

GANDHI

Pegasus Books LLC
80 Broad Street, 5th Floor
New York, NY 10004

Copyright © 2011 by Jad Adams

First Pegasus Books cloth edition 2011

Library of Congress Cataloging-in-Publication Data is available.

ISBN: 978-1-60598-171-0

10 9 8 7 6 5 4 3 2 1

Printed in the United States of America

Distributed by W. W. Norton & Company, Inc.
www.pegasusbooks.us

For Julie

Contents

Maps

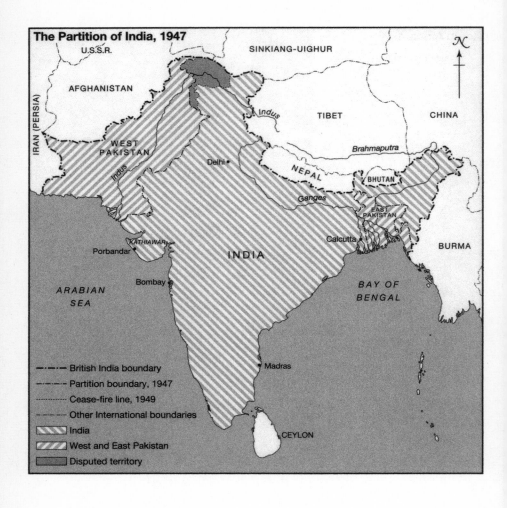

The Partition of India, 1947

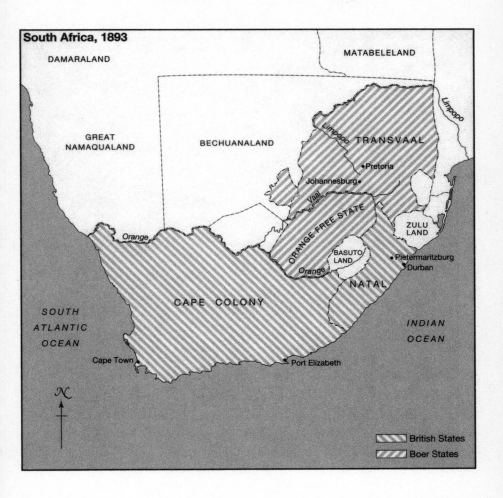

South Africa, 1893

INTRODUCTION

'My life is its own message.'[1]

The world-changing event of 1930 was recorded in every national newspaper and newsreel: in an act of defiance Gandhi had challenged the British Empire by taking untaxed, contraband salt from his own land.[2] Accounts report how he then cleansed himself in the sea, pictures of the time showing the tiny white-clad individual against the pure-white salt flats, a symbol of purity challenging the greatest empire the world had known. As he held up the white crystals for all to see, the nationalist poet Sarojini Naidu cried out, to the acclamation of the crowds: 'Hail, deliverer!'

The iconic image is, as usual in these cases, a fake, a concoction of journalists, film-makers and adulatory biographers. Gandhi did go to Dandi, but the images and accounts of it are a carefully thought out, stage-managed set-piece. The famous picture shows Gandhi three days after he arrived, picking up salt at nearby Bhimrad, ten kilometres from the coast and twenty-five from Dandi. Sarojini Naidu was present when he reached Dandi but she did not utter the often reported cry (which would have been a disappointingly trite utterance, for her).[3] The great photographic moment was a re-enactment for the cameras of the event that had taken place on a muddy beach where the salt was not visible and the act therefore less apparently symbolic.

Gandhi's achievement was not in defying the law to gather salt (peasants did that with impunity all the time): it was in announcing that he was going to break the law, then marching for twenty-four days to do it, giving the media plenty of time to comment and orchestrate their coverage.

1

His political colleagues had been bemused, never considering salt in the slightest bit important; likewise the British authorities, who made no show of strength because of the pettiness of the act. But Gandhi knew the importance of symbolism. He was the most spiritual of men, praying twice daily and incessantly murmuring the name of God, and his attention to diet extended to counting the number of raisins he ate. But more significant than any of his spiritual knowledge was his awareness of image. His oddly assorted clothing reflected the way he had striven to make himself the message: the top-hat and spats of a London barrister, the plain shirt and dhoti of an indentured labourer, the homespun clothes of those who rejected British cloth imports. Finally, when he had an army of supporters clad in homespun yarn, he appeared wearing almost nothing, nude but for a loincloth. This was the image that went around the world – one near-naked holy man against an empire. He became an icon. At that time only Charlie Chaplin and Adolf Hitler had achieved such worldwide recognition for their image, such that everyone knew exactly what they stood for.

Gandhi's life is the ultimate challenge for a biographer: it was so multifaceted, and there is so much surviving contemporary information about it. Many people demonstrate two aspects of interest in their lives. A national leader may have an incandescent political career and a lurid sex life, but nothing else worthy of comment. It is not unusual to encounter social reformers who have a complex relationship with food, or with religion; many people famous for their achievements have a tumultuous family life. Gandhi's political life, spiritual life, family life and sex life were all fascinating; his relationship to food could fill a volume in itself.

In all these areas, Gandhi's own testimony survives, his collected works run to one hundred volumes: books, articles, letters and speeches. For some world figures such as Homer there is no reliable biographical information, for some such as Abraham there is little, for Gandhi there is a superabundance. Gandhi knew what use would be made of this material, and he was not encouraging: 'My writings should be cremated with my body. What I have done will endure, not what I have said or written.'4

Notwithstanding his warning, this biography is based on primary sources, on his own writing and that of people who were close to him.

Chief of these were his secretary between 1917 and 1942, Mahadev Desai, who wrote a nine-volume diary, and Desai's assistant and later the principal secretary, Pyarelal, who was with Gandhi from 1920 until his death. With his sister Sushila Nayar, Gandhi's doctor, Pyarelal wrote a ten-volume biography. Of all the other material used here the work of eyewitnesses, particularly in diaries or near-contemporary accounts, is taken as paramount, in preference to later interpretations.

Gandhi's own two autobiographies, one on his life to the 1920s and the other on his South African experiences, are a guide not so much to the events (though sometimes they are the only record) but to the relative importance he placed on the various aspects of his life. Thus much less emphasis needs to be given to the law and politics when Gandhi was a student in London than to his vegetarian diet, because that was what obsessed him. In South Africa the life of the ideal communities he set up and his own celibacy were to him the most important part of his work. The battle with the government over Indian rights was what he *did*, the struggle with his sex drive was what he *was*. Like many very ambitious men, Gandhi was highly sexed: the interest for the biographer is how he tried to contain this sexuality, and how rivetingly candid he could be about it in his own writing.

Any reliance on Gandhi's own writing immediately opens up question of trust: did he tell the truth? His autobiography is subtitled *The Story of My Experiments with Truth*, but what kind of truth was it that he believed in? Any politician could say they experimented with the truth, which would be a euphemism for lying.

There is some evidence that the incompetence Gandhi showed in his early public life has been exaggerated, giving a more dramatic impression of his later resounding successes. Later historians have found his contribution to South African politics greatly overstated. His followers were certainly left disappointed after his supposed agreements with the South African government unravelled. It is not over such matters or their interpretation that the real question of Gandhi's veracity emerges, however. In terms of mere fact, Gandhi's truth is a selective one not so much for what he wants to conceal as for what he wants to explore in his past: his moral development. The *Autobiography* started as a series of instructive articles in his newspaper *Young India*, where each separate

3

chapter had to stand alone with its own moral. The work is therefore fashioned as a series of lessons, as 'the trials of Gandhi' or 'Gandhi's progress' after one of his favourite books, Bunyan's spiritual biography *The Pilgrim's Progress*. Gandhi is less concerned with the factual accuracy of an incident than with its spiritual meaning.

For Gandhi the striving for truth was not an attempt to reach unquestioned factual accuracy, but a stretching out towards spiritual perfection. For him, truth was eternal and, conversely, if something were transient it could not be true. 'Often in my progress I have found faint glimpses of the Absolute Truth, God, and the daily conviction is growing on me that He alone is real and all else is unreal,' he wrote.[5] Gandhi's truth *was* the divinity: 'Truth is God, or God is nothing but Truth.'[6] He explained the steps by which he had reached this position: 'Instead of saying "God is Truth" I now say "Truth is God" ... There was a time when I doubted the existence of God. Even at that time I did not doubt the existence of Truth. This Truth is not a material quality; it is pure consciousness. Since it orders the whole universe it is God.'[7]

The truth, as it functioned in everyday life, was not immutable, even when religious questions were under consideration. Gandhi pronounced on the vexed question of intercaste relationships in the 1920s: 'Prohibition against intermarriage and inter-dining is essential for a rapid evolution of the soul.'[8] The following decade he had modified his view: 'Restriction on inter-caste dining and inter-caste marriage is no part of the Hindu religion. It is a social custom which crept into Hinduism when perhaps it was in its decline.'[9] By the 1940s he was saying: 'I do not at all approve of marriages within the same caste', and began actively discriminating against caste marriages in the most forthright manner.[10] He blessed a marriage between a Brahmin professor and an untouchable woman, 'and further declared that thereafter his blessings would not be available to any wedding couple unless one of the parties was a Harijan [untouchable]'.[11]

He explained to those bemused by his positions: 'I am not at all concerned with appearing to be consistent. In my search after Truth I have discarded many ideas and learnt many new things ... What I am concerned with is my readiness to obey the call of Truth, my God, from moment to moment, and therefore, when anybody finds any inconsistency between any two writings of mine, if he has still faith in my sanity, he would do well to choose the later of the two on the same subject.'[12] More straightforwardly, he explained: 'My aim is not to be consistent with my previous statements on a given question, but to be consistent with truth, as it may present itself to me at a given moment. The result has been that I have grown from truth to truth.'[13] Hence the biographer's dilemma in interpreting Gandhi's writing about his own life.

Even non-violence was qualified – he was willing to call off civil disobedience in 1930 in return for acquiescence to a list of demands including the right of Indians to bear arms. He explained at the start of the Second World War: 'If Poland has [the] utmost bravery and an equal measure of selflessness, history will forget that she defended herself with violence. Her violence will be counted almost as non-violence.'[14] His willingness to see civil war in India in the 1940s horrified the British with whom he was negotiating.

He stated clearly that he had learned from the great religions 'that we should remain passive about worldly pursuits and active about godly pursuits, that we should see a limit to our worldly ambition and that our religious ambition should be illimitable.'[15] He made daily references to other religions, sang Christian hymns and was subjected to public abuse for using quotations from the Koran in his prayer meetings, but his core beliefs remained entirely Hindu. It is apparent that he did not find the cosmological systems of other religions at all satisfactory – only Hinduism had the answer to spiritual oneness. He took reincarnation as a factual matter; writing to Tolstoy in 1909 he said: 'Reincarnation or transmigration is a cherished belief with millions in India, indeed in China also. With many, one might almost say, it is a matter of experience, no longer a matter of academic acceptance. It explains reasonably many mysteries of life.'[16]

The personal part of the cosmology, for Gandhi as for other devout Hindus, was a movement of the spirit through seemingly limitless refinements to reach perfection. Gandhi described it as 'self-realisation, to see God face to face, to attain moksha. I live and move and have my being in pursuit of this goal.'[17] Moksha is the term for freedom from the cycle of rebirth and death; release from it was hardly a modest aim, but one which Gandhi saw within his reach: 'I am impatient to realise myself, to attain moksha in this very existence. My national service is part of my training for freeing my soul from the bondage of flesh. Thus considered, my service may be regarded as purely selfish. I have no desire for the perishable kingdom of earth. I am striving for the Kingdom of Heaven which is moksha.'[18]

This is the clue to Gandhi's sometimes contradictory behaviour: he was an intensely ambitious man, but this was no ordinary ambition. He did not personally care about salt, and was trying to eliminate it from his diet; he campaigned for the indigo workers when he did not approve of dyeing cloth; he supported the mill workers when he was opposing the use of mill-produced cloth; he wanted Indians to rule India but had no time for elections and assemblies; he enjoyed the fulsome support of the rich while promoting the values of poverty. None of it really mattered; the aim was not in the achievement of these transient things, but in accruing spiritual power. As he said, it was the life itself that was the message. The ambition was not for fairness for labourers or Indian independence – these were transitory demands. Gandhi's objective was nothing short of spiritual perfection.

1

Childhood and Marriage

'You are standing near the corner of a public road,' wrote Gandhi, remembering the India of his childhood at the time of the winter festival of Divali. He continued:

Mark the shepherd trotting in his milk-white suit, worn for the first time, with his long beard turned up beside his face and fastened under his turban, singing some broken verses. A herd of cows, with their horns painted red and green and mounted with silver, follows him. Soon after you see a crowd of little maids, with small earthen vessels resting on cushions placed on their heads . . . Then observe that big man with white whiskers and a big white turban, with a long reed pen thrust into his turban. He has a long scarf wound round his waist with a silver inkstand adjusted in the scarf. He, you must know, is a great banker.[1]

This was the world into which Mohandas Karamchand Gandhi was born on 2 October 1869 in the harbour town of Porbandar. He was of the Vaishya caste of merchants, artisans and landowners, ranking third in the spiritual hierarchy of the four major divisions of Hindu society, after the Brahmin and Kshatriya but above the Sudra. Of this caste, he was from a subsection, the Bania, who were usually merchants – so many were that the British took to using the term Bania to mean 'merchant'. Within this group, with the usual complexity of Indian social organisation, Gandhi's family were of a further subdivision, the Modh.

Gandhi says his forebears had originally been grocers but by the time he was born they were settled into public service. Since the time of his grandfather Uttamchand Gandhi, the men in his family had been prime ministers in the princely states of Kathiawar, the peninsular part of Gujarat that juts out into the Arabian Sea. It was the same part of the province from which the merchant family of Mohammad Ali Jinnah, Gandhi's great adversary, came.

Mohandas Gandhi was the youngest of three sons and one daughter born to Putlibai, the last wife of Karamchand Gandhi who was prime minister of Porbandar at the time of Gandhi's birth. He was later to be prime minister of Rajkot and of Vankaner. There were some two hundred princely states in Kathiawar, but only fourteen of them had what passed for an independent political system, allowed to function so long as they remained within limits set by the British political agent who acted as their 'adviser'.

The qualities that Gandhi admired in his father were that he was truthful, brave and generous. On the negative side, he remarked that his father was short-tempered and 'to a certain extent he might have been given to carnal pleasures'.[2] Gandhi reflected these traits: he was certainly brave, the more so for having had to overcome shyness even up to adulthood; he was very generous with his skills, in helping those such as the South African Indian labourers; and he took a preoccupation with the truth to metaphysical levels. His definition was that the truth he aspired to was 'truthfulness in word, but truthfulness in thought also, and not only the relative truth of our conception, but the Absolute Truth, the Eternal Principle, that is God'.[3]

On the other hand, of the traits he singled out as those he did not respect in his father, Gandhi was rarely short-tempered with members of the public, though he was often so with his wife and other members of his family. Perhaps partly from a desire to distance himself from his father's 'carnal' nature, Gandhi made a point of being abstemious about alcohol, tobacco and meat-eating; and he carried out exercises to control his sexual appetite. He was to take such sexual exercises, and public reports of them, to levels that many considered obscene.

His father was religious in a general sense, without training or regular ritual until the end of his life when he took to reading the great religious and philosophical poem the *Bhagavad Gita* daily. Gandhi's mother was a far more profound influence in this area. He remarked:

'If you notice any purity in me, I have inherited it from my mother, and not from my father.'[4] She was exceedingly religious – Gandhi wrote of her 'saintliness'.[5] This expressed itself in going to the temple daily, maintaining both spiritual and physical cleanliness via rituals in bathing and defecation; never eating without saying prayers; and keeping the fasting period over the four months of rains, the Chaturmas. Gandhi noted that 'to keep two or three consecutive fasts was nothing to her'. She contrived ingenious new fasts for herself; during one Chaturmas, instead of eating one meal a day she would eat only every alternate day; another time, she would not eat unless she had seen the sun. This was a test to the young Gandhi, who would stand staring at the sky while the sun was obscured by rain in order to rush in and tell his mother as soon as the sun had come out, so that she could eat that day. She would run out to see with her own eyes, but if the sun was no longer visible she would keep to her vow. 'That does not matter,' she would say, 'God does not want me to eat today', and she would return to her duties. The effect on Gandhi was to instil in him the perception of a close connection between religious observance and everyday life, something he would always display as a mature man. He was introduced into the discipline of fasting, which is an integral part of the Hindu and Jain religions (as it is, with its variations of Lent and Ramadan, in the Christian and Muslim religions). Gandhi was to take fasting to a new level.

It was from Putlibai that Gandhi acquired his meticulous regard for cleanliness and neatness. There was also some universalist element in her influence, as her parents had been members of the Panami sect which aims at combining the best elements of Islam and Hinduism. Putlibai was, however, an orthodox Hindu in matters of caste. She told her children they were not to touch the 'untouchable' boy who cleaned the lavatories; if they had accidental contact with an untouchable, they had to take a ritual bath; if that were not practicable, touching a passing Muslim would pass on the uncleanness. As he grew older, he came to argue with Putlibai: 'I told my mother that she was entirely wrong in considering physical contact with Uka [the untouchable] as sinful,' he recalled.[6] Gandhi considered that if God was everywhere, then God was in the untouchable too. His Hinduism was monotheistic: all the gods of the pantheon were aspects of a single divine entity.

Gujarat was one of the main homes of members of the ancient Jain religion for whom the principle of non-injury to living beings is sacrosanct, and who also stress spiritual independence and non-violence. The Jains are significant scholars, having founded some of the most ancient libraries in India. Gandhi did not take up the passion for learning in early life; he did not, for example, read the *Bhagavad Gita* until he was in his twenties, in 1890, and then he read it in an English translation. He showed an entirely natural tendency to take what he found attractive from his influences and discard the rest; in his case this was unusual in that what he wanted was the moral message, not the adventure that was also to be found in religious stories.

He was moved by improving tales from Hindu literature, feeling that they were not mere fancies, but moral examples to copy. He singled out the stories of Shravana, who was so devoted to his aged parents that he carried them on pilgrimage; and that of King Harishchandra, who never told a lie and always kept his word. Harishchandra's moral fortitude led him into situations in which he had to give away his kingdom, then to sell his wife and son and finally himself into servitude. This behaviour was praised by the gods, and his virtue rewarded. Gandhi remarked that he was haunted by the story and wished to go through the trials of Harishchandra for the sake of truth.

When Gandhi was about seven, his father moved the family to Rajkot where he had been appointed prime minister and a member of the Rajasthanik Court, which had been set up by the British to settle local disputes. Gandhi was therefore exposed to the operation of government, both of the British and of the princely states. Until the very end of Gandhi's lifetime two-fifths of the territory of India and one-fifth of the population were under the governance of local rulers. The rest was ruled by the British directly with the Viceroy, at the top of the administrative hierarchy, representing the Crown.

Gandhi later remarked that he was probably an indifferent pupil – all he could remember about his first school was having difficulty with multiplication tables. Nor was there anything memorable about his studies at primary school. He remembers himself as being so shy that he would make sure to be at school as it opened and run home as soon as the school day finished in order that he did not have to talk to anyone, for he feared their ridicule. He was small and frail, afraid of ghosts, thieves and snakes, and could not go to bed without a light. His nurse told him in times of fear to repeat 'Ramanama' – the name of God. He never forgot this lesson, and in later life described the practice as 'a sun that has brightened my darkest hour'.[7] He was heard to repeat the name of God aloud at times of physical attack.

Gandhi had three siblings: an elder sister, Raliatbehn who was born in 1862, and two brothers, Laxmidas (1863) and Karsandas (1866). His early playmates were his family members, particularly Karsandas. Together they chafed at the restrictions put on their independence, nurturing their resentment that they had to ask permission for everything they did. They started smoking, first discarded ends thrown away by an uncle, then they took to stealing money from a servant (presumably accessible because of the expectation of honesty in the house) in order to buy cigarettes. Their puerile lack of judgement was demonstrated by their next exploit – they were so frustrated by their lack of freedom that they decided to kill themselves and obtained the seeds of a poisonous plant from the jungle. But they lost courage and did not take the seeds; Gandhi later said this exploit led him to think little of threats by others to commit suicide.

While he was still a child Gandhi's parents set about finding a wife for him, following the usual practice in Kathiawar (and other parts of India) of 'betrothal' to a suitable girl. He was betrothed three times, the death of the first two girls demonstrating why this custom prevailed: it was wise to 'reserve' a future spouse for fear there would be none left of appropriate caste and social standing when the time for marriage came.

Betrothal was an established practice in a place where marriages were arranged by parents. Gandhi had been betrothed for the third time when he was seven in 1876, but may not even have been told about it. Child marriage was not a necessary part of this proceedure, though it was culturally acceptable. Gandhi's marriage at the age of thirteen was the subject of continuing disgust to him. He described it as one of the 'bitter draughts' he had to swallow in the course of setting down the truth about his life. 'I can see no moral argument in support of such a preposterously early marriage,' he wrote.[8]

Indeed, Gandhi had utter contempt for Hindu marriage customs, which he related to waste, not seeing any pleasure or even apparently any point in it.

> The parents of the bride and bridegroom often bring themselves to ruin ... they waste their substance, they waste their time. Months are taken up over the preparations – in making clothes and ornaments and in preparing budgets for dinner. Each tries to outdo the other in the number and variety of courses to be prepared. Women, whether they have a voice or not, sing themselves hoarse, even get ill, and disturb the peace of their neighbours. These, in their turn, quietly put up with all the turmoil and bustle, all the dirt and filth, representing the remains of feasts, because they know that a time will come when they will also be behaving in the same manner.

This is not merely a criticism of child marriage but also seems to show intolerance of the attention given to marriages – part of Gandhi's general impatience with the things that ordinary people find important. He also shows here a trait that would develop in adult life: an intolerance of the marriage bond itself, suggesting the relative unimportance of the relationship with spouse and family compared with a more transcendental union with the deity, and a connection to humanity at large.

Gandhi's wedding in 1883 was particularly unfortunate for one not too impressed with the things of this world, as his family decided to marry him, his brother Karsandas and his cousin of similar age in a triple ceremony. In this way the cost would be shared between Gandhi's father and uncle, and the expenditure and trouble would be over all at once – a boon for the two men, who were advancing in age and wanted to dispatch the business of marrying off their last children as expeditiously as possible.

As the wedding approached, his father was kept at work by official business until, in the end, he had to make the five-day journey from Rajkot to Porbandar in three days. His coach toppled over and Karamchand was severely injured, but as all the plans were already made the wedding took place, in a hall hired for the purpose. His father's injury later gave Gandhi another reason to reflect on his wedding with distaste, but at the time it simply meant interesting clothes, music and cere-monies and 'a strange girl to play with'. He was taken out of school for his marriage, missing about a year of education in preparation for the event.

Kasturbai Kapadia was the same age as Gandhi. She was born in April 1869 so at the time of their marriage in May she was fourteen, he thir-teen. Gandhi later saw fit to 'severely criticise my father for having mar-ried me as a child' (though the criticism was not made in his father's presence). At this time in Britain the age of consent was thirteen and the age of marriage was twelve for a girl and fourteen for a boy; a mar-riage such as Gandhi's could have taken place in Britain, though in fact custom precluded such early marriages. Gandhi's was far from being a child marriage by Kathiawar standards – most girls were married by the age of eight.

Kasturbai too (the form Kasturba was used after she assumed con-trol of her own household) had been born in Porbandar, to a trader in cloth, grain and cotton and one-time mayor of Porbandar, Golkaldas Kapadia, and his wife Vraikunwerba. They also were of the Modh Bania sect (indeed, Gandhi and Kasturbai would not have been married by their parents if they had not been compatible in this way). Their home was close to that of the Gandhis, though they would not have played together as they grew up. When he was not at school Gandhi was free to go into the streets to follow a ceremonial parade or climb trees in the nearby courtyard temple, whereas Kasturbai was not sent to school or allowed to play outside but kept at home learning how to be a mother and housekeeper. The improving stories she would have been told were of good wives such as Anasuya who remained chaste when her virtue was tested, and Sita who was faithful to her husband Rama through many tribulations.

Kasturbai brought with her a cedar chest filled with new clothes and a teak box containing gold jewellery. Before the wedding the bodies of the bride and bridegroom were anointed with turmeric, almond, sandal-wood and cream by family members of the same sex. In a Sanskrit cere-mony held at a time that was propitious according to astrological predictions, the young couple took their first seven steps together, speaking lines on the significance of each until, on the final step, Gandhi proclaimed that step signified 'that we may ever live as friends' and Kasturbai responded: 'It is the fruit of my good deeds that I have you as my husband. You are my best friend, my highest guru, and my sovereign lord.'[9]

That night, he reported, they were too nervous to face each other, though his brother's wife had explained to him the basics of sex and he hints that someone must have coached Kasturbai. 'Oh, that first night,' he writes, 'two innocent children all unwittingly hurled themselves into the ocean of life.'[10] Gandhi's later repudiation of his sexual nature makes him reluctant to describe any but a few details of his 'carnal desire'; he writes: 'I propose to draw the curtain over my shame.' In fact he seems to have had a normal healthy sexual appetite, the expression of which had, despite his youth, been sanctioned by local custom and by his family. The revulsion was something he brought to the affair himself, in later reflection.

It was not as if the young people were all alone against the world – very far from it: they lived in Gandhi's family house in Rajkot, a household under the control of his beloved mother. Fortunately for the young bride, Putlibai was not the tyrannical mother-in-law so resented by new brides. Young husbands and wives were supposed to ignore each other during the daylight hours: expressions of affection were considered indecent; they were together only in their small bedroom. Lacking experience in the field of marriage, Gandhi would read small pamphlets discussing conjugal love, thrift, child marriage and other such themes. He remarked: 'It was a habit with me to forget what I did not like, and to carry out in practice whatever I liked.' One principle he gleaned from these pamphlets was the duty of a husband to be faithful to his wife. He embraced this notion, and extended it to her, insisting on her fidelity. This was no burden, but he began to be jealous of any commitment other than to himself, to insist on her staying in the house, telling her she could not go anywhere without his permission. She refused to accept such unreasonable restrictions and continued going to the temple and on visits to friends. 'More restraint on my part resulted in more liberty being taken by her,' Gandhi wrote, 'and in my getting more and more cross.' This adolescent playing on the authority of a husband was redeemed, in Gandhi's eyes, because his severities were based on love and his wish 'to make her live a pure life, learn what I learnt'.

Kasturbai had had no formal education, and was illiterate, so Gandhi set about improving her. He came up against barriers, for she was 'not impatient of her ignorance', so what teaching he had time for, in the evenings, 'had to be done against her will'. As well as her reluctance, he also regretted that 'lustful love' left him no time for instruction. Her education remained rudimentary, something Gandhi later blamed on their active sex life: 'I am sure that, had my love for her been absolutely untainted with lust, she would be a learned lady today.'

After the break for his marriage Gandhi continued at high school, where he had progressed to being an above-average pupil and had earned the affection of his teachers. He was rarely punished, but if he was, the shame of having merited it he felt to be worse than the penalty. In time the medium of instruction became English and he also progressed to learning Sanskrit, which he found difficult but eventually rewarding as it was the language of the Hindu holy books.

Gandhi rebelled no more than the usual adolescent against this upbringing: he was led into bad habits in the company of a friend of his brother, Sheikh Mehtab, an older boy whom Gandhi had the conceit to imagine he could reform. He said as much to his wife, his mother and his brother, who advised against his association with the boy. Mehtab appears in the *Autobiography* as a dark double of Gandhi – embracing all the evils that Gandhi samples but resists, he is the tempter in the morality tale that is Gandhi's life. He is not named in the *Autobiography*, doubtless because when the recollections were published, in the 1920s, Gandhi did not want to highlight the fact that one of the few entirely negative characters in his life was a Muslim at a time when he was promoting Hindu–Muslim unity.

Mehtab, hardy and athletic, attributed his strong constitution to eating meat. He also attributed the dominance of the British over India to their diet. This was not an outlandish view. A verse of the time translates:

Behold the mighty Englishman
He rules the Indian small,
Because being a meat-eater
He is five cubits tall.

Gandhi was impressed by this cure for national ills: 'It began to grow on me that meat-eating was good,' he said, 'that it would make me strong and daring, and that, if the whole country took to meat-eating, the English would be overcome.'[11] Thus as a teenager he was already thinking of ridding India of the imperial presence – and he already thought diet had a large part to play in politics.

His parents were of the majority, Vaishnava, form of Hinduism, in which meat-eating was proscribed, and the influence of Jainism with its extreme respect for all forms of life was strong. One day, goaded by the urge for 'food reform' and the thrill of making a new departure in life, Gandhi sat on a riverbank with Mehtab and tried to eat some goat's meat with his bread. It was tough and he was sick; he had a sleepless night, with dreams of a live goat bleating inside him. His friend persevered, Gandhi convinced himself that meat-eating was a duty, and in the setting of an attractive dining-room and given meat delicacies cooked by a chef, Gandhi found a taste for these dishes. The meat-eating phase lasted for perhaps half a dozen meals spread over a year, when he was fourteen or fifteen. Meat was no longer physically offensive to Gandhi by the end of this time, but lying to his parents and deceiving them as to why he had no appetite for family meals he found unbearable. His resolution of this dilemma – not wanting either to lose his friend or to lie to his parents – was to assure Mehtab that, though it was essential to eat meat and to take up the cause of national food reform, he would not do so until his parents were dead so he would not have to lie to them.

These chapters of his autobiography read like 'the temptations of Gandhi': he tells of how he was misled into smoking, stealing, meat-eating and sex but found ultimate sanctity in rejecting these diversions from the true path. He even remarks that the suspicions he developed about Kasturbai were nurtured by Mehtab, as if Gandhi himself was not responsible, did nothing wrong except when tempted. In recounting this time, fifty-five years later, he recalled that Sheikh Mehtab 'kept me under his thumb for more than ten years. On his suggestion, I came to doubt the character of Ba [Kasturbai]. I broke her bangles, refused to have anything to do with her and sent her away to her parents.'[12]

Sheikh Mehtab was the son of a jailer employed by the British, and so of a far less wealthy family than Gandhi's. Why did this friend spend so much money on Gandhi? He took him for restaurant meals and once even paid for him to visit a brothel. There has to be a suspicion that Gandhi was a more than willing participant in these social adventures: he felt frightened – 'he threatened me many times,' he said – but also admiring and in awe of Mehtab.[13] He was far from the only sensitive youngster who was led astray by bad company. In the brothel the shy young man could not perform: 'I went into the jaws of sin, but God in his infinite mercy protected me against myself,' he wrote; 'I was almost struck blind and dumb in this den of vice.'[14] He sat on the bed near a prostitute but was tongue-tied; he does not say what efforts she made to stimulate him, but in the end she lost patience and, insulting him, showed him the door. He took the trouble in recounting this to say there had been four 'similar' incidents in his life – presumably ones in which he may have had sex outside of his marriage – 'and in most of them my good fortune, rather than any effort on my part, saved me'.

These teenage misdemeanours were all petty transgressions, but of biographical interest because of Gandhi's guilty pondering over them. Most people (and most legal systems) are content to overlook minor transgressions committed when moral faculties are not fully formed. Gandhi the man was interested in the development of this moral process; he wanted to know how it had changed him. The comparative value he placed on his transgressions is interesting. He repeatedly returns to sex (including sex within marriage) as shameful; he dwells at length on the sin of meat-eating; yet he passes over in one line the act of stealing pennies from a poor man, which many people would consider beneath contempt. Gandhi says this happened when he was twelve or thirteen – he is more concerned about his theft at the age of fifteen of a gold piece from his brother. This crime troubled him so much that he swore never to steal again and to make a confession to his father. He could not bring himself to speak, so he wrote it down and handed the paper to Karamchand, expecting him to be volubly angry. In fact his father wept and said nothing, leaving a deep impression on Gandhi who concluded that 'a clean confession, combined with a promise never to commit the sin again, when offered before one who has the right to receive it, is the purest type of repentance . . . From that day, truth-telling became a passion with me.'[15]

Karamchand had been ill for some time, and his son had to return home from school to take his turn in nursing him; he had never fully recovered from his injuries in the coach crash at the time of the wedding, and had a fistula on his neck that was unresponsive to treatment. An English surgeon had recommended an operation but the family's local physician had advised against it. Gandhi saw to his father's medicines, dressed his wound and fed him. Sometimes his duties would be relieved by other members of the family, including Karamchand's brother, who came to visit and would insist on sleeping by the sick man's bedside.

He took over on the night of 16 November 1885, sending Gandhi to bed. The teenager was eager to have sex with Kasturbai, whom he woke up for the purpose. In a few minutes, however, a servant came to the door. Gandhi sprang out of bed to be told, 'Father is no more.' He ran to his father's room to see Karamchand dead. He bitterly regretted that his father had not died in his arms – 'it was my uncle who had this privilege.'[16] Gandhi compounded his grief for his father's death with guilt that he had not been present and with the 'shame of my carnal desire even at this critical hour of my father's death, which demanded wakeful service'. He could never forgive himself for having been 'in the grip of lust' at that moment. Even at the age of fifty-six when he wrote his memoir of the event, he was still dwelling on it: 'It took me long to get free from the shackles of lust, and I had to pass through many ordeals before I could overcome it'. Gandhi added that Kasturbai had been pregnant at the time, and the child she bore lived only a few days. This too he blamed on himself: 'Nothing else could be expected. Let all those who are married be warned by my example.'

The family now had a serious problem: the pension Karamchand had received from the ruler of Rajkot no longer arrived and Gandhi's elder brothers held only minor legal positions. They did not have the command of English necessary for a senior government post like their father's, now that the British were so prominent in the political system. Karamchand had spent money as he had earned it; he left some property but little else.

The family now looked to Gandhi to carry their fortunes forward. He would have to get into higher education and land a well paid job to help support them. He was an above average though not a spectacular student at high school, which he attended with the help of scholarships. He was one of four applicants who passed the matriculation examinations for Samaldas College, where he was admitted in January 1888 at the age of nineteen.

He was lonely and homesick at college in Bhavnagar, ninety miles from Rajkot, where he was living alone for the first time in his life. Lessons were conducted in English, which was a struggle for him; the teaching was pitched at a level higher than his, so he could not follow well and his marks were poor. Time earlier lost from his studies for his wedding and while tending to his father in his illness cannot have aided Gandhi's performance as a student. He was to progress in later life by applying discipline and determination to his studies, but he was never a gifted scholar.

Kasturbai was pregnant again, with their first son who would survive, Harilal, so thoughts of impending fatherhood may well have also had an effect on him. At the end of the first term when he returned home he discussed his problems with the family, whose fortunes depended so much on his efforts. In the absence of Karamchand the family was relying for counsel on a friend, Mavji Dave, who was a learned Brahmin with more than a little worldly wisdom. He said that if Gandhi overcame his obstacles and continued to study at college he would get a BA degree, but that would not qualify him for high office – he would not be able to follow his father and become a prime minister. What he should do was to go to London and study to be a barrister at the Inns of Court. A three-year course would bring great rewards.

There were barriers to overcome: the cost would be three or four thousand rupees, a fortune for a family that had struggled to send the youngest son to college ninety miles away. There was also the fact that an orthodox Hindu should not cross the sea for fear of ritual pollution, and his mother's very real fears that Gandhi would mix with women, drink alcohol and eat meat if subjected to the temptations of London life. If Kasturbai had an opinion, it is not recorded; her son was born in the spring of 1888 while preparations were being made for Gandhi's future.

Gandhi described thinking to himself: 'If I go to England not only shall I become a barrister (of whom I used to think a great deal) but I shall be able to see England, the land of philosophers and poets, the very centre of civilisation.'[17] Thirsting for experience, he 'jumped at the proposal' to send him to London, though he was uncertain whether he should study for the law or for medicine, which he preferred. His family were firm on this, however, not wishing for religious reasons for Gandhi to have anything to do with dissection; also, they considered that medicine would not be so suitable if he was to follow in his father's footsteps as a prime minister. But the choice of career did not suit Gandhi's nature – it took a long time before he was even a passable lawyer. On the other hand, he was naturally attracted to healing: he took every opportunity to engage voluntarily in health-related work – in tending to the wounded in wartime, in sanitation work, in nursing his friends and family and trying out his home remedies for their ailments.

If he was aiming for a post in the Indian administration, it was reasonable to look first to the British for assistance in his studies as they controlled not only British India but the princely states, via their political agents. There was a British agent in Porbandar, where the family was known because of Karamchand's work and where his brother Tulsidas lived. Gandhi therefore went to Porbandar and called on his uncle, hoping for a letter of recommendation to the political agent, but he was unsuccessful. Tulsidas was unhappy with the appearance of Indians who returned from England as barristers. He said they adopted a European lifestyle – their clothing, food, smoking cigars – and it was all distasteful to him.

Gandhi therefore wrote direct to Frederick Lely, the political agent, who invited the young man to his home. The official had made no arrangement for a special audience with Gandhi, but saw him nonetheless there and then. Gandhi bowed low and delivered the few sentences he had prepared for this, his first interview with an English gentleman, speaking (somewhat foolishly for someone who wished to study in England) in Gujarati. Lely simply told him: 'Pass your BA first and then see me. No help can be given you now.'[18] While it is comical to think of this administrator lightly casting aside Gandhi, who would later have so much to do with the dismantling of British India, from his own point of view Lely had made a sensible decision. For the best return, Lely's limited funds needed to be spent on excellent scholars, and Gandhi was a poor candidate. He had chosen to try to go to England because of difficulties with his studies in India; though Lely doubtless did not know this, his attitude was calculated to winnow out such candidates. Furthermore, Gandhi came with no recommendation except that he was his father's son, and Karamchand's other two sons had not excelled themselves.

Gandhi returned to Rajkot crestfallen, thinking of his options. His elder brother Laxmidas in whom he had always put his faith should be able to help. Perhaps, Gandhi thought, he could sell Kasturbai's jewellery. Back home, he now faced renewed opposition from his mother, still fretting that Gandhi would be subject to moral temptation in England. She asked the advice of a Jain monk friend who had been a Modh Bania before he had converted. His solution was to put her son under oath. Gandhi duly vowed not to touch wine, woman or meat while he was away, and his mother gave her permission. 'Sleeping, waking, drinking, eating, walking, running, reading, I was dreaming and thinking of England,' he recalled.[19] With some self-knowledge he wrote at the age of nineteen: 'I am not a man who would, after having formed any intention, leave it easily.'[20]

He and his family spent the spring and summer of 1888 contacting friends and family to raise the necessary money. Finally there was sufficient – it was all the money the family of Karamchand had. It was so rare for a young man from Rajkot to go to England that his high school held a send-off in his honour. He had prepared a few words of thanks, but was so shy and unused to public performance that he could scarcely stammer them out. 'I remember how my head reeled and how my whole frame shook as I stood up to read them,' he wrote.[21] His farewell to his family, at his home on 10 August, was even more harrowing. He wrote: 'My mother was hiding her eyes, full of tears, in her hands, but the sobbing was clearly heard . . . I was among a circle of some fifty friends. "If I wept, they would think me too weak; perhaps they would not allow me to go to England," soliloquised I; therefore I did not weep, even though my heart was breaking.' Last came the leave-taking from Kasturbai. Since it was contrary to custom for him to see or speak to her in the presence of friends he had to see her in a separate room. 'She, of course, had begun sobbing long before. I went to her and stood like a dumb statue for a moment. I kissed her and she said "Don't go."'[22]

Laxmidas and Gandhi's friends, including Sheikh Mehtab, travelled with him as far as Bombay where the brothers stayed at the home of their sister Raliatbehn. At that moment the Indian Ocean was stormy, a ship had recently been lost, and it was felt advisable for Gandhi to wait for a few weeks before he travelled. While he was there, as soon as other Modh Bania caste members heard of his expedition he could not go out without being pointed and stared at, or jeered at by passersby.

The head man of the community, who had been on good terms with Gandhi's father, focused the unease of the Modh Bania. He called a general meeting of the caste, to which Gandhi was summoned. The head man presented his prejudices as religious obligations: 'Our religion forbids voyages abroad,' he said, explaining that it was not possible to live among Europeans without compromising Hinduism. Gandhi recounted the vows he had made to his mother and said he felt the caste should not interfere. The head man swore at him and declared: 'This boy shall be treated as an outcaste from today. Whoever helps him or goes to see him off at the dock shall be punishable with a fine.'[23]

With Gandhi now an outcaste, and others who supported him threatened with the same, the young man's situation was precarious. 'Even the chosen few who had supported me through thick and thin left me alone,' he said.[24] He became more anxious than ever to sail, in case some other problem impeded him. This was prescient, for when he found a ship and asked his brother-in-law for the money that had been left in his safekeeping for Gandhi, the brother-in-law refused. He said he could not afford to lose caste – he must not help Gandhi to travel. Gandhi solved this religious impasse by asking a friend to loan him the money for his passage and for clothes. His brother-in-law repaid the loan, thereby not helping Gandhi directly, and religious purity was inviolate.

He sailed from Bombay on 4 September 1888. For the first time he was in the company of British people; all but one of the others in the second-class saloon where passengers mixed were British (though he wrote that they were 'English', which was a common confusion in his work). He shared a cabin with the only other Indian.

In India Gandhi had worn a long cloth jacket over cloth trousers, and a turban. His hair was tied in a shikka, or knot, but he abandoned this for the trip to London, fearing it would expose him to ridicule. Wanting to blend in as far as possible with British society, he bought British clothes including a necktie which he 'abhorred' – but which he 'delighted in wearing later' – and a jacket which, as it was shorter than the Indian equivalent, stopping above the behind, he 'looked upon as immodest'.[25] There is a picture taken of him with slicked-down hair and a clear parting, wearing a three-piece suit with a wing collar and a bow tie, looking very much the middle-class Englishman.

This was his first time in the company of a mass of British people and he did not do well: he was unaccustomed to speaking English and he could not follow their remarks, nor reply even when he understood. He had to frame every sentence in his mind before he could bring it out. He could not use knives and forks and was not bold enough to enquire which dishes at mealtimes were meat-free.

He was advised by Indian friends before he left that he would not be able to face the British climate without eating meat; he was also warned that without liquor he would be numbed with cold and that smoking was obligatory. A kind fellow passenger who accompanied him to the dining-table also advised him that he would have to start eating meat, now or in England, but he resisted. On board, he was surprised and fascinated by everything; he found lavatories bemusing – 'We do not get water there and are obliged to use pieces of paper.'[26] On first entering a lift, in London, he thought it was a small room in which he was to wait, until it began to rise. When he stepped ashore at Tilbury on 29 September he was inappropriately dressed for the weather, in a white flannel suit, the only one of the passengers so attired. Thus inexperienced and unprepared, he took a train to London.

The relationship of India to Britain was (and continues to be) a complex one, eliciting a variety of responses on each side. At base, Britain was an occupying foreign power. The British had displaced other

European powers in the race to dominate India, but had also displaced the Moguls, the previously successful conquerors. Twelve years before Gandhi's birth the 1857 mutiny of Indian troops had aimed to expel the British and to re-install the decadent Mogul emperor (though the former was a more clearly defined aim than the latter). The mutiny had been sparked by rumours that rifle cartridges – the ends of which had to be bitten off – had been prepared with the use of pork or beef tallow, and so were taboo to Muslims and Hindus respectively. This rumour (and others, including that cook-house flour had somewhat improbably been contaminated with cow and pig bone-meal) found a ready audience in resentful soldiers who had previously mutinied over other matters. Those who spread the rumours had succeeded in uniting India's Hindu and Muslim populations in a common cause of complaint – this was the grail of nationalist agitations that was never again to be so firmly grasped: Gandhi was one of many who failed to unite the religions of India into anti-British feeling, except for very short periods.

After the 1857 rebellion had been suppressed, the British Crown took direct control of the nation under a viceroy appointed by the queen. Britain gained an Indian market for her goods, particularly cotton; there were jobs for British expatriates, especially for those of ability but limited means, to run the railways, to build roads and bridges and to become officers in the army. By 1930 there were some 7,500 retired British officials drawing £3.5 to £4 million in pensions from the Indian revenue. India supplied a vast standing army and massive reserves of volunteers who could be called upon to go anywhere in the Empire to defend British interests.

India gained relative internal peace, post, road and rail systems and other infrastructure, and a continually developing administrative and legal system. The disparity between what these two nations gained from the relationship is obvious: once India had its functioning infrastructure, there was no more need for the imperial power. For Britain, however, there was no end in sight to the need for money, a market and an imperial army.

The vast majority of Indians who were engaged in agricultural work had had no more contact with the British than they had with their own princes – the patterns of village life were woven without much reference to rulers. Indian reactions to Britain among the middle class varied widely, from violent antipathy at one extreme to a loyalty that extended to adopting British manners, dress and attitudes at the other. Most were selective, as was Gandhi in the 1880s, taking what seemed valuable from Britain in terms of modernity, but also largely maintaining religious and social traditions.

The long-standing lesson of the 1857 mutiny was that violence would not succeed in expelling the British, who would always be militarily stronger. Gandhi was always an Indian nationalist. What he eventually brought to the scene was a uniquely Gandhian approach to nationalism that had been crafted over the twenty-six years he spent out of India (excepting short periods) after he first left the subcontinent's shores in 1888. At this time, adopting Western ways along with a Western education was still the way forward.

2

London Lessons

When Gandhi arrived in London the aristocratic Lord Salisbury led the Conservative party as prime minister; the previous year Queen Victoria had celebrated fifty years on the throne. The stately buildings in Whitehall ultimately administered four hundred million people. London was the greatest city in the world, at the centre of the first truly global empire.

Viewed from that perspective, the Empire seemed unbreakable, a thing to wonder at rather than to attack. But the cracks were already apparent. The ongoing unrest in Ireland had already convinced the most far-sighted that home rule was the only solution. The London match-girls, amongst the most downtrodden and ignorant workers, had successfully held a strike to improve their pay and conditions earlier in 1888. The year after Gandhi arrived the dockers would strike, halting trade through the centre of the Empire.

These manifestations of discontent may seem remote from the self-image of the shy student from Kathiawar who landed at Tilbury, but Gandhi is known to have followed the Irish progress to independence through the press; he would seek, and receive, an audience with Cardinal Manning to congratulate him on his conciliatory role in ending the dock strike. He also met the match-girls' leader Annie Besant in London, and later worked beside her for Indian independence when she took her own path to mysticism in Madras.

British culture as centred on London offered other manifestations of uncertainty. The established Church continued its struggle against the forces of rationalism as represented by the Darwinists, and the best-selling author Marie Corelli was writing books discussing the masculine and feminine nature of God, reincarnation, and the role of the occult in evolution. The London that Gandhi had entered brimmed with insistent new ideas – of the socialist Social Democratic Federation, the Society for Psychical Research, the Theosophical Society and the Anti-Vivisection Society. He could not have arrived at a time of greater challenge and excitement than the last decade of the nineteenth century.

On his arrival Gandhi went by train to central London with a companion he had met on the boat, to the luxurious Victoria Hotel, which had been recommended to them. His new friend accepted the first rooms offered at the first price – six shillings a day. To give an idea of the value of money: there were twenty shillings to the pound and the dockers had been striking for a minimum wage of half a shilling (sixpence) an hour – though they often got only three hours' work a day.

A network of Indian expatriates supported newcomers, and Gandhi carried letters of introduction to several people to ease his entry into British society. One of his contacts was Dr Pranjivan Mehta, who was studying law as well as taking an advanced course in medicine. When he called to see Gandhi in his hotel on his first night there, he felt the young man was something of a barbarian – he was touching Mehta's clothes with puerile interest, and his English was poor. Mehta was also concerned at the cost of the hotel, and arranged for Gandhi to live with an English family that took in boarders.

Gandhi's hotel bill for the few days he was there was for £3, which shocked him; he had around £400 for his entire three-year trip. He had been eating in the hotel even though he found the food unpalatable, and was surprised that he still had to pay for dishes he had ordered even if he had not eaten them.

Gandhi was to have a problem finding food – the English landladies' boiled vegetables without seasoning were all but inedible. They were also intended as an accompaniment to a meat dish. He was too shy to make his needs better known and would fill up on bread but would not ask for more vegetables. He was at an extra disadvantage because he still considered meat-eating was essential to achieve national freedom; his vegetarianism was a result only of his vow to his mother to abstain. He was urged to abandon the promise – 'What is the value of a vow made before an illiterate mother, and in ignorance of conditions here?' a friend asked, but for Gandhi a vow was inviolable.[1]

He wept with homesickness during this time of boarding with different families, in Richmond and West Kensington. But he started reading newspapers, an important contribution towards the political education of someone who had not previously had any acquaintance with current affairs.

After taking some time to orientate himself in the new country, Gandhi enrolled at the Inner Temple, one of the four Inns of Court. The qualifications for being called to the Bar were to pass examinations in Roman and common law and to attend a number of dinners at the appropriate Inn. There was little by way of formal training; most depended on personal study. Gandhi does not seem to have particularly enjoyed the medieval Inns of Court, though he spent many days working in the library of the Inner Temple, thus saving on coal to heat his rooms. He ate the compulsory dinners in the Inner Temple Hall where, surprisingly considering his difficulty elsewhere, it was possible to order vegetarian fare. He discovered abstinence had its rewards: as each table was supplied with the same amount of wine, he was a welcome guest at the tables of those who enjoyed it, since they could drink the ration supplied for him. He bought and studied the recommended books, discovering that many students got by using tutors or cramming notes, never having to read the textbooks – 'question papers were easy and examiners were generous'.[2] His study of English common law, incorporating criminal and civil law, gave him an appreciation of the concepts of equal rights before the law, indicating that there were values within which the government must operate.

His struggle to find suitable food ended when he came across a vegetarian restaurant, the Central on St Bride Street, off Farringdon Street, where he began to eat, feeling that 'God had come to my aid.'[3] He bought a copy of the proselytising *A Plea for Vegetarianism* by Henry Salt. Salt was a socialist, a former Eton schoolmaster who wore sandals (unusual at the time) and attempted to live the simple life with his wife, a Sanskrit scholar called Kate Joynes, on the smallest amount of money possible.

Gandhi was glad to have found a vegetarian meeting place, but looked with disdain at vegetarians who were obsessed with their health and talked of nothing but disease. He was moving towards the incorporation of vegetarianism into a spiritual scheme of his own devising, but one which would draw much from his London experiences. As noted earlier, he had previously considered vegetarianism a moral necessity but a meat diet to be 'scientifically' superior. He was now converted to the superiority of the vegetarian diet, joined the London Vegetarian Society in 1890 and met with other enthusiasts. He began to read vegetarian magazines and was invited by the editor of *The Vegetarian*, Josiah Oldfield, to attend the International Vegetarian Congress in September 1890. Within this network Gandhi discovered a great freedom: he could eat in vegetarian restaurants and travel around the country using vegetarian-orientated accommodation, as advertised via the society. He later moved into rooms at Oldfield's residence in Bayswater. Gandhi commented enthusiastically about his friend: 'I have seen him work at the rate of sixteen hours or more per diem. He was, when I saw him last, living on bread, figs and water.'[4] Oldfield said: 'Those were happy days, of consciousness that we were helping to make the world better.'[5]

By 1891 Gandhi was defending vegetarianism in articles in *The Vegetarian* and ascribing the weakness of India to other causes, including child marriage which supposedly produced weak offspring and a strain on the young parents.[6] In his search for perfect nutritional equilibrium he was prey to every food fad, whether or not there was any rational basis for it. 'There was in those days,' he records, 'a body of opinion which regarded tea and coffee as harmful and favoured cocoa' – cocoa, then, it was.[7] The seed for all his future experiments in diet, he recorded, was sown in London (presumably he did not include his Indian experiences with meat-eating as experiments). He also invented diets of his own, giving up starchy foods, living on bread and fruit alone, then on cheese, milk and eggs.

Gandhi's involvement with what were thought of as food cranks disconcerted Dalpatram Shukla, another Kathiawari in London, who wanted his young friend to become a sophisticated man of the world. One evening he took Gandhi to the theatre, preceded by a restaurant meal at which he was embarrassed when Gandhi called the waiter to ask if the soup was vegetarian. Gandhi decided in response to his friend's discomfiture at his 'making a scene' that, though he could not relent over meat-eating, he would nevertheless become an English gentleman.

He therefore upgraded his wardrobe, at considerable expense. He bought a top-hat and an evening suit and set about reforming his manners. He was advised he had to learn to dance and to speak French, so he signed up for lessons. He found dancing difficult, so bought a violin and hired a teacher in order to acquire a taste for Western music. He also engaged an elocution teacher. This 'infatuation', as he called it, lasted around three months, after which he dispensed with the services of all his teachers – typically, again taking an extreme position. In fact elocution lessons for someone not a native English speaker would at the time have been of real value – the fact that he did not think he needed them meant he did not see his future as including making speeches in English, but one of working in the Indian courts or in Indian public service as his father had. Despite dispensing with the 'charm school' accessories he retained a 'punctiliousness in dress'; and he did so for years, he maintained – certainly throughout his time in Britain he was the image of the 'brown Englishman'.[8] An Indian in London described him at this time: 'Gandhi was wearing a high silk top hat brushed "burnish bright", a stiff and starched collar (known at that time as the Gladstone), a flashy tie displaying all the colours of the rainbow, under which there was a fine striped shirt. Gandhi wore a morning coat, a double-breasted vest [wasitcoat], dark striped trousers to match, patent leather boots and spats. He carried leather gloves, and a silver-mounted stick.'[9]

He was now becoming more concerned about the dwindling of his funds. Living with a family was proving too expensive, so he took rooms, probably in Store Street; he would walk to wherever he had to be, covering distances of eight to ten miles a day, and started cooking some of his meals at home. He enjoyed the discipline of progressively reducing his expenses: 'I kept account of every farthing I spent, and my expenses were carefully calculated.' He was eventually able to live on around a shilling a day for food.[10] He also reduced the variety of foods he was eating, as a matter of discipline rather than expense, and stopped using the spices sent to him from India, becoming instead enamoured of boiled spinach.

He once fell ill with bronchitis and a doctor was sent for who advised

Gandhi he must eat meat for his strength. He brought beef tea to the supine Indian and told him he must either drink it or die. 'I had to reply,' recalled Gandhi, 'that if it were God's will that I should die, I must die, but that I was sure it could not be God's will that I should break the oath that I made at my mother's knee before I left India.'[11]

He also decided on a course of study to fill the time when the Bar examinations were not absorbing him, and took the London Matriculation, a general exam that increased his store of general knowledge at no particular cost. He organised his timetable to the minute and worked hard at subjects such as Latin and science; though he failed the examination the first time he took it (flunking the Latin paper), he repeated the papers and passed in June 1890.

Every student should go to England to study because so much could be learned, he remarked, not because of what was there but what was not: 'Whilst he is in England he is alone, no wife to tease and flatter him, no parents to indulge, no children to look after, no company to disturb.'[12] Gandhi was already seeing personal freedom in terms of being free from his family, something that would be a continuing theme in his dealings with his relations.

Gandhi did not move in literary circles when he was in London (as his later friend Sarojini Naidu did), but he read some of the fiction of the day including Oscar Wilde's *Picture of Dorian Gray*, later remarking: 'A great crime committed by a man has been known to change his face in such a way as to stamp the crime on it', as if the truth of literature could be read as literal fact – just as he also recounted the events of Indian religious stories as if they were about historical characters.[13] Of the writer he commented: 'Wilde saw the highest Art simply in outward forms and therefore succeeded in beautifying immorality.'[14]

In December 1890 he sat for the Bar finals, which took place over four days, and early the next year he found he was one of the three-quarters of candidates who had passed. He was required to stay in London to complete the requirements for the Bar, but was now free to step up his involvement with the Vegetarian Society.

Gandhi had letters of introduction to four people, including Dadabhai Naoroji, a Parsi intellectual and cotton trader who was also from Gujarat. Naoroji was to become the first Asian member of parliament, representing Finsbury Central from 1892 to 1895 (his election campaign would be helped by Mohammad Ali Jinnah, who was at that time studying law in London). Gandhi did not present his letter to Naoroji until very late in his stay in London, feeling he had no right to trouble such a great man, and though the veteran accepted his young admirer warmly, Gandhi could not bring himself to take up Naoroji's offer of assistance.

The British Committee of the Indian National Congress was founded in July 1889 but Gandhi does not seem to have attended any of its meetings; he did, though, attend meetings of the London India Society that discussed 'political, social and literary subjects relating to India' and acted to acquaint the public in England of Indian opinion 'on all important questions that might arise from time to time'.[15] The society had been set up by Naoroji in 1865 so it was a mature institution by the time Gandhi attended its meetings. Naoroji visualised the constitutional progress of India through the just and fair administration of the British, guided by their sense of fair play. It was a position that took at face value the Liberal project of enlightened rule. When India was not well governed, Naoroji criticised it as 'unrighteous and un-British'.[16]

Gandhi's main activity in London was with the Vegetarian Society. He was elected to the executive committee in September 1890, but he proved a disappointment to them: though he was fine at talking to individuals, he was too shy to open his mouth in a committee meeting. 'It often happened that just when I mustered up courage to speak, a fresh subject would be started,' he wrote.[17] The Vegetarian Society confirmed his belief in diet as a reforming force. He also encountered there opponents of alcohol, and felt confident in proclaiming that in India 'One of the most greatly-felt evils of British rule is the importation of alcohol – that enemy of mankind, that curse of civilisation'; he was later to similarly curse tobacco.[18]

The society was largely funded by a wealthy ironworks owner, Arnold Hills, who practised his own brand of paternalistic capitalism and promoted extreme puritanism in matters of tobacco, alcohol and sex. His form of Christianity, which has been said to have been influential in Gandhi's thinking, was of the perfectibility of man: people could become like Jesus by controlling the body's unruly appetites. In *Essays on Vegetarianism* Hills promoted a 'Gospel of Vitality' which involved eating 'vital foods' such as uncooked fruit, vegetables, nuts, pulses and grains to cultivate 'vital force'. He believed that cooking impaired the power of the sun's rays that were stored in foods and advised eating vegetables raw. He explained: 'it is not enough to abstain from the indulgence in dead and stimulating foods; under the gospel of Vegetarianism, we listen to the beatitudes of Vital Food and Vital Drink'.[19] Gandhi tried an experiment in vital food in Bombay in 1892 and in Pretoria in 1893, but it was hard to digest and left him feeling hungry and sick – the sort of reaction that must tell even the most enthusiastic experimenter that something is wrong.

Part of the preservation of vital force in Hills's view was in refraining from sex, except specifically for procreation. Sex 'has been given for its own special purpose, and for no other. It may not be abused for pleasure; it may not be indulged for passion.'[20] It was at the Vegetarian Society (and in Hills's tracts in *The Vegetarian*) that Gandhi first encountered this doctrine of extreme puritanism with regard to sex, a principle that was not present in his family's Hinduism. Even more extreme was another belief of Hills that celibacy should be maintained even after marriage, so-called 'chastity within the marriage bond'; this was to form a mainstay of Gandhi's organisation of his own model societies in later life.[21]

A leading member of the Vegetarian Society was Thomas Allinson, a doctor of medicine and the founder of naturopathy which promoted health through exercise, fresh air, a vegetarian diet and the avoidance of alcohol, tobacco, coffee and tea. Thus far everything fitted with Hills's views, but out of sympathy for the over-fecund Victorian woman borne down by repeated pregnancies, he also promoted birth control. Gandhi became involved in the argument between these two, which culminated in a motion for the expulsion of Allinson from the society. Gandhi tended to sympathise with Hills in opposing birth control, but he thought it was improper for Hills to exclude a man 'simply because he refused to regard puritan morals as one of the objects of the society'.[22] Gandhi put his thoughts in writing and went to the committee meeting with his speech in his pocket, but again he did not feel bold enough to present it, and the chairman had it read by someone else. Allinson lost the day and was expelled; later he was struck off the Medical Register for his advanced views, and he set up the whole-grain bakery that still bears his name.

In London, at least from his own account, Gandhi seems to have indulged his preoccupation with food, but he does not record extensive ponderings on sex, such as would preoccupy him in later life. Once at a vegetarian conference in Portsmouth in 1890 he was put up in a lodging house that also operated as a brothel. When conversation in the parlour took a racy turn, Gandhi remembered the vow he had made to his mother and fled the scene, though he remarked that it was 'the first occasion' on which a woman, other than my wife, moved me to lust'.[23] Apart from this he reports little by way of sexual diversion except visits he would make every Sunday to the home of an elderly lady who had befriended him, and who was eager to introduce him to young women and to impress on him the merits of marriage. 'Flirting' was encouraged, and he was often left alone with one young woman in particular. Finally he could bear it no longer and, still too shy to trust himself to speak in person, he sent a letter to his hostess confessing that he was married with a son, saying: 'Will you forgive me? I assure you I have taken no improper liberties with the young lady.'[24] The old lady responded with good humour, and he continued to be invited to her house. Gandhi felt his punctilious regard for the truth had freed him from moral disaster. It is, incidentally, worth remarking on the absence of racial prejudice evinced in his encounters with ordinary British families during his time in London. If there was unpleasantness, he does not remark on it, in sharp contrast to his later descriptions of his South African experiences.

It was in religion that, separated from the orthodox Hinduism of his caste, Gandhi made the most progress while in London. He contrived to acquaint himself with the world's major religions and even read a book promoting atheism. He read parts of the Bible, given to him by a vegetarian Christian. He found the Old Testament sent him to sleep but delighted in the New, particularly the Sermon on the Mount. His studies in this field were without much system. He read about Mohammed in Carlyle's *Heroes and Hero Worship*; about Buddha in Edwin Arnold's popular poem *The Light of Asia*; and would first be introduced to the *Bhagavad Gita* in another of Edwin Arnold's verse translations, *The Song*

Celestial. Gandhi had such confidence in Arnold that he believed its sentimental depiction of Buddha with animals demonstrated his superiority over Jesus, because of Buddha's thereby proven love for all life, not merely for humans. In fact such scenes as Buddha carrying a sick lamb were Arnold's invention and have no basis in Buddhist texts. Gandhi started a vegetarian club in Bayswater when he lived there, with himself as secretary and Oldfield as president, and he invited Arnold, also a vegetarian and living locally, to be vice-president; the club went well for a time, before Gandhi moved from the area. He must have met Arnold on several occasions, but there is no record of it.

Gandhi was introduced to the original Sanskrit version of the *Bhagavad Gita* by two members of the Theosophical Society, Bertram and Archibald Keightley, an uncle and nephew whom he probably met through his vegetarian connections. They were reading Arnold's translation but wanted some idea of whether the translation was a good one so asked Gandhi's help. He had to admit that he had not read the poem in any form and his knowledge of Sanskrit was poor, but he could put what scholarship he did have at their service. Thus it was that he became acquainted with the work that was to be his guide in future life, the exemplar of spiritual truth for him and the subject of daily reading.

The Keightleys (who are described as 'both unmarried', perhaps a euphemism for homosexual) made their West London home available to Madame Blavatsky, the founder of theosophy, and introduced Gandhi to her. He read Blavatsky's *Key to Theosophy*, which strengthened his attachment to Hinduism. Though he hardly knew her, Blavatsky was significant in Gandhi's life for two reasons: first, because she headed an organisation that promoted Hindu thought in England, and therefore reinforced his conviction that the values of his homeland were not to be discarded in a rush to 'modernise'. Second, theosophists were also having an influence on the Indian independence movement, devotees playing a prominent role in the founding of the Indian National Congress.

Helena Petrovna Blavatsky was born in Russia in 1831 of prominent parents and took to travelling early in life, including to India and Tibet. Thus religiously invigorated, she settled in the United States, there meeting a former colonel, Henry Olcott, who was writing on spiritualism. Together they and some like-minded individuals founded the Theosophical Society in 1875 in New York. The society was dedicated to a universal brotherhood of humanity without regard to sex, race or creed. It aimed to encourage the study of comparative religion, philosophy and science and to investigate unexplained laws of nature and the powers said to be latent in man. The group moved to India and in 1882 set up their permanent headquarters in Adyar, near Madras. Despite being somewhat discredited by the exposure of fake psychic phenomena, theosophy exerted a powerful influence, particularly on social reformers of a spiritual bent such as Annie Besant whose reading of Blavatsky's work converted her from atheism – something that impressed Gandhi, for whom books were always a strong influence. He also heard Besant speak in London, and was struck by her final comment that she would be 'quite satisfied to have the epitaph written on her tomb that she had lived for truth and died for truth.'[25] On Blavatsky's death in 1891, Besant became one of the organisation's leaders and was elected president in 1907. Part of theosophy's message was that the highest wisdom in the world belonged to the East, and was not all contained in the past but maintained in the present day by living masters, or mahatmas.

Gandhi writes that he did not join the theosophists, but independent evidence attests to his having become an associate member on 26 March 1891, one of a number of instances when Gandhi's *Experiments with Truth* diverges from the truth as it is generally understood.[26]

Spiritually, Gandhi was following his own path towards perfectibility, remarking later that it was at the age of twenty or twenty-one, when he was in London, that he first aspired to attain 'a state of mind [which] cannot be affected even in dire circumstances or at the moment of death.'[27] In pursuit of this goal he sought a guru, or spiritual guide, to enthrone in this heart, as he put it. He felt that there must be 'ceaseless striving after perfection. For one gets the Guru that one deserves. Infinite striving after perfection is its own reward. The rest is in the hands of God.'[28] It almost goes without saying that such a strong-willed character as Gandhi never did find anyone to be his perfect spiritual guide; he would continue as a lone seeker, offering his insights to others.

Gandhi's knowledge of European countries other than Britain was limited, but he went to Paris for the World Exhibition in May 1889 and spent a week there. He ascended the Eiffel Tower and visited Catholic churches, where he was impressed by the devotion of the worshippers, just a closed door away from the noise and bustle of the capital's streets.

Before leaving for India he gave a farewell dinner to members of the Vegetarian Society but, as so often, was too shy to give a speech: he said his mind went blank when he rose to deliver his prepared words and he felt he had embarrassed himself, but contemporary records demur. In fact, Gandhi frequently presents himself as more shy and incapable than he actually was: in spring and summer 1891 he several times gave his paper 'The Foods of India' to audiences interested in vegetarianism in different parts of southern England or spoke on other matters, though he does remark that in Ventnor he was overcome with shyness and a colleague had to read his paper.

His vegetarian friends responded thus to his departure: 'there was no sign of sorrow, because all felt that though Mr Gandhi was going back to India, yet he was going to a still greater work for vegetarianism, and that on the completion of his law career and his final success, congratulations to him should take the part of personal wailings.'[29] Vegetarianism, dietary experiment and fasting were at least as important to Gandhi himself as non-violence, which is popularly considered to be his legacy.

Gandhi's vegetarianism was not separate from his general world view; he advised other Indians: 'The Vegetarian movement will indirectly aid India politically . . . inasmuch as the English Vegetarians will more readily sympathise with the Indian aspirations (that is my personal experience).'[30] He believed in the principle, supported by British Liberals, of increasing Indian participation in government, taking the best from British civilisation and presenting in return the best of the East.

He left London strengthened by his vows to his mother which, under great pressure, he had managed to keep, plus a knowledge of formal organisations through the Vegetarian Society and of religious proselytising through the theosophists and Arnold Hills. He also left it with ideas, promoted by Henry Salt and in the work of Edwin Arnold, of human perfectibility: that a person by his own efforts could develop spiritual power. What is lacking from records of this time is any strictly political thought or any contribution towards improving the working of the law. There was no evidence from his time in London that Gandhi, twenty-two when he left, would become a great political leader, and certainly none that he would become a great lawyer. He was called to the Bar on 10 June 1891, enrolled in the High Court on the 11th, and on the 12th he left the country via Tilbury on the steamship *Oceana*. 'It was not without deep regret that I left dear London,' he said.[31]

3

Adventures in Natal

Gandhi's brother Laxmidas met him at the dock in Bombay. His return to India was to sadness, as his mother had died at the age of forty-one, shortly after learning of his success in his studies. The family had kept from him the fact of Putlibai's death earlier in 1891, feeling there was no benefit in telling him while he was abroad. Now almost the first thing he said was 'How is mother?' Laxmidas at first avoided the question but later that evening Gandhi asked again. His grief, he said, was 'even greater than over my father's death' but he was proud of the self-control that allowed him to act as if nothing had happened.[1]

The family continued to suffer the excommunication from caste that Gandhi's visit to Britain had brought them, but one section of the Modh Bania were prepared to readmit him once he had been through a ritual cleansing. Whatever they thought before he left, having an English-educated lawyer among them would do the caste group no harm. It had been Putlibai's wish that he be readmitted so Gandhi acquiesced and his brother arranged the purification in the Godavari River; and for the next step, a dinner for all the elders of the caste whom Gandhi, stripped to the waist, served. Another section of the caste refused to readmit him, and he therefore continued to suffer a ban on visiting his in-laws. Kasturbai and their son Harilal had also been subject to this restriction in Gandhi's absence, though they disobeyed it and visited her parents, doubtless with some level of secrecy. Gandhi declared he would either visit his in-laws openly and honestly or not at all, so it became not at all. He was never a very family-orientated man and so it was probably no great hardship to be forbidden to visit.

He makes little of his reunion with Kasturbai after the three-year absence. Nothing, it seemed, had changed between them; he had intended to teach her to read and write but again his need for sex at the times they were alone together intervened – 'my lust got in the way', as he put it. His attitude towards her was in some respects as bad as ever: 'I continued my squeamishness and suspiciousness in respect of every little thing,' he wrote; 'once I went to the length of sending her away to her father's house, and consented to receive her back only after I had made her thoroughly miserable.'[2] He seemed to have changed when she returned after a month, and the suspicions (and the lessons) ended. Perhaps he was merely preoccupied with other things. Their second son, Manilal, was born the year after Gandhi returned, in October 1892. He enjoyed becoming acquainted with Harilal, now almost four, and he took in hand his instruction and that of the other children of the household. He instituted a programme of physical exercise to 'make them hardy'.

Laxmidas was proud that now Gandhi had returned, the family was going to move up in the world, and he wanted their living habits to match their aspirations. He had high hopes for his brother's success; Laxmidas had many friends and a generous personality, and expected to get work for Gandhi via this wide social network. Gandhi's journey and studies in London had cost nearly 13,000 rupees, far in excess of the 5,000 originally estimated. In addition, Laxmidas had spent freely in the expectation that his brother's return would revive the family fortunes. He had attempted to create an English atmosphere in the house in Rajkot: tea and coffee were regularly served, and crockery, which had been for special occasions, was now in general use. New furniture had been bought. Gandhi's arrival prompted other 'reforms' by Laxmidas including the introduction of cocoa and porridge and European dress.

Gandhi's guilty secret was that he was actually a very poor lawyer: he was acutely aware of his lack of experience and of his general inadequacy. He had no confidence in his own abilities and felt he was ill versed in the ways of the world. A senior in the profession reassured him that it took no unusual skill to be an ordinary lawyer – common honesty and industry would suffice. He asked about Gandhi's general reading and advised, sensibly, that it was meagre: he had no knowledge of the world, not even of the history of India. Gandhi did as he was told and read some books on physiognomy offering what passed for a scientific approach to human nature, but his plodding approach to learning would never change.

The brothers, had, moreover, overreached themselves in their efforts to make Gandhi a high earner. He had read Roman law in Latin and understood the common law of England but knew nothing of the law in Kathiawar. As a British-educated barrister, however, it was customary to charge ten times the fees of a locally educated man, who could do the job better. Gandhi therefore went to Bombay, studied Indian law and tried to obtain cases. Here he learned that a new barrister could wait five or more years before his career took off.

No briefs came to him and he was so fastidious as to refuse to employ touts to seek out work. To save money he walked to and from the courts, though he still had to maintain standards by keeping a household and wearing European dress. He again for a short time experimented with the 'vital food' advised by Arnold Hills – eating just raw fruit, nuts, grains and pulses. He attended the High Court in Bombay daily but did not have sufficient knowledge to follow the cases and would doze off. He tried to get work as a teacher, but without a BA he was at a disadvantage. He did some free work which built his confidence but his first appearance at court was a disaster. He was appearing for the defendant in the Small Causes Court; when the time came to examine the plaintiff's witness, he recounted, 'I stood up but my heart sank into my boots. My head was reeling and I felt as though the whole court was doing likewise. I could think of no question to ask. The judge must have laughed, and the vakils [court pleaders] no doubt enjoyed the spectacle.'[3] Gandhi sat down and told the agent he could not conduct the case; he returned his fee and hastened away from the court in shame. He was not to go to court again until he had left India.

Gandhi could no longer justify the expense of keeping an establishment in Bombay and moved back to Rajkot, now working with his brother who had set up as a lawyer in partnership with more experienced man. Gandhi now worked drafting applications and other legal documents, in which capacity he was not obliged to address the court.

Gandhi's indebtedness to his brother led him into the worst mistake of his professional life. When Laxmidas had been secretary to the heir to the throne of Porbandar he had overlooked the theft by the young man of some state jewels. Indian princes were not allowed to sequester the property of their state for personal use and the matter was being looked into by the British political agent Charles Ollivant. Gandhi had met Ollivant in London and had a passingly friendly relationship with him. Laxmidas seized on this and urged him to use his influence with the Englishman. Gandhi resisted, telling Laxmidas to submit a petition in the proper way – if he were innocent, he would be vindicated. Laxmidas persisted, telling Gandhi he did not know the world, and certainly did not know Kathiawar: 'Only influence counts here. It is not proper for you, a brother, to shirk your duty when you can clearly put in a good word about me to an officer you know.'[4]

With reluctance Gandhi sought an audience with Ollivant, visited the important man in his office and reminded him of their acquaintance. He began to speak about the case. Ollivant resented even the suspicion that he could be prejudiced by a personal appeal: 'Your brother is an intriguer,' he said. 'I want to hear nothing more from you. I have no time. If your brother has anything to say, let him apply through the proper channel.' Gandhi should have apologised and left but instead compounded the offence by continuing with his story. 'You must go now,' the political agent said, but Gandhi begged to be allowed to continue, whereupon Ollivant sent for his peon (attendant) who placed his hands on Gandhi's shoulder and sent him out of the room.

Instead of reflecting on what had happened, Gandhi was outraged at his treatment and immediately sent a note saying: 'You have insulted me. You have assaulted me through your peon. If you make no amends, I shall have to proceed against you.' This foolishness elicited the response: 'You were rude to me. I asked you to go and you would not. I had no option but to order my peon to show you the door. Even after he asked you to leave you did not do so. He therefore had to use just enough force to send you out. You are at liberty to proceed as you wish.'

Gandhi was miserable and confused as to his future path. What could he now do? His brother could not help, so he asked for the advice of a senior barrister, one Pherozeshah Mehta, who told him to do nothing – he would gain nothing by proceeding against the political officer, and could ruin himself. Gandhi took this good advice, but now he was really in a fix as most of his work in the region would be in the political agent's court. He felt he had to get away from the poisonous atmosphere of Kathiawar.

While Gandhi was struggling with this question of how to make a living, Laxmidas heard of a Porbandar merchant firm, Dada Abdulla & Company, that had built up a business in South Africa and needed a barrister to help with a big case. The fee would be good, with first-class travel and all living expenses paid. Dada Abdulla, who was based in Natal while his brother ran the business in Porbandar, had a trading empire operating between India and South Africa where he ran his own fleet. Though barely literate, Abdulla had made his fortune several times over, notably in the gold rush of 1888–90 when he was able to buy gold at thirteen rupees to the pound. He needed a man such as Gandhi as an intermediary between his lawyers, who spoke no Gujarati, and himself (having only poor English). Gandhi, proficient in both languages, legally qualified and familiar with the trading milieu (he came from the Gujarati merchant caste, after all), was in the right place at the right time.

In April 1893 he set sail for Africa, leaving Kasturbai with Harilal, now five, and Manilal, just six months old. It was with some regret that he said goodbye to Kasturbai: the maturity he had developed in London was finally bearing fruit in his relationships, and they had been getting on better in recent months.

When the steamer reached Durban, the main port of Natal, he was met by the elderly Dada Abdulla, who viewed this smartly dressed young man in his frock-coat, striped trousers and black turban with some suspicion. Clearly, Gandhi was going to have to prove himself. He immediately noticed the contempt with which Indians were treated by Europeans in South Africa. The political manifestation of this contempt, rather than case law, was to underlie his major work here.

Asians were resented because they seemed an unstoppable force – there was an apparently inexhaustible supply of migrants from India and China; in South Africa their ability to live frugally and work hard meant they prospered, their supportive family structures providing the ideal setting for raising children. If the Europeans let them, they feared the Asians would soon outnumber the whites and outperform them economically. Neither the Asians nor the Europeans paid much attention to the native Africans who, at the end of the nineteenth century, were politically inchoate.

After a day or so spent settling in, Gandhi was taken by Dada Abdulla to the Durban court. When the magistrate saw that the young lawyer was wearing his Western dress with a turban, he told him to remove his headdress. Gandhi thought this a preposterous request, refused, and walked out of the court. Court reporters noted the event and Gandhi's insistence on wearing his turban in court made headlines in the local press. His arrival was thus widely advertised within days of his setting foot in the country. It was not obvious to him how he should proceed in dealing with this matter – he wondered whether he should henceforth wear British dress entirely, but as Indian waiters and other serving people who had adopted Christianity did so, this would be seen to be breaking faith with those Indians who had retained their culture while in Africa. He therefore maintained his combination of frock-coat and trousers plus turban.

His grounding in Roman law served him well in South Africa where many of the laws were based on Dutch law, which had taken elements of Roman jurisprudence as its foundation. However, Gandhi knew nothing of accounts, the subject on which the case he was dealing with turned, so he bought a book and taught himself as much as he needed to know. Once he was up to speed, he was sent to Pretoria in the Transvaal where the case between Dada Abdulla and Tyeb Khan Mohammed was to be heard. Tyeb Khan Mohammed occupied in the Boer republic of the Transvaal the same position of trading seniority that Dada Abdulla had in the British colony of Natal.

In the 1890s, South Africa comprised four areas. The two British ones were the Cape Colony, which was self-governing under the Crown; and Natal which was a Crown colony. The two Boer republics were the Transvaal and the Orange Free State. There could be racial discrimination in any of these places, but for Indians the most severe was to be found in the Orange Free State, where they were forbidden to live. In the Transvaal they were tolerated, but poorly treated. When Gandhi was travelling to Pretoria, he was moving from a more or less tolerant British regime to a draconian Boer one. For the part of the journey that was

by train, he travelled in a first-class compartment as far as Pietermaritzburg, the capital of Natal, at which point a European passenger
boarded and sought two railway officials to have him taken along to the
van compartment. As Gandhi would not leave voluntarily a compartment for which he had paid the appropriate fare, they summoned a
policeman, who threw him out and his baggage after him. He still would
not go to another, inferior compartment. The train left and he sat all
night in the cold, dark station waiting-room; his overcoat was in his
luggage but the railway officials had that, and he did not want to invite
further insult by asking for it.

Gandhi had little experience of racial prejudice. Doubtless he met
with some in London, but not enough to be worth remarking on in his
letters or memoirs. In Britain foreigners were regarded with indifference or welcomed as physical representations of the breadth of the British
Empire. They added to the colour and variety of London life; they were
visitors who had come to enjoy and contribute and then to leave. Among
the girls he met and at the Vegetarian Society Gandhi, far from being
reviled, encountered curiosity to the point of fascination. His stay at the
heart of empire had given him an experience of people of different types
and backgrounds getting on together, of the tolerance and decency of
cosmopolitan society. The British considered themselves the superior
nation, their pre-eminence evinced by their imperial dominance. Whites
so outnumbered non-whites that there was no perception of a threat.
In South Africa, however, non-white people vastly outnumbered whites;
white domination needed for its maintenance not just force but an
ideology based on racial superiority. In South Africa Gandhi was witnessing, at the end of the nineteenth and the beginning of the twentieth
centuries, the creation of a unified racial state. The Boers, via the Dutch
Reformed Church, had a thoroughly worked-out scriptural justification
for their racial stratification of society, which to them had quite as much
validity as, for example, the Hindu imposition of 'untouchability' on
their society. The white masters could convince themselves that they
were not perpetrating a system of injustice, but doing the work of God
in keeping the races separate.

Indians fitted between the black African and white populations as
racial and cultural intermediaries. They were Muslim businessmen (who

were often referred to as 'Arabs', though they were not), Indian Christians who were in the service industries, Parsi clerks, and Hindus who for the most part came as indentured labourers. Under this latter system an Indian workforce was imported to serve five years of tied labour. The arrangement came about because the Europeans found Africans unwilling to work for wages in the regimented fashion necessary for modern production, and the shortage of opportunities back in India led to many Indians remaining after their period of work. As this community grew and settled, a merchant class became attracted to the area, paying their own passage from India. However, because of the labouring origin of the community they were collectively called 'coolies'. In South Africa Gandhi was not a man respected for his travels or his education or because he had been born into a family in public service; here he was a 'coolie barrister'.

Gandhi debated the whole night at the Pietermaritzburg station whether he should forget this job and return to India, or whether he should go on to Pretoria, fighting for his rights. The hardship he experienced, he felt, was superficial, only a symptom of the deep disease of colour prejudice. Later he described his inner struggle as the one experience that had changed the course of his life: 'My active non-violence began from that date.'[5]

In the morning he sent a telegram to the general manager of the railway, and to Dada Abdulla. Dada Abdulla also contacted the railway authorities and sent a message to Indian traders at Pietermaritzburg to go to the station to meet Gandhi. Dada Abdulla's reputation was such that his will was done and Gandhi had a parade of traders visiting to give him comfort and tell him their stories of similar insults over which they had been unwilling to fight. In the evening the next train arrived with a first-class berth reserved for Gandhi – the protests had brought a result. Being the agent of a powerful man such as Dada Abdulla added practical power to moral indignation; it was a lesson well worth knowing.

When Gandhi arrived at Charlestown and proceeded on the next leg of his journey, which had to be by stagecoach as there was no rail link, he experienced another display of racism. First he was told, mendaciously, that his ticket was 'cancelled', then when he stood his ground he was allowed to approach the coach but the conductor refused to allow him to sit inside. The conductor normally sat next to the driver but he gave this seat to Gandhi and sat inside the coach. When the coach stopped, however, the conductor wanted to smoke and ordered Gandhi down. 'Sami, you sit on this,' he ordered, telling his passenger to sit on the running-board.[6] Gandhi refused to sit at his feet, but was prepared to sit inside. The conductor began to strike him and tried to drag him down. Now the passengers started to protest, thereby teaching Gandhi a valuable lesson – that injustice played out in public is likely to stimulate protests from the apparently disinterested. The passengers were prepared to allow Gandhi to sit with them rather than witness a beating. But rather than tolerate such a breach of racial protocol the conductor ordered a black servant who was sitting on the other side of the coachbox to sit on the footboard, and Gandhi took the servant's place.

When he reached Johannesburg, in the Boer territory of the Transvaal, it was night. Gandhi called a cab and was taken to the National Hotel but they said they had no room. He went to the home of an Indian associated with Dada Abdulla's company and was welcomed there, where more people told him tales of insult and unjust treatment. They laughed that he had expected the National Hotel to give him a room and told him that when he set off for to Pretoria he would have to travel third-class.

He ordered a first-class ticket and picked it up from the station master who, by chance, was a European but not a Boer and was not inclined to refuse him, but he could not speak for the railway guard. Sure enough, when the guard came to collect tickets in the first-class compartment he ordered Gandhi to go to third-class. Again, it was an ordinary passenger who protested, the only other person in the compartment, an Englishman who defended Gandhi's right to travel first-class with the appropriate ticket.

In Pretoria, he again found trouble when seeking a hotel but a black American traveller directed him to one run by an American. He was allowed a room, but not to dine with other guests; he must eat in his room. Later, instead of a waiter arriving with his dinner, the patron came: 'I was ashamed of having to ask you to have your dinner here,' he said. He had spoken to the other guests and none objected to Gandhi's dining with them, so he joined them.[7]

These details of petty racial prejudice are worth noting because it was here that Gandhi observed the state as it functioned on the ordinary level. The problem was not so much major laws that oppressed a racial group in particular areas of life, but everywhere, every interaction between the whites and other races was oppressive – an oppression which was mitigated from case to case by decent people for whom such a state of affairs was clearly an abomination. Gandhi was personally offended, but more importantly he was morally outraged. Worse than this, he was ashamed of his Indian fellow sufferers for putting up with such treatment.

Gandhi showed himself an excellent lawyer in preparing the facts of Dada Abdulla & Co.'s case, which entailed the huge sum of £40,000. Having mastered the case, however, he realised that if it went to court it could ruin both the plaintiff and the defendant, Tyeb Khan Mohammed, who were relatives. Lawyers' fees were devouring all their resources and their time was so occupied with the case that they could do little else. Gandhi successfully persuaded them to hand the case over to arbitration at which his client won (perhaps he would not have suggested arbitration if he had felt his client would lose). Gandhi then succeeded in negotiating an agreement between the parties which allowed payment by instalments, so the loser did not have to go bankrupt. He remarked joyfully: 'I realised that the true function of a lawyer was to unite parties riven asunder.'[8] He would not find universal agreement on that assessment, but he received the respect of influential men in his community for his skills; he had become a person to whom others would listen.

His solicitor in the case (Gandhi was a barrister who would plead in court, having been prepared by a solicitor) was Albert Baker, a lawyer and director of the South African General Mission that worked to bring Africans to the Christian Church. Baker was a fundamentalist Christian of the best type: he believed salvation could come only by accepting Jesus as the son of God, but preached his doctrine with an indifference to colour or rank that transcended the divisions of South African society. Baker helped Gandhi to find a place to stay, and Gandhi, eager to learn about other religions, attended prayer meetings with Christians, who attempted to convert him – without success, though he read the books his new friends offered him. At this time he was said to have read about eighty books on religion.[9]

As he could be harassed by the police while out at night, a Quaker friend took him to meet the State Attorney Dr F.E.T. Krause, who had been called to the British Bar via the same Inn as Gandhi. He was sympathetic and gave his young colleague a letter saying he could be out of doors at all hours. He also introduced Gandhi to his brother, the public prosecutor in Johannesburg. Gandhi was thus creating a network via the law and his Christian friends that would prove invaluable in his work for the Indian community.

Gandhi writes that early in his life in Pretoria, while he was working on the Dada Abdulla case, he determined to get in touch with every Indian living there with a view to understanding their lives and improving them. 'My first step was to call a meeting of all the Indians in Pretoria and to present them with a picture of their conditions in the Transvaal,' he wrote.[10] To this end, he made the acquaintance of his client's adversary Tyeb Khan Mohammed, the most powerful Indian in the Transvaal – he does not suggest that such contact was unusual behaviour for a lawyer, which is an indication of what an unusual member of his profession he was.

So he called a meeting in June 1893 at the house of a Muslim whose acquaintance he had made. Most of those present were Muslim merchants, whom he urged to forget communal, religious and provincial distinctions in a common Indian interest. He stressed the idea that business and truth were not incompatible, and that religion and practical affairs should go hand in hand. In his first recorded moral preaching to what would become his community he declared that he was 'awaken[ing] the merchants to a sense of their duty, which was twofold. Their responsibility to be truthful was all the greater in a foreign land, because the conduct of a few Indians was the measure of that of the millions of their fellow-countrymen.'[11] Secondly, they needed to clean up: he drew their attention to the Indians' poor sanitary habits 'as compared with those of the Englishmen around them'; and finally he urged them to learn English, offering his services to those few young men who wished to do so.

In other words he gave them a pep talk rather like those delivered by head teachers to their charges impressing upon them that they were ambassadors for their school or, in this case, for their nation, and that they had to set aside bad habits. Why they consented to be so addressed about the morality of their trade and of their daily lives is questionable. Curiosity must have played a part, about a man who had been educated in England and had been brought to South Africa in the expectation that his abilities would be useful. The fact that he was already in the confidence of the most powerful men in the community also helped him to gain an audience.

Gandhi offered a complete self-improvement package: moral uplift (truth in business), practical advance (sanitation) and education (learning English). It is telling that it was the British he wanted to impress with his raising of the living standards of his compatriots, rather than the Boers, in one of whose republics he was speaking. Perhaps he thought the Boers were too much of a hard case to crack whereas the British were more tractable and open-minded, or perhaps he was using 'Englishmen' as a generic term for 'white'.

Doubtless Gandhi addressed the subjects he said he did. However, in his autobiography he omits any political context so as to make his engagement with the Indian traders entirely a matter of moral leadership; it is a characteristic of his biographical writing that it reflects his concerns at the time of writing, in this case the 1920s, rather than applying a historical perspective. His own writings and, even more strongly, later pictures of this period present South Africa as a *tabula rasa* before he began to make his impression upon it, as if he alone were able and willing to fight against the racial oppression of the Indians, who had apparently done nothing for themselves before his arrival. In fact there were already powerful Indian self-help organisations acting within the community, and there had already been some engagement in political activity.

As Gandhi told it, he became the reluctant hero of the next stage in the story of South African democracy. He had completed his work on the Dada Abdulla case and was to return to India. When he arrived in Durban, in Natal, he chanced to see a paragraph in a newspaper under the headline 'Indian Franchise'. It concerned a bill then before the House of Legislature of Natal which sought to deprive Indians of their right to elect members of the legislative assembly. At a farewell dinner given for him he drew this to the attention of Dada Abdulla, who replied: 'What can we understand in these matters? We can only understand things that affect our trade. As you know, all our trade in the Orange Free State has been swept away. We agitated about it, but in vain . . . What can we know of legislation?'[12] He explained that the Indians had registered to vote in order to support Harry Escombe, a European lawyer who had worked as a legal adviser to Abdulla's firm, and it was because of their involvement in this that moves had been taken to disenfranchise them.

It is clear that Dada Abdulla, despite protesting his lack of interest, did know something about the politics of South Africa. White settlers were resentful of the success of Indian traders, and Indians had consequently been expelled from the Orange Free State; they were understandably anxious about their position in Natal and the Transvaal. They did not need a Gandhi to tell them their future was uncertain. Dada Abdulla headed the Durban Indian Committee that met on an ad hoc basis to discuss subjects affecting the trading community. The year before Gandhi's arrival the committee had sent a list of grievances to the Natal Colonial Secretary which had been dismissed out of hand. This may have accounted for apparent Indian indifference over the franchise bill – they knew there was no official regard for their opinions.

They were encouraged by Gandhi's eloquence, however, and other guests joined in, begging him to stay – 'and we will fight as you direct us'. The merchants seemed quite aware of the significance of the bill, which might well be a prelude to an attack on their commercial interests. Gandhi, as a currently unemployed lawyer who was fluent in English and Gujarati and well connected in the community among both the Indians and the English, was ambitious to make his mark. The traders offered him fees for his services, which he refused, saying he should take no fees for public work. This was a typically magnanimous gesture on Gandhi's part but one that put all those for whose interests he worked in his debt, whereas accepting payment would have made him their servant.

Gandhi immediately displayed the organisational zeal and attention to detail that were to distinguish the next fifty years of his public life. The bill disenfranchising Indians was about to pass its second reading.

He therefore first called for more time to prepare his case, sending a telegram to the Speaker of the assembly asking him to postpone discussion of the bill. The Speaker responded well to this audacious request and gave the Indians two more days. Gandhi then wrote a petition arguing that Indians 'had a right to the Franchise in Natal', had it copied by hand and the merchants went out in their own carriages or hired vehicles to obtain as many signatures as possible. Newspapers printed the petition and responded positively to it. The bill went on to pass its second reading, but Gandhi counted it a victory that the community had been mobilised and organised a larger petition calling for the bill to be vetoed at its next stage. Teams of volunteers gathered ten thousand signatures for the new petition and presented it to Lord Ripon, Secretary of State for the Colonies. In response Ripon disallowed the bill for introducing a specifically racial distinction into the franchise, and another, murkily worded bill was passed which admitted to the rolls only voters whose native countries had the parliamentary franchise – Indians had only a municipal franchise in their homeland and so were excluded in South Africa.

Gandhi was persuaded to stay in Natal by his fellow countrymen, who implored and flattered him, and he finally consented. He continued to insist on receiving no payment for his public services but contended that he needed at least £300 a year to run an independent household. He felt he could not add to the credit of his community unless he lived in a style appropriate to barristers. He would stay if they guaranteed that income from legal work; about twenty merchants therefore awarded him a retainer, and Dada Abdulla furnished his new home, Beach Grove Villa, a two-storey house with an iron front gate and a veranda overlooking the beach in Durban.

Gandhi later claimed that he saw practice as a lawyer as 'a subordinate occupation' to public work but, having found his vocation in representing public protest movements, he still had to remain in practice to make a living. The Law Society of Natal opposed his application for admission to the Supreme Court as a barrister, but Gandhi had sensibly asked two Europeans for the necessary letters of recommendation to vouch for his good character. He had his application presented by the now Attorney General Harry Escombe, who had been an adviser to

Dada Abdulla & Company and was Gandhi's next-door neighbour at his new residence. The Law Society asked for further particulars about Gandhi, which were supplied, after which it continued to oppose his application. When it was finally heard the court declared it could see no distinction in law between whites and non-whites and allowed him admission. He was, however, asked to remove his turban and this time he was prepared to do it: it was one of those occasions when Gandhi compromised a small issue of principle in pursuit of the fruits of more important battles. His dress at this time included a European suit, a wing collar, a tie and polished shoes.

The Indian traders founded the Natal Indian Congress on 22 August 1894 to 'cope with the legislative activity, of a retrograde character, of the first Responsible Government of the Colony with regard to Indians'.[13] Though membership was open to 'any person approving of [its] work' the annual fee of £3 limited its membership to the relatively wealthy. Gandhi took to collecting the subscriptions and discovered the truism of voluntary organisations: that it is easier to extract money when there is an exciting event on which to focus; the maintenance of the organisation stimulated no such enthusiasm.

The Muslim traders had a community of interests in their businesses but Gandhi struggled to have them see their collective identity as Indians. The Natal Indian Congress had as one of its objectives the alleviation of the suffering of the indentured labourers, who were Hindus; Gandhi also urged his compatriots to accept that Christian Indians were Indians too. 'I felt this class should be claimed as our own,' he said; 'did they cease to be Indians because they had become Christians?'[14] Gandhi was only theoretically successful in his attempts to widen the remit of the Congress's work. The organisation in fact emphasised protection for the trading and social status of Indian businessmen which meant they were an essentially conservative organisation that was not inclined to challenge the existing social order. The Congress had to ensure that traders continued to enjoy the privileges that their wealth and entrepreneurial abilities merited. By the same token the assumed racial inferiority of 'coloureds', those of mixed race, and of Africans was written into the traders' attempts to maintain their own position.

Whether Gandhi appreciated these contradictions at the time is uncertain. Politically he recognised the divisions Europeans imposed on the society they ruled. As he said to an audience in 1896: 'Ours is one continual struggle against a degradation sought to be inflicted upon us by the Europeans, who desire to degrade us to the level of the raw kaffir whose occupation is hunting, and whose sole ambition is to collect a certain number of cattle to buy his wife with and, then, pass his life in indolence and nakedness.'[15] He appealed to Lord Ripon, Secretary of State for the Colonies, not to allow the ill-treatment of the Indians, which would cause them to 'degenerate, so much so, that from their civilised habits, they would be degraded to the habits of the aboriginal natives'.[16] In writing about the Africans nearly thirty years later, in 1924, he would comment: 'It is only vanity which make us look upon the Negroes as savages. They are not the barbarians we imagine them to be.'[17]

The spiritual equality among Gandhi's nonconformist Christian friends contrasted with the inbuilt inequality of Hinduism, in which a person was born a Brahmin or an untouchable and had to live out his or her life according to the rules laid down for the respective groups. Gandhi later thought of his own racial humiliations as 'the reward' for untouchability. He remarked after an English barber in Pretoria had refused to cut his hair: 'We do not allow our barbers to serve our untouchable brethren. I got the reward for this in South Africa, not once, but many times, and the conviction that it was the punishment for our own sins saved me from becoming angry.'[18] He was certainly promoting an ecumenical approach to life, dining with Christians, Muslims and Parsis and even inviting an untouchable to live with him. It is notable that Gandhi thinks of *himself* as experiencing a humiliation as a punishment for the collective 'sins' of Hindus. Why should that have been, unless he felt himself marked out for some role as a man of destiny?

Another theme in his life, that of caring for the poor, now begins to be mentioned in his record whereas it had not been a feature earlier. Gandhi had previously, in Kathiawar, London and South Africa, been concerned with the middle class – first public servants, then lawyers, then merchants. 'Service of the poor has been my heart's desire,' he remarks, not obviously relating this to any time period. He tells in his autobiography of how in 1894 as a twenty-five-year-old lawyer he received a visit from a Tamil indentured labourer who had been severely beaten by his employer who had broken his two front teeth. Gandhi, using the interpreting services of his clerk who was also a Tamil, sent the wretched man to a doctor who certified his injuries, then took him to a magistrate who issued a summons. Armed with this, Gandhi went to the man's master, a leading European citizen of Durban, and gave him his options: to be prosecuted or to release the indentured servant from his employ. The European, doubtless amazed at Gandhi's temerity, took the latter course and Gandhi found a decent European (no Indians kept indentured labourers) with whom the man could serve out his term.

The incident shows Gandhi's commitment to taking the moral course of action in the public sphere – and his confidence that the British authorities would support him in a just case, which was an important part of his advocacy. He talks of indentured labourers now considering him as their friend and a stream of them pouring through his office, so he 'got the best opportunity of learning their joys and sorrows'.[19]

The government in Natal attempted to impose an annual tax of £25 on indentured Indians who wished to stay in South Africa after their period of indenture had expired. The objective was to make it unprofitable for them to remain and prevent the further development of the Indian minority who, it was feared, were prospering in such a way that might threaten the small white community. The Natal Indian Congress opposed the tax at any level. Their opposition doubtless contributed to its reduction to £3 per adult, though it was still a bitterly resented imposition that was not remitted for almost twenty years. Much more in line with the Natal Indian Congress's core concerns, as a middle-class pressure group, was the proposal by the government to introduce a bill 'providing that no person of Asiatic race, birth or descent should be allowed to take out a licence for the purpose of trading as a storekeeper', which was dropped in 1894.[20]

Gandhi, and the Indians in South Africa generally, had confidence in the justice of British rule. Believing it to be on the whole beneficial to the ruled, they sang the national anthem at their meetings. The Indians of Natal and the Transvaal sent an address to Queen Victoria on her Diamond Jubilee in 1897, drafted by Gandhi, which said, 'We are proud to think that we are your subjects, the more so as we know that the

peace we enjoy in India, and the confidence of security of life and prosperity which enables us to venture abroad, are due to that position.'[21]

Gandhi, as a citizen of more than one world, could see how the Europeans viewed the Indians: he remarked on 'our indifference to the laws
of hygiene and sanitation, our slowness in keeping our surroundings
clean and tidy, our stinginess in keeping our houses in good repair'.[22]
This made him a rather more balanced nationalist than the many who
remarked on the victimhood of their race or argued for the superiority
of their own culture. He was also undergoing experiences that led him
to question the accuracy of received notions about the superiority of
the upper castes. When, briefly back in India in 1896, he volunteered
to work on a sanitation committee at a time of plague in Rajkot, he
found the standards of hygiene of the rich to be disgusting; the poor
were at least prepared to improve their condition, while the homes of
the untouchables were clean, however lacking in possessions.

Gandhi had a cook at Beach Grove Villa, various of his clerks boarded
with him and he often had English and Indian guests, so his house was
an embryonic form of the communities he was later to set up. His trusting
nature was again exposed as a weak point when he invited Sheikh Mehtab,
his old childhood friend, to live with him when Mehtab arrived in Natal.
Gandhi took him in as a companion and effectively as manager of his
household. He was always attracted to bad boys – he felt he could reform
them. He does not seem to have been inoculated by his experiences in
his youth against Mehtab's sly character.

Gandhi took heed one day when Mehtab criticised an office clerk
who was also staying at Beach Grove Villa, becoming suspicious of the
clerk, who at the first suggestion of mistrust angrily left the house, and
Gandhi's employment. Gandhi's cook took it upon himself to expose
Mehtab. He fetched Gandhi from his office, not telling him why he
wanted his master home early for lunch that day. When they reached
the house the cook led him upstairs to Mehtab's room. Gandhi knocked
loudly on the door and Mehtab opened it – he had been having sex
with a prostitute. Gandhi immediately cast him out, saying he would
never have anything to do with him again. Mehtab threatened to 'expose'
him, at which empty threat Gandhi said he would call the police. His
former friend left. Gandhi was distraught: he felt that 'in the attempt to

reform him I was ruining myself'.[23] His final word on the 'the long tale, pleasant as well as pathetic', of his relationship with Mehtab was that 'he continued to worship me from a distance'.[24]

Objectively, the offence was less serious than Gandhi made it out to be: sexual licence does not, as Gandhi seemed to think, denote an irredeemably vicious character; his response was extreme, as it usually was with sexual matters. It was the case, however, that in conservative South Africa it would have put him outside respectable society if he permitted his house to be used for assignations with prostitutes. There is also the element of miscegenation: the prostitute was probably African – Indian men vastly outnumbered Indian women in South Africa – so such sex would be doubly disparaged in the racial state.

Gandhi puts this episode of misplaced trust in a cosmic setting: 'God came to the rescue... The cook had been almost a messenger sent from heaven.' The wise cook (who, incidentally, was said to be very bad at his job) also left Gandhi's employment, complaining that Gandhi was too easily misled. Doubtless for the same reason the innocent clerk, whom he had suspected, would not be reconciled with Gandhi even after he had apologised.

Gandhi resumed his experiments with 'vital food', eating only raw vegetables, cereals, fruit and nuts until ill-health forced him to revert to a more sensible diet. He would always consider, though, that control of the needs of his body would lead to control of the outside world – a very dubious proposition. His sanctimonious streak irritated even those who had shown him friendship. At one time he had a standing invitation to have Sunday lunch with a simple Christian family who were good enough to accommodate his dietary requirements, yet he was still unable to resist exhorting their five-year-old son to vegetarianism: 'I spoke derisively of the piece of meat on his plate and in high praise of the apple on mine.'[25] This, together with his comparing Buddha with Jesus, unfavourably to the latter, led to their mutually agreeing he would visit them no more.

After three years in South Africa Gandhi returned to India for a visit, taking the opportunity of travelling by boat to Calcutta, for self-improvement as usual: he found an Urdu-speaker among the other passengers to help him learn the language, which was mostly spoken among the Muslims of India. He also bought a self-help book to teach himself Tamil so he could communicate with the Indians of the Madras area, from which most of the indentured labourers came.

Later on this journey, when he missed his train at Allahabad he characteristically used the time fruitfully and sought an interview with the editor of one of India's leading newspapers, the *Pioneer*. He was impressed by Gandhi and said he would publish material on the Indians in South Africa, though he would not commit the paper to support the Indian cause there. Gandhi was pleased, asking for no more than a fair hearing; he believed the facts alone would win the argument. This meeting encouraged him to feel there was an audience for his work, and back in Rajkot he engaged in his first major writing project, a description of the conditions of Indians in South Africa; he took a deliberately subdued tone as he did not wish to be accused of exaggeration and he knew that distance would anyway lend power to his argument.

He had ten thousand copies printed of *The Grievances of the British Indians in South Africa: An Appeal to the Indian Public*, which became known as the Green Pamphlet from the colour of its cover. Gandhi had copies sent to every newspaper and party leader in India. For the work of wrapping the leaflets and addressing them he used the volunteer labour of his sons and local children. The *Pioneer* covered the leaflet, as its editor had promised, publishing an article based on it, that was picked up by Reuters news agency in London and distributed in a truncated form by them, to Natal among other places. It was Gandhi's first appearance on the international stage, though it did not name him: 'A pamphlet published in India declares that the Indians in Natal are robbed and assaulted, and treated like beasts, and are unable to obtain redress.'[26]

With the active assistance of Pherozeshah Mehta, the barrister who had previously advised him and who was a leading member of the local authority the Bombay Corporation, Gandhi organised a public meeting in Bombay. Mehta, the dominant figure in nationalist politics, would be knighted for services to the British Empire in 1904. He advised the young man not to extemporise as he had intended, but to write out his speech and print it. Pherozeshah chaired the meeting and encouraged the still hesitant Gandhi to speak up. Eventually he gave the prepared speech to a supporter who was a fine orator, and the audience received it with enthusiasm. Gandhi travelled around India meeting influential people and educating them as to the conditions of Indians in South Africa. By thus working on behalf of the Natal Indian Congress he was demonstrating his qualifications for national campaigning when he returned more permanently to India. He made a point of meeting the two leading contenders for Pherozeshah's position of pre-eminence in the nationalist movement: Bal Gangadhar Tilak and Gopal Krishna Gokhale. He found Tilak uncongenial but said he 'fell in love with' Gokhale who was impressed by Gandhi and assured him of his support.[27]

He went on to Madras, impressing the Tamil people with his tale of the beaten labourer whose indenture he had transferred to a decent employer. In Calcutta he faced an uphill struggle in interesting people who felt they had troubles enough of their own. He was attempting to organise a public meeting in the city when he received a cable from Durban calling him back to South Africa.

He had returned to Rajkot where he had been reunited with his wife whom he had not seen for three years, and his two sons, to whom he was a stranger. With her eldest sister-in-law head of the Gandhi household, Kasturbai had been living as an inferior wife. She knew little of Gandhi's life. Since she was illiterate he did not write to her; she would have heard his formal letters to his brother read out. From this she would have known that he was prospering and that from his successful law business he was able to pay off the debts incurred on his behalf for his education. His self-assurance and evident success must have pleased Kasturbai. He told her he was ready to take her back to South Africa with him and she would doubtless have been thrilled to know she was getting her own house at last, even if in another country.

Gandhi travelled with his wife, his sons and Gokaldas, son of his widowed sister, on the *Courland*, a ship owned by Dada Abdulla & Company; their passage was supplied by the owner, gratis. The most respected Asians in South Africa were Parsis, so Gandhi had his wife dress in the fashion adopted by Parsi women: a long sari, long-sleeved blouse, socks and shoes; the boys wore Parsi coats and trousers. Thus he hoped his family would be considered respectable. He had Kasturbai practise wearing shoes and socks on the deck of the ship from Bombay to South Africa, insisting she wore them all day, which she found onerous. He also taught them to eat with utensils, sitting at a table and coming to terms with the unaccustomed bland European food.

The crossing was stormy but Gandhi was a good sailor and he was able to move among the passengers, encouraging and comforting them. After eighteen days the *Courland* and another ship of Dada Abdulla's that had shared the crossing arrived at Durban. Health officials came aboard and ordered that the ships be held in quarantine – this was standard procedure if a vessel came from an area where there had been plague. The ships' captains and owners dutifully acceded, but after five days the quarantine was extended. It became clear to Gandhi from reports that reached him from Dada Abdulla & Co. that the bacillus being denied entry into South Africa was himself. The scaremongering story was that Gandhi was coming back bringing hundreds of new immigrants who would be fighting for their rights. The charges of racial discrimination laid in the Green Pamphlet had been circulated in Natal, initially because of the Reuters report based on the *Pioneer* article, but coverage continued with accounts of Gandhi's speeches in India.

The government wanted to intimidate the immigrants into returning to India or, more realistically, keep them at bay until public attention had turned elsewhere. Huge meetings of angry whites were called in Durban, under the banner of organisations with names like the European Protection League and the Colonial Patriotic Union, which issued threats to Dada Abdulla & Co. to induce them to turn the ships around; there were even offers of compensation for the company if it did so. The quarantine lasted over the Christmas period. On Christmas Day Gandhi and his family were invited to dine with the captain. Gandhi made an after-dinner speech, talking earnestly on 'Western civilisation' when in fact the occasion called for a lighter touch. 'I deplored the civilisation of which the Natal whites were the fruit, and which they represented and championed,' he later remembered. [28]

He bore heavily the burden of the danger he had brought to the company. He knew he had led the generous Dada Abdulla on a course that would oblige him to fight for principle, rather than simply trading, and he had jeopardised the lives of his own family and the other passengers, for threats were being made that the passengers would be drowned before the mob would allow them to land. Any pretence that the question was one of quarantine had long since passed; the quarantine officer admitted that he was receiving his orders direct from the government. Finally on 11 January 1897, after being detained for twenty-three days, the *Courland* and the *Naderi* were allowed to dock and the passengers to disembark. Crowds of white demonstrators assembled to prevent the immigrants coming ashore. Harry Escombe was able to disperse them only by giving an assurance that the 'Indian question' would be dealt with in an early session of parliament.[29]

Gandhi had been advised by a message from Harry Escombe, who had no wish to see public disorder over Gandhi or the immigrants, that he should not himself disembark until dusk and that the port superintendent would escort him and his family home. Dada Abdulla & Company's lawyer Frederick Laughton, however, suggested that Kasturbai and the children should go to the house of a Parsi friend, Jivanji Rustomji, while Gandhi and Laughton would enter the port on foot. He was concerned about the dignity of the enterprise and Gandhi's pride was touched – he did not want to enter by stealth as if he were ashamed of the views he had put forward or afraid of his enemies.

So he went ashore with Laughton, but as soon as he did so some children recognised him and started shouting his name. Around half a dozen men joined them, Laughton hailed a rickshaw in which to escape, but the frightened rickshaw boy ran away.

The crowd quickly grew, Laughton was grabbed and separated from Gandhi, who was then pelted with stones and other missiles – someone snatched his turban and others kicked and pummelled him. He began to faint and caught hold of the railings in front of a house to steady himself but the blows kept coming. Jane Alexander, the wife of the Durban police superintendent, saw the commotion and, armed only with her parasol, stepped in between Gandhi and the mob to protect him, shouting 'Cowards!' at his assailants. As they could not harm him without harming her, the mob desisted.

An Indian who had seen the attack ran to the police station to alert them, and a police posse was sent out to escort Gandhi and disperse the crowd. Richard Alexander, the superintendent, suggested he take refuge in the police station but Gandhi, failing to understand crowd behaviour, declined the offer with 'They are sure to quiet down when they realise their mistake. I have trust in their sense of fairness.'[30] So, escorted by police, he went in broad daylight to Jivanji Rustomji's home where his wife and children were already waiting; doubtless, they greeted the sight of the bruised and bloodied Gandhi with horror.

The mob now knew where Gandhi was and as night drew on, a crowd gathered outside the Parsi merchant's house as word spread of their target's presence there. They called for Gandhi to be delivered to them, and threatened Rustomji. Superintendent Alexander arrived with reinforcements but realised the situation was beyond him, and feared the mob would raze the house to the ground. He sent a message to Gandhi that if he wanted to save Jivanji Rustomji's house, and his own family, he should escape in disguise. Gandhi had been asked this twice before – by Harry Escombe when he was on the ship and by Alexander when they were passing the police station. Now Alexander had got the measure of the man: by appealing to his interest in protecting others, he finally had Gandhi do the sensible thing and lie low under police protection.

Alexander kept the crowds occupied by leading them in a song that went 'Hang old Gandhi/On a sour apple tree', while inside the house Gandhi was dressed in a police uniform with a helmet improvised out of a tin pan held on his head by a shawl. Thus disguised and accompanied by two detectives he slipped out through a neighbouring warehouse, through the still violent crowd and into a waiting carriage. Once the superintendent had been informed of his safe arrival at the police station, he told the crowd that Gandhi had escaped them. When some refused to believe his story, Alexander invited them to appoint a few representatives to search the house. After submitting the hospitable Rustomji to this indignity, the mob at last broke up.

Harry Escombe later offered to prosecute Gandhi's assailants, if he could identify them, but Gandhi refused, somewhat querulously telling Escombe that the crowd's leaders were to blame as well as Escombe himself for failing to guide his people. Gandhi accused him of believing that he, Gandhi, had made statements exaggerating the reprehensible behaviour of the whites in Natal, whereas he should have waited for the evidence. Ignoring Gandhi's charge, Escombe now saw a way to draw this ugly incident to a close. He told him that if he did not press charges it would help him in restoring quiet and enhance Gandhi's reputation. Wily administrators such as Escombe were already learning to play Gandhi, appealing to his most 'Gandhian' instincts, which would also serve their interests.

Gandhi had not, from this adventure, grasped the message (though that is implicit in his later account) that discretion was the better part of valour and that he should have taken Harry Escombe's advice and crept out of his friend's house after dark. The proposition that sometimes the authorities act in the best interests of law and order was not one that he favoured. The moral he drew from the event was the typically Gandhian one that a public display of forgiveness to his attackers would be so remarkable that it would make the Durban Europeans ashamed of their conduct.

His decision not to prosecute had an immediate international effect: for the first time Gandhi came to the attention of the British Empire. In India, the Viceroy expressed concern at the attack on him; in London the Colonial Secretary Joseph Chamberlain called for the perpetrators to be punished. In order to release Escombe from his legal obligations, Gandhi signed an affidavit to the effect that it was his own decision not to prosecute. In fact, the publicity gained was far in excess of what would have been garnered from a court case. The Natal newspapers gave Gandhi space to explain that he had had nothing to do with organising the two shiploads of immigrants, and most were anyway not staying in Natal but heading for the Transvaal. Most importantly, nothing he had said abroad was more inflammatory than anything he said, freely and repeatedly, in Africa itself. The attention he received gave some of the Europeans cause for reflection, and also attracted clients to his law practice.

Gandhi turned this public attention to good account by making an appeal for membership and funds for the Natal Indian Congress. His experiences in South Africa had allowed him to develop a dynamic model for campaigning organisations: they should not have permanent funds, he contended, because that leads such organisations to become institutional and not responsible to the public for whom they are set up. Instead, current expenditure should be funded from subscriptions voluntarily donated from year to year, thus obliging organisations to justify themselves continuously and restraining them from becoming bigger than the causes that gave rise to them.

The publicity surrounding Gandhi also stimulated the opposition, who successfully brought in the Immigration Restriction Bill and the Dealers' Licences Bill to restrict immigration and trade, aimed primarily at Indians. The Dealers' Licences Bill in particular affected the big merchants who were the only committed supporters of the Natal Indian Congress, which now came to revolve around court cases that challenged refusals to renew old licences or to transfer licences to new premises.

The Gandhi family soon moved from the hospitable Rustomji home to Beach Grove Villa which had been closed during Gandhi's absence and where for the first time in her life Kasturbai was in charge of her own household and took the name Kasturba, which indicated her seniority. She was able to understand what a respected individual her husband had become; people were always visiting him for advice. But her home was not her own for long. Gandhi invited some of his law clerks to lodge with them, and even at one time took in a leprous beggar. The man had come begging and Gandhi, indulging his passion for nursing, dressed his wounds and invited him to stay, but his needs were greater than could be provided by an ordinary household and so he took him to a government hospital for indentured labourers. Later Gandhi would increase his health-care experience by volunteering at a small hospital for two hours every morning, leaving his routine legal work to an assistant.

Gandhi's position would have allowed him to place his children in a European school, but he did not want to benefit from favours not extended to other Indians. He anyway regarded the mission schools as inadequate, and doubtless feared they might feed his children a spiritual diet of Christianity. He therefore did not send his sons to school but engaged an English governess. Not satisfied with her instruction, he attempted to teach the children himself, but came home too late in the evening or was expecting the boys to be up too early for such exercises to be adequately described as education. Harilal, at least, spent some time at boarding school when the family returned to India. Gandhi wrote in his *Autobiography* about his failure to have his children properly educated: 'All my sons have had complaints to make against me in this matter.' He was similarly chastised by friends over this aspect of his children's upbringing, but he persisted in believing that if he had allowed them an education that other children could not have he would have 'deprived them of the object lesson in liberty and self-respect that I gave them at the cost of literary training'.[31] He thus convinced himself that he made the sacrifice of their education for their own spiritual sakes.

Kasturba found bowing to Gandhi's moral principles intolerable, even as she tried to be an obedient wife. 'I regarded myself as my wife's teacher and so harassed her out of my blind love for her,' he wrote. He had decreed that all residents of Beach Grove Villa must empty their own chamber pots, an activity that would never be undertaken (or even noted) by a Brahmin woman – an untouchable would deal with the family's excrement. If the pots were neglected, Gandhi had decided that he and Kasturba would do it rather than ask a servant – presumably to shame the occupants in the house into carrying out this chore next time. One day a clerk, a Christian but of a family of untouchables, was newly staying with them. He did not know the house rules and left his chamber pot under his bed. Kasturba knew Gandhi would empty it, and the only thing worse than doing it herself was allowing her husband to so defile himself. She therefore carried the chamber pot down the stairs and emptied it, weeping with anger that her life had come to this.

Gandhi saw her, and was angry too: he wanted her to go about the task gladly. He called to her: 'I will not stand this nonsense in my house.' 'Keep your house to yourself and let me go,' she shouted back. Gandhi writes that he forgot himself, caught her by the hand and dragged her to the gate, opened it and intended to push her out. She cried out: 'Have you no sense of shame? Must you so far forget yourself? Where am I to go? I have no parents or relatives here to harbour me. Being your wife, you think I must put up with your cuffs and kicks. For heaven's sake behave yourself, and shut the gate. Let us not be found making scenes like this.'[32]

He was ashamed, though of what is not clear – of his anger at a trivial domestic chore? That she had made him angry? Of his overreaction? He writes later of how 'the wife, with her matchless powers of endurance, has always been the victor'. He does not seem to have relented on the principle – perhaps he excused her doing night-soil duty in future, but there is no indication that he questioned the principle of a domestic regime so draconian as to touch on comedy: he was asking her not just to deal with faeces but to look happy about doing it.

As a lawyer Gandhi never defended falsity, refusing to be a willing party to deception. As this became known, judges tended to trust him, though over the course of his career he lost several thousand pounds in fees on account of rejected briefs. In addition, he felt it beneath him to sue for unpaid fees, which also cost him dear. Nevertheless, he soon became a successful lawyer with twelve staff, but this only made Gandhi feel more strongly than ever the pull of the spiritual, away from the life of luxury he was currently enjoying. His solution was to reduce household expenses so as to free up more money for public works. This started with dismissing the servants. He gives no indication that he considered alternative views: that wealth had its obligations and one of those was the employment of others; that he should allow other people to work at their own level to leave him the time to do public works that they respected; that he gave others pleasure in allowing them to serve him in the best way they could. For Gandhi, only the personal spiritual search mattered: the path to spiritual enlightenment led through small acts of self-reliance; the family was going to participate too, so Kasturba and the boys would also do household tasks.

Gandhi learned to do his own laundry, just as he had earlier learned to cut his own hair after being rejected by the English barber – as he put it, 'I freed myself from slavery to the washerman, I threw off dependence on the barber.'[33] Some of his experiments in self-improvement were risible, such as his first attempt at hairdressing and over-starching his collars, but when he determined that a course was right he was impervious to ridicule.

During these years in South Africa Gandhi was reading the Theosophical Society's English translations of the Upanishads, and (doubtless influenced by his Parsi friends) he read *The Sayings of Zarathustra*. He was also influenced by more popular works: Washington Irving's biography of the Prophet Mohammed and his successors; and he reread *The Light of Asia*, Edwin Arnold's fanciful poem on the life of Buddha, and the Koran in translation.

Leo Tolstoy's didactic works influenced him particularly. He read *The Kingdom of God Is Within You*, which discussed the Sermon on the Mount and presented Jesus not as the figure of divine ransom for man's sins but as a seer offering practical guidance on the way to live a spiritual life. Tolstoy was a significant model especially in the development of non-violence in his thinking. (Gandhi was not interested in Tolstoy's superlative fiction, while the latter's self-improving and spiritual work is not rated highly in the literary canon.)

Gandhi described himself as acting, in his early years in South Africa, as 'agent for the Esoteric Christian Union and the London Vegetarian Society'. He actively promoted the Union as representing 'the unity and common source of all the great religions of the world' and disparaged 'the utter inadequacy of materialism which boasts of having given the world a civilisation which was never witnessed before' but which had in fact given humanity 'the most terrible weapons of destruction, the awful growth of anarchism, the frightening disputes between capital and labour, and the wanton and diabolical cruelty inflicted on innocent, dumb, living animals in the name of science'.[34] He recommended the Union as 'a system of religion which teaches universality, and is based on eternal verities and not on phenomena or historical facts merely'.[35] He could see 'unmistakeable signs of a return from the materialistic tendencies, which have made us so cruelly selfish, to the unadulterated esoteric teachings of not only Jesus Christ, but also of Buddha, Zoroaster and Mahomed'.[36]

Gandhi does not seem to have come across (or at least been directly influenced by) the nineteenth-century internationalist religion Baha'i, which represents Krishna, Jesus, Mohammed and other religious figures as prophets of the one God. The monotheistic view of the divine, while acknowledging the contribution of the prophets of all religions, was common currency among thoughtful, spiritual people in the late nineteenth and early twentieth centuries. While accepting the value of other religions and combing their literature for supportive texts, Gandhi also maintained a belief in the Hindu notion of the cycle of life and rebirth, and of spiritual improvement with the ultimate aim of moksha:

escaping from the cycle of life and death. His restless search for spiritual improvement, including his experiments with diet and sex, was very much a Hindu preoccupation.

In May 1898 Kasturba had a third son, Ramdas. Gandhi assisted the doctor at the delivery – his quest for self-improvement had led him to study a book on childbirth. After this difficult birth Kasturba was confined to bed with anaemia, and Gandhi looked after her, their new baby and the older boys. A fourth son, Devdas, was born on 23 May 1900; the labour began quickly, there was no time to summon help, and Gandhi delivered the child himself. It was another difficult labour, and his witnessing Kasturba's suffering contributed to his decision to have no more children. Gandhi had sufficient knowledge of contraception, garnered during his time with the Vegetarian Society in London, but he was also moved to believe that self-control was a finer means of preventing conception than other methods.

Later, he could not remember why he had developed an enthusiasm for chastity in marriage, except that it came to him when he was in South Africa. He moved towards a vow of chastity, known as brahmacharya (though the term encompasses a wider spiritual meaning, it is generally used to mean chastity). He believed he had been influenced in this by his communication with Raychandbhai, a Jain businessman with spiritual leanings whom he had met in Kathiawar after he returned to India from London, and with whom he corresponded. Gandhi's letters from South Africa reflect the spiritual conundrums he was addressing: 'What is the soul? Does it perform actions? Do past actions impede its progress or not?' he wanted to know. 'Is it possible for a person to know for certain, while he is still living, whether or not he will obtain moksha?'[37]

He cites no particular exchange in which marital chastity was broached, but rather he pondered his relationship with his wife, as if the condemnation of 'lust' was already taken as part of the equation. 'Did my faithfulness consist in making my wife the instrument of my lust?' he asked. 'So long as I was the slave of lust, my faithfulness was worth nothing.' Kasturba's opinion was not sought at this time; 'she was never the temptress,' Gandhi remarks. She had shown no great interest in sex and he gives no indication that he made any attempt at pleasing her.

They started to sleep in separate beds, and Gandhi would go to bed only after he had exhausted himself with work. He still failed to maintain his self-imposed self-control, and did not take the brahmacharya vow for several years.

When he was discussing these thoughts thirty years later he revealed a spiritual dogmatism: 'It is the height of ignorance to believe that the sexual act is an independent function necessary like sleeping or eating. The world depends for its existence on the act of generation, and as the world is the play-ground of God and a reflection of His glory, the act of generation should be controlled for the ordered growth of the world.'[38] This peculiar notion, that the control of sex influences the functioning of the world, had its roots in these first efforts at sexual renunciation in the late 1890s in South Africa; it was to have its bizarre culmination in India in 1947. Gandhi's attempts to control his high sex drive and to condemn expressions of sexuality in others would bring his political activity into disrepute.

The causes of the Boer Wars lay within the conflicts between the two white tribes that had descended on southern Africa, displacing the Zulus who were the previous conquerors of the area. These were the Boers, of Dutch descent, who were fiercely protective of their independence, and the British, whose loyalty was to their Crown. The conflict was heightened by the Transvaal president Paul Kruger's denial of political rights to newcomers who had been attracted by the discovery of gold in Boer territory. The white newcomers, mainly British, were permitted to work but were heavily taxed; they were also refused the franchise, which was based on a residency qualification that was continually raised so as to be beyond their reach. Thus Kruger attempted to further partition the racial state, subdividing it between the favoured whites who were of Dutch descent and Afrikaans-speaking and the English-speaking British whites.

Kruger's forces attacked Cape Colony and Natal in September 1899. Gandhi had personal sympathy for the Boers out of respect for their independent spirit, but he sided with the British for a number of reasons. He had a genuine affection for them, and a belief in their generally benign influence. Despite instances of injustice, the rule of law and a belief in common decency were integral to the imperialists' notions of themselves and their mission in creating and ruling the Empire. With the British, he could appeal to a common standard of fairness. He also felt that demanding rights as a British citizen involved obligations in times of war, and that accepting those obligations strengthened the Indians' right to remain in South Africa. Further, he believed that India could achieve independence within the British Empire, so it was his duty to his people to stay friendly with them; the Boers could offer nothing in regard to India, only to give better treatment to Indians in their own lands, and they had shown no inclination to do even that.

There was a further reason why Gandhi wanted to serve the British interest in wartime: it was generally believed that the Indian was a coward who would not take risks or look beyond his immediate self-interest. Gandhi determined to challenge this, and he therefore created an ambulance corps recruited from the Indian community, and arranged training in nursing for volunteers. Both the Dada Abdulla Company lawyer Frederick Laughton and the Natal Attorney General Harry Escombe supported the plan, but the government of Natal, grateful though it was, informed Gandhi it had no need of their help.

The war went against the British in the early months, however, and it was quickly realised that Gandhi's corps would be valuable. He had assembled some eleven hundred men under forty leaders, of whom he was one, with the rank of sergeant-major. They came from the Hindu, Muslim and Christian communities and were both free and indentured (the indentured came courtesy of their masters). They were not expected to work under fire, but during the disastrous action at Spion Kop in 1900 they were asked to recover the British wounded from the field and so worked within the firing line. They would march up to twenty-five miles a day, carrying the wounded on stretchers. The Indian merchants, who were the mainstay of the Natal Indian Congress, recognised a chance to demonstrate their worthiness as citizens and donated money to support the corps and to buy gifts for distribution to the wounded.

Vere Stent, a British journalist born in South Africa, recalled seeing the stretcher-bearers on the road from Spion Kop:

After a night's work, which had shattered men with much bigger frames, I came across Gandhi in the early morning, sitting by the roadside eating a regulation army biscuit. Every man in General Buller's force was dull and depressed, and damnation was heartily invoked on everything. But Gandhi was stoical in his bearing, cheerful and confident in his conversation, and had a kindly eye. He did one good . . . I saw the man and his small undisciplined corps on many a battlefield during the Natal Campaign. When succour was to be rendered they were there. Their unassuming dauntlessness cost them many lives.

This last comment is a journalistic flourish: Gandhi specifically states that none of his men took a bullet and that the Indians in the war 'suffered hardly any loss of life'.[39]

The corps was disbanded after six weeks, when the war took a different course and the commanders decided to wait for reinforcements rather than launch any further frontal attacks. Gandhi received the British Empire War Medal and the corps was mentioned in dispatches. This official recognition and the appreciation of the Indian volunteers by the soldiers led Gandhi to believe that they had entered a period of better prospects for the Indian community. When British victory was assured (after a war waged with exceptional brutality) the former Boer republics of Transvaal and the Orange Free State were expected to liberalise their laws, thereby making conditions easier for Indians.

Thus after the war Gandhi felt he could leave South Africa because the Indians no longer needed his services and also – with typically Gandhian logic – because he was becoming too successful in South Africa and not following a spiritual path. His supporters in Natal lamented his impending departure at farewell meetings, where he was showered with gold, silver and diamond gifts. This caused a moral problem for Gandhi, as he had always argued that he worked for the community without remuneration. He suffered a sleepless night after he was presented with these gifts. He had simplified life in the family home, dispensing with ornaments and other non-essentials, so how could he now be seen wearing a gold watch or a diamond ring? He himself might decide to give the gifts away, but how could he persuade Kasturba who had been given, among other things, a gold necklace?

Ever the wily lawyer, Gandhi first converted the children to his way of thinking. He enlisted Harilal and Gokaldas who were thirteen and Manilal who was nine to persuade Kasturba. His wife knew his tricks, however, and said: 'You may not need [the gifts]. Your children may not need them. Cajoled, they will dance to your tune. I can understand your not permitting me to wear them. But what about my daughters-in-law? They will be sure to need them. And who knows what will happen tomorrow? I would be the last person to part with gifts so lovingly given.'[40]

Gandhi responded that when the time came for the children to marry they would be grown up and able to look after themselves. If their brides needed jewellery, she could ask him again then. At this she exploded: 'Ask you? I know you by this time. You deprived me of my ornaments, you would not leave me in peace with them. Fancy you offering to get ornaments for the daughters-in-law! You who are trying to make sadhus [itinerant holy men] of my boys from today! No, the ornaments will not be returned.' When she asked what right Gandhi had to take a necklace given to her and he replied that it was given because of his work, she reminded him how *she* worked for him, particularly for the people he brought to the house: 'You forced all and sundry on me, making me weep bitter tears, and I slaved for them.'

Eventually he 'somehow succeeded in exhorting a consent from her', Gandhi wrote. His account of the event (the only one extant) is not written out of self-recrimination: he remarks that he never regretted the step of returning the gifts (in fact they were placed in a trust fund to be used for public work). Of course, nothing Kasturba said would have made the slightest difference: Gandhi had not only made up his mind, he had already drafted the deed of trust giving away the jewellery before he even spoke to his children.

While the event is of biographical interest, it is also of historical importance because it shows how Gandhi came to his decisions and the pointlessness of arguing with him: he assumed a position of absolute rectitude from the start, treating any objections as merely challenges to be overcome by greater acts of spiritual determination. The leaders of the Indian National Congress and representatives of the British government were later to observe this approach with some bewilderment.

When the renunciation of the gifts became known, it of course enhanced Gandhi's stature in South Africa and also, more importantly, in India, where he was intending soon to make a splash at the Calcutta session of the Indian National Congress and propel himself into the forefront of Indian public life.

The family left for Bombay in October 1901.

4

Challenge and Chastity

The Indian National Congress had been set up to give political representation to the middle class that was emerging in Indian society in the
late nineteenth century. It was started by Allan Hume, a British
theosophist who had worked for the Indian Civil Service until he resigned,
irritated at being denied promotion because he was too pro-native. At
his suggestion a meeting of Indians had been held in Bombay in 1885
at which the proceedings began with a declaration of loyalty to Britain
and a statement that their objective was not political independence but
a better deal for Indian professionals. The Congress quickly took on the
aspirations of educated Indians and absorbed such organisations as Dadabhai Naoroji's Indian National Association. Thereafter the lawyers and
administrators of Congress met once a year to discuss how to acquire
a role in government.

Though Congress aimed to represent all educated Indians, fault lines
were evident from its inception. Muslims tended to view the organisation sceptically because of its Hindu majority, despite the presence
in its ranks of such Muslim activists as Mohammad Ali Jinnah.
Orthodox Hindus, on the other hand, were suspicious of the westernised outlook of Congress – they would have preferred a Hinduised
discourse that put the preservation of their tradition at the centre of
political life. Nor was Congress in its early years of any interest to the
common people; it made no attempt to address issues such as poverty
and the lack of essential services in health and education. Over the
years Gandhi was to struggle with all these issues, attempting to unite
in Congress's activities the three interest groups: the masses of India

whose principal concern was day to day existence, Muslim activists and orthodox Hindus.

Having settled his wife and children at the family home in Rajkot, Gandhi went on to his first Congress meeting in Calcutta. He used the train journey to lobby travelling delegates on behalf of a resolution advancing the interests of South African Indians. The lordly Pheroze-shah Mehta told him they could do nothing for Indians in the colonies when they did not have rights in their own country.

At the conference venue Gandhi made his customary inspection of the sanitary arrangements and as usual found them disgusting. He complained to the volunteers who had come to help with the meeting but they were not interested, considering such work to be fit only for untouchables. Gandhi asked for a broom and cleaned a latrine. Later he invited volunteers to help him clean faeces from the veranda outside the dormitory where they were staying, where delegates had defecated during the night. They declined, so he found a broom and did it himself.

Gandhi made a point of seeking out leading Congress members and renewing his acquaintance with some such as Tilak and Gokhale whom he had previously met. For Bal Gangadhar Tilak, also known as 'Lokamanya' (beloved of the people), Western institutions were a means to an end – to independence and a reassertion of Hindu national character. Tilak had entered active politics when the British raised the age of consent to twelve in 1891, after a child bride had died of sexual injuries; such interference with religious practice could not be tolerated. He later served a prison term for incitement to murder after publishing inflammatory articles quoting the *Bhagavad Gita* saying that no blame could be attached to anyone who selflessly killed an oppressor, after which a British administrator was assassinated. Gandhi admired but kept his distance from Tilak.

Far more amenable to Gandhi's approach was Gopal Krishna Gokhale, head of the moderates, who admired the means and methods of the West and worked within, though not for, British structures. He campaigned for social justice (via such organisations as his Servants of India Society – it was not a Congress priority) and acted more as a Gladstonian Liberal than as an Indian nationalist. Indeed, he modelled much of his approach on that of Gladstone. Gandhi hero-worshipped him, calling him 'my political guru' and treating him as a political father-figure, though Gokhale was only three years older than him.[1]

Gandhi's first experience of constitutional democracy was not a positive one. There were lengthy speeches on major resolutions, all of which had some well-known leader to back them. The final resolutions, which the subjects committee came to late at night when everyone wanted to get away, were rushed through without real consideration. Gandhi's resolution on support for the South African Indians had the backing of Gokhale, who spoke up for Gandhi when the meeting was almost over. With that mark of approval – rather than any objective sense of the importance of the motion – he was permitted to speak for five minutes. He started, but in these unfamiliar surroundings the facility he had acquired for public speaking in South Africa departed him; he read the resolution and began his introductory remarks, but despite all his lobbying he had not taken the time to study procedure. When the bell was rung to signal that he had used three minutes of his time he assumed it was telling him that his time was up, and sat down. He felt hurt because he had seen important delegates speaking for half an hour and no bell had been rung for them. His resolution was accepted but, as none were rejected, this was a qualified success. Both Gandhi and the Congress had a good deal to learn about running a successful political meeting. Nor had he endeared himself to the leadership by blaming the Indian National Congress for not acting to defend Indians in the Transvaal and Orange Free State, concluding that 'had no steps been taken in Natal, the position would be infinitely worse there today than it is'.[2] In other words, had Gandhi not organised the Indians in Natal their situation would be as bad as that in the Boer republics, which was a questionable proposition at best.

Gandhi had hoped to make an impression at Congress but this first foray into national politics had not been encouraging. In Calcutta after the Congress session he stayed with Gokhale, who introduced him to important people and praised his habits of self-reliance. Gandhi made so bold as to advise his mentor on his way of life, explaining the virtues of the simple life such as that of walking rather than taking a carriage or a train. Gokhale listened indulgently but did not change his lifestyle.

Seeing animal sacrifice at a temple of Kali in Calcutta made Gandhi reflect that 'the life of a lamb is no less precious than that of a human being', a belief he shared with the Jains of his native Gujarat.[3] He had read about the Hindu reforming organisation the Brahmo Samaj, and now met some of its members. Later, he travelled to Benares (Varanasi) where, as usual when he visited holy sites, he was disgusted by the filth. While there, he called in to see Annie Besant, leader of the theosophists, thus maintaining his contact with the religious movement that had informed his own views.

He left Gokhale in order to make a tour through India from Calcutta to his home in Rajkot during which – in a way that would be recognised as pure Gandhi – he chose to travel third-class on the trains. He carried a food box given him by Gokhale, a long coat to keep him warm, a canvas bag and a water jug; he was at this time still wearing the coat and trousers of a Parsi. He had travelled both third- and first-class in Europe and found little difference between the basic amenities. In India Gandhi was appalled at the indifference of the railway authorities to the comfort of third-class passengers, and at the dirty and inconsiderate habits of the passengers themselves which included smoking, spitting and throwing rubbish on the floors. Gandhi's idea of improving matters was to propose that 'educated men should make a point of travelling third class and reforming the habits of the people.'[4]

Gokhale had told Gandhi to settle down in his own home area, to work as a barrister and make a contribution to the work of Congress. He arrived back in Rajkot in February 1902, then settled in Bombay, which was a better location for political action. He was diffident about resuming practice, remembering his past failures and having no love for the conventions of the Bar, but he found that his experience in South Africa and his diligent attention to the Indian Evidence Act had produced a good lawyer out of unpromising material.

Without the obligations of earning a living he would never have taken to the law; but he practised medicine – his own form of it – simply because he enjoyed it and could immediately see its value. During this trip to India ten-year-old Manilal was stricken with both pneumonia and typhoid. There was no effective treatment except to keep the patient comfortable and strong enough for the immune system to fight off the infections. A Parsi doctor told Gandhi his son needed eggs and chicken broth. Gandhi told him that as the family was strictly vegetarian, it was out of the question to give him either. The doctor advised him not to be so hard on his son, but he felt that it was only in such cases that a man's faith was truly tested. Gandhi decided personally to administer to Manilal hydropathic treatment as set out in the work of a German writer, Louis Kuhne, who saw disease as the result of 'morbid matter' entering the body. Treatment was the elimination of this matter by water baths, wrapping the patient in wet sheets and other bathing-related practices. To this Gandhi added fasting, which 'could also be tried with profit', so Manilal was put on a diet of orange juice and water together with frequent three-minute hip baths.[5] Gandhi was genuinely haunted by fears that he was foisting his fads on his children, but the child's fever broke and Manilal recovered, confirming Gandhi in his confidence in the 'nature cure'. He was further to confirm the curative abilities of his remedies when he treated the broken arm of eight-year-old Ramdas with an earth poultice. He henceforth used earth, water and fasting for a variety of ailments.

Gandhi's legal practice in India was soon providing him with a living; his South African clients in particular stayed in contact, supplying him with work that needed to be done on the subcontinent. On leaving South Africa, Gandhi had promised to return if he were needed. Just as he was settling in he heard that the British Secretary of State for the Colonies, Joseph Chamberlain, was visiting South Africa as part of wound-healing exercises after the Boer War. the Indian community wanted to present their case to Chamberlain and felt they needed Gandhi to help them with it.

So Gandhi left his family in November 1902 and sailed off, expecting to be away for less than a year. The war had ended with the expectation of all four colonies uniting under one government; in the event, there was no quick progression to union but each colony continued with its own legislature and the Boers refused to have anything to do with the British central government. This was the situation that confronted Chamberlain.[6]

As the Boer War had supposedly been fought in order to promote just rule in South Africa, the Indians thought they had a reasonable chance of a fair hearing. There was a good deal of confusion over this, but many Europeans as well as Indians believed that anti-Indian ordinances had gone with the Boer defeat – certainly, anti-British laws had been repealed. Chamberlain received Gandhi's Natal delegation coldly, however. The government had made no policy statement on the position of Indians: that of the 'natives' was considered paramount. Chamberlain acknowledged that the Indians' grievances appeared genuine but stressed that the imperial government had little control over self-governing colonies, and if the Indians wanted to live in an area dominated by Europeans, they had best try to placate their immediate masters.

Having made such representation in Natal, Gandhi aimed to head next for the Transvaal, where the Boers were still predominant, in order to represent Indian concerns about their treatment. But permits were needed to travel to the Transvaal, and Indians found it hard to obtain them. Gandhi asked his old friend Alexander, the police superintendent, who obtained a pass for him.

When Gandhi arrived, the 'Asiatic Department' was set to arrest him – until they found he had a permit, which enraged them. The Assistant Colonial Secretary then received Gandhi and other delegates, and rudely explained that Gandhi would not be allowed to see Chamberlain. In the event, Gandhi's place was taken by another Indian barrister but Chamberlain was no more encouraging in Pretoria than he had been in Natal. It was an experience that would make many want to leave the region and not go back. Characteristically, given his courage in the face of danger and his willingness to enlist for a long struggle, the setback led Gandhi to feel he must stay in South Africa, particularly in the Transvaal where the oppression was worst. He set up a practice in the legal district of Johannesburg with four Indian clerks and a Scottish secretary. Soon he was to found a party, the British Indian Association. In rejoining the battle in Africa he was to present himself as a servant of the people moving from 'larger' service in India to a smaller region where he was needed more.[7] In fact, he had met with no great success in public work in India and he was finding in South Africa the political and professional opportunities that had been denied him in his home country.

His first political job in South Africa was to clean up the Asiatic Department, which was run by people whose experience of government had been gained on the Indian subcontinent and who were contemptuous of those whose interests they were supposed to protect; at least some of them were actively corrupt. After permit restrictions had been relaxed for Europeans it became apparent that Indians and other Asians, such as the Chinese, were obliged to pay bribes to officials, putting an unfair burden on them. It also meant that permits to travel and work in the Transvaal were awarded on the basis of ability to pay rather than the needs of the territory.

Gandhi collected evidence of the bribes and took it to the police commissioner, who listened patiently – it was the second time Gandhi had found a senior police officer in South Africa to be just and fair. He examined Gandhi's witnesses and was satisfied with the evidence but lamented that it was difficult to get a white jury to convict a white offender against non-whites. Gandhi refined his evidence and narrowed the case down to two officers against whom he had irrefutable proof, and warrants were issued against them. One of them absconded but the police commissioner brought him back. They were tried, but despite the evidence the jury acquitted them. Gandhi was becoming disgusted with the whole legal system, but the case had drawn attention to genuine abuses and both officers were eventually dismissed from their posts. The importance of honesty was reaffirmed and the Indian community reassured. Furthermore, Gandhi's position was considerably enhanced, bringing him more business.

Gandhi now again brought his family to South Africa. He felt he must take personal responsibility for them for two reasons: he wanted to tell his brother he would remit no more money to him, and he was about to cancel the insurance policy he had taken out earlier in order to protect his family in the event of his death. Gandhi had struggled spiritually with his obligations towards family. He had formed a study group with some theosophists, looking at Hindu scriptures in both translation and the original (as he had done when he was in London). The *Bhagavad Gita* now became the subject of the primary in-depth study of his life. He took to learning sections by heart while he did his morning ablutions, and in this way committed thirteen chapters to memory. He came to regard the *Gita* as 'an infallible guide of conduct. It became my dictionary of daily reference.' This is far from remarkable, since people of a spiritual bent do the same in respect of the Torah, the New Testament or the Koran. What is different about Gandhi is the way he wanted to interrogate the scriptures until they gave answers he felt applicable to him. 'How was one to divest oneself of all possession?' he asked. 'Were not wife and children possessions? . . . Was I to give up all I had and follow Him?'[8]

It is difficult to escape the conclusion that his family was treated like so much baggage of which he had to be divested if he wanted to reach spiritual perfection. People who are, or who have pretensions to be, great spiritual leaders have been known to renounce their families: Jesus did so, as did Buddha, though Mohammed did not – his mission was aided and encouraged by his wife Khadijah.

Gandhi's practical difficulty was that his brother Laxmidas, as head of the family, was looking after Gandhi's wife and children for which he was sending him money. Gandhi now decided that God would take care of them, so he wrote to his brother, who had supported him through all his studies and early struggles, to tell him he had given him all his savings and he should expect nothing more, as future earnings would be utilised for the good of the community. Laxmidas was deeply offended and felt Gandhi was reneging on a sacred duty to care for his family. Gandhi wrote, in a cold letter addressing Laxmidas as 'Respected Sir', that the whole community was his family. This is very similar to the answer Jesus gave when told he was forsaking his mother and brothers (Matthew 12: 46–50), but Gandhi does not refer to it.[9] Similarly, it was in what he represents as a moment of weakness that he had taken out the life insurance policy. Now he cancelled it, feeling that such a thing would rob his wife and children of their self-reliance, and that God would provide.

This dealing over his family's future was probably the most dishonest thing Gandhi ever did in his life – he knew very well that it was not God directly, but his brother Laxmidas, who would look after his wife and children in the event of his death, but his spiritual pride led him to renounce his bonds with his brother. His obligation to contribute to the family economy was clear: he had reaped the benefits of familial obligation when he was studying and struggling as a young lawyer, then instead of contributing towards the support of the next generation as custom and generosity decreed, he had discarded such obligation. Now that he had the freedom to spend as he wished, some of the public uses to which he put his money were questionable. For instance, he borrowed £1,000 from a client's account, with his permission, to support a venture for a large vegetarian restaurant in Johannesburg, but the business failed and Gandhi had to pay his client back from his own pocket.

Gandhi was always scrupulous with his accounts and expected others to be so. When a legal clerk, James W. Godfrey, had apparently lost ten shillings on the day's accounts, Gandhi held him responsible. 'He went carefully over all the accounts,' said Godfrey, 'and found that the book keeper had made a mistake, apologised profusely to me and punished himself by starving himself for three days. He said he had done me a grave wrong and had to punish himself.'[10]

Laxmidas continued to act as head of the family, and in January 1903 had arranged the betrothal of Harilal, who was fourteen, to the eleven-year-old daughter of a lawyer friend of the family. Gandhi's dismay can only be imagined – presumably Laxmidas had anticipated it and was asserting his authority over his capricious brother. Gandhi finally gave his consent when it was agreed that the marriage would not take place for many years. They married in 1906 when Harilal was almost eighteen and his bride, Gulab Vohra, almost fifteen. Laxmidas arranged an expensive wedding but when he asked Gandhi to reimburse him he declined. With less than paternal benevolence Gandhi wrote: 'It is well if Harilal is married; it is also well if he is not. For the present at any rate I have ceased to think of him as a son.'[11]

Kasturba and the other boys, Manilal, Ramdas and Devdas, arrived in South Africa early in 1904, thereby fulfilling a promise Gandhi had made to her when he had left India that either he would be back there within a year or she would come out to him. In spring that year, plague broke out in an Indian settlement and Gandhi worked in a makeshift infirmary. For the first time Kasturba directly contributed to his work, visiting Indian women in their homes to explain basic hygiene measures and how to detect plague symptoms. She had finally found a way to get through to him and he began to show the first glimmerings of respect for her.

Gandhi was described at this time as 'bright and cheerful and full of the joy of life'.[12] A British journalist, Arthur Hawks, who visited him, described entering 'a very plainly furnished office, about twelve feet square' where he met 'a little man, apparently forty years old, with a small black moustache on a face not specially dark in colour, but very bright in understanding. His voice was of the singular softness which seems to distinguish all Indians. From the opening of the conversation I was struck by his exquisite English – as natural in flow as if he had never spoken another tongue and as mellifluous in diction as it was in inflection.'[13]

Gandhi's new project in South Africa, which absorbed any spare money, was a press. Early in 1903 he had been approached by a printer and community activist, one Madanjit Vyavaharik, to help with the launch of *Indian Opinion*, a weekly newspaper that was to be published in English, Gujarati, Tamil and Hindi. It was first published on 4 June 1903, but soon found the range of languages too much to handle and reverted to English and Gujarati only. Its declared objective was for 'an Imperial and pure ideal . . . to bring the European and the Indian subjects of King Edward closer together'.[14] In spring the following year Vyavaharik, who wanted to return to India, offered the journal to Gandhi in return for loans Gandhi had made him. So Gandhi was now in control of the enterprise.

He was thirty-three years old and ambitious for influence; he had been a successful lawyer and respected in his community, but he had not been able to prevail upon Chamberlain and the authorities to accede to his point of view (or even to receive him, in the Transvaal). He had made little stir in nationalist politics in India. He simply had to move his personal project to another level: *Indian Opinion* would be the vehicle for this. The newspaper presented not so much Indian opinion as Gandhi's. He wrote for it every week, and it therefore contained the essence of his thoughts while he was working on the ideas that would make him world-famous.

The newspaper covered current events concerning the Indian community in South Africa and abroad. Foreign subjects chosen for coverage were those that were felt to reflect on the Indian scene in South Africa: the strikes in Russia in 1905; unrest over the partition of Bengal in 1906; and celebratory pieces on the Japanese victory over Russia in the Russo-Japanese War of 1905. Gandhi's future colleague Jawaharlal Nehru, thousands of miles away at Harrow School, was similarly moved by news of the first Asian defeat of a European power. Its meaning for the end of the European empires in the East was to unfold gradually over the next forty years: Japanese expansion was to form the backdrop to all regional independence movements.

Indian Opinion contained uplifting features on the lives of great Western reformers such as Elizabeth Fry, Florence Nightingale, Abraham Lincoln and Leo Tolstoy. Gandhi also gave helpful social tips such as 'Avoid, as far as possible, blowing your nose or spitting on the street or paved walks or in the presence of others . . . One should not belch, hiccup, break wind or scratch oneself in the presence of others . . . if one's spittle gets blown on to others, it annoys them . . .'[15] He penned moral injunctions against such practices as the use of tobacco: 'The evil effects of this habit become really dangerous when it spreads among juveniles. They learn to steal and commit other crimes. They deceive their parents and ruin their health. They become irritable, and by the time they become adults they lose their strength of mind.'[16] In this Gandhi was following Tolstoy, whose views on tobacco he quoted: 'the worst of all intoxicants inasmuch as a man addicted to it [is] tempted to commit crimes, which a drunkard never dare[s] to do.'[17] It is characteristic of Gandhi that, once he had accepted Tolstoy as a spiritual guide, he accepted as accurate his pronouncements on merely factual matters too.

In a quest for spiritual perfection Tolstoy had divested himself of his estates and wealth and endeavoured to live the simple life of a peasant, much to the consternation of his wife and family. It was this Western (and Christian) influence rather than anything specifically Indian that informed Gandhi's progress over the next ten years.

Politically, Gandhi repeatedly stressed the failure of the merchant elite to unite and organise, recognising their obligations to the wider community. As Maureen Swan has noted, Gandhi was 'looking always for a deficiency in the individual' rather than in institutions and the wider political climate.[18] On the positive side, there was no doubting his genuine wish to elevate his community. His failure to engage with the articulate activists in the black and coloured communities, however, meant his work was committed to subdividing the racial state to separate Indians from other non-whites. Gandhi was as much a racial purist as the Boers. He wrote in September 1903: 'We believe as much in the purity of race as we think they do, only we believe that they would best serve the interest, which is as dear to us as it is to them, by advocating the purity of all races and not one alone'. Indicating that if given citizenship rights Indians would know their place, he continued, 'We believe also that the white race in South Africa should be the predominating race'.[19] An association with the elite and racially exclusive did not fit badly with Gandhi's view of the spiritually superior man, his body purified by the right food and the chastity, his mind rarefied by contemplating the moral value of every action.

Journalism was a unifying force for the Indian community, but just as importantly, a bridge between them and those Europeans who could respect cogent arguments in print. It was through his writing that Gandhi met Henry Polak, a Jewish-English journalist who frequented the vegetarian restaurant where Gandhi ate lunch and dinner. Polak had been converted to vegetarianism by reading Tolstoy, so he and Gandhi had much in common. Polak introduced himself by complimenting Gandhi on his written criticisms of the government over the recent plague.

On the day he met Polak for the first time, in October 1904, Gandhi had to go to Durban to sort out the finances of the *Indian Opinion* press. Polak accompanied him to Johannesburg station and gave him a book of essays, John Ruskin's *Unto This Last*, to read on the journey. Gandhi found the book impossible to put down: it seemed to answer all his questions about how to put into practical effect his spiritual yearnings. The message he received from it was the Christian socialism that had become increasingly attractive in Europe in the last half of the nineteenth century: its basic premises were that the good of the individual is contained in the good of all, that there is dignity in labour and all labour is of equal value, that a life of labour is a life worth living, that each person should be able to keep himself from his own labours, that the pursuit of luxury for its own sake is to be disparaged. Ruskin's 'there is no wealth but life' is perhaps his most celebrated statement. His reputation was tarnished in the twentieth century by scholars pondering on his private life – in particular, his unconsummated marriage and his emotional attachment to little girls – but in the nineteenth century, when such things were less discussed, he was an influential visionary of culture and social organisation, promoting education, self-reliance and self-respect among the working class.

There was an endearing adolescent quality about Gandhi – reading a book that inspired him, he would often find it offered the answer to his problems and just had to put its ideas into practice immediately. He writes: 'I determined to change my life in accordance with the ideals of *Unto This Last*.'[20] Thus started Gandhi's experiments with ideal communities.

Ideas of socialist self-help had been developed in Britain by such pioneers as Robert Owen and Edward Carpenter; the latter thinker's book *Civilisation: Its Cause and Cure* was also avidly devoured by Gandhi. Socialist beliefs were discredited in the second third of the twentieth century by brutal experiments in state socialism, but they were very much the progressive alternative in the late nineteenth and early twentieth centuries. In a further development in Britain, William Morris dwelt on notions of the spiritually elevating power of art, which should be available to all. This was something that did not particularly interest Gandhi; in his model religion took the place of art. The spiritual message of work and self-reliance had evolved as a corrective to the predominantly class-based view of British society that saw manual work as low and undignified, the 'intellectual' work of the middle class as more elevated and the workless state of the landed aristocrat as best of all.

When he arrived in Johannesburg he found the press's finances in an even worse state than he had imagined. He had just installed an Englishman, Albert West, as head printer, another skilled worker whom he had met through the vegetarian restaurant and who had left a safe job in a Johannesburg print shop to follow Gandhi. The profits anticipated from *Indian Opinion* had not materialised, but West was a solid enough character to want to overcome the difficulties rather than merely complain about them. The situation he explained to Gandhi was this: subscriptions were not being collected, bills were not being paid; the newspaper was making a loss and was projected to do so for the foreseeable future. Gandhi's solution, inspired by Ruskin's book, was to move the press to a small farm on which everyone would labour to produce food for the community; everyone would draw a basic salary of £3 per month regardless of nationality, colour or the labour they performed, and *Indian Opinion* would be produced as an offshoot to this experiment in alternative living.

Albert West was enthusiastic (despite the £3 salary being £7 less than his agreed rate). 'To say I approved of the proposal suggests a certain amount of wishful thinking,' he commented later. I was certainly in love with the idea, and my love for Gandhi was sufficient to make me want to succeed in this venture.'[21] Chaganlal Gandhi, a cousin who had come over with Gandhi and was working at the press, agreed to follow the master in whom he too had put his faith. Maganlal, another cousin who was soon to become a favourite of Gandhi, also joined, though their wives were more orthodox and found communal living a trial: amongst other duties, they had to purify the brass utensils used by Gandhi's Muslim friends by putting them in the fire. Most of the ten or so workers already employed at the press rejected the new scheme, but rather than terminating their contracts Gandhi determined to keep them on their original salaries so long as they would move with the press. The editor of the paper, another Gandhi supporter and activist called Mansukhlal Nazar, was not prepared to move to the farm but was willing to continue as editor from Durban.

Gandhi now advertised for a piece of land near the railway line in Durban and soon he and West were examining a hundred acres near the station at the town of Phoenix that Gandhi bought for £1,000. The land was overgrown and snake-infested but there were fruit trees on it and a collection of dilapidated farm buildings. His old friend Jivanji Rustomji placed large corrugated-iron sheets and other building materials at his disposal, and some Indian building workers who knew Gandhi from their service in the Boer War helped to erect a shed for the press. The heavy printing equipment had to be moved from Durban to Phoenix using four wagons and sixty-four bullocks, and they had to ford three rivers to reach the settlement.

People worked all the daylight hours, sleeping in hastily pitched tents, erecting the shed, installing the press and making roads and irrigation ditches. During this time only one issue of *Indian Opinion* had to be printed by an outside press. For the first Phoenix edition, working to a strict deadline, the type was set and the paper prepared for a run that had to be printed and hand-folded ready for the morning train, for national distribution. When the press was ready to run, however, the engine failed. West was in tears; everyone feared the first Phoenix edition would not appear on time.

The only alternative was to use a wheel that had to be hand-turned and required four men to perform the task – it was so laborious that they had to work in relays. The printers were exhausted, but so were the carpenters who had been working all day on the buildings: they were now sleeping, and West was loath to disturb them. Nonetheless, Gandhi woke them and, using his special skills of persuasion, asked them to start turning the heavy wheel. They agreed and worked all night, Gandhi working beside them while West sang hymns to keep their spirits up; the edition went off in time. It was a lesson to Gandhi in how to push people beyond the supposed limits of their endurance – asked to make a further sacrifice, they willingly acquiesced.

In order to follow the plan of self-sufficiency the land was parcelled out so that each worker, Gandhi included, had three acres on which to build a corrugated-iron houses for himself. Gandhi would have preferred mud huts or peasants' brick houses but they would have cost more than corrugated-iron ones. The settlement's atmosphere was enthusiastic and happy, partly because of its experimental nature and the feelings of optimism surrounding it, and because Gandhi had not yet evolved the regulations that were to curse his future settlements. He did not try to impose chastity, for example, or the rigorous food disciplines that could make life miserable.

Back in Johannesburg Gandhi told Polak about the Phoenix settlement – in effect, the fruits of his reading *Unto This Last* – a revelation that doubtless increased Polak's admiration for his new friend. Polak forthwith handed in his notice at the magazine he worked for and went to work at Phoenix. Gandhi soon had need of an assistant in Johannesburg, however, so he invited Polak to join him, living at his home, and set about training him to be an attorney. He encouraged him to bring his fiancée Millie from England and a few months later was best man at their wedding; he was at this time encouraging his supporters to marry and have a normal family life. Millie had met Polak at the South Place Ethical Society in London; they had been delaying their wedding on financial grounds, but Gandhi assured them he would look after them.

When the Polaks were installed in Gandhi's house Kasturba had to put up with the novel experience of sharing her working areas with another woman who did not know her language or share her approach to family organisation. Recognising Gandhi's attachment to Polak, she used to call him Gandhi's 'first-born' – a not particularly subtle comment on the difference between the affection he showed for his children and that for his disciples.[22]

With the introduction of the Polaks into Gandhi's home in Johannesburg came a further drive for simplicity: he purchased a hand mill so that his family could grind their own flour to make bread. His sons also helped in the laundry and, inevitably, with the sanitary arrangements. Manilal and Ramdas, twelve and seven in 1904, were still not sent to school, but Gandhi improved on his previous efforts at educating them by asking them to work with him every day, talking to them on the five-mile walk to the office and giving them school work to do when they got there. He addressed the children exclusively in Gujarati, although Polak argued that fluent English-speaking would give the boys an advantage. Gandhi contended that knowledge of their home language would be to their country's good: having grown up in South Africa, it was important that, back in India, they did not seem like foreigners.

Gandhi encouraged some of his extended family and his friends to move to the Phoenix settlement and was soon working out a way to get Kasturba and the boys there. The opportunity was afforded him by the Zulu rebellion that came about in Natal early in 1906 when a Zulu chief, enraged by the imposition of yet another tax, advised his people to refuse to pay it and speared the tax collector. An expeditionary force went out to 'subdue' the Zulus. Though Gandhi's sympathies were with the Africans, his loyalty was with the British Empire, and applying the same logic he had used over the Boer War he asked himself what would be best for the Indian community. Indians were still considered cowardly scoundrels and Gandhi was anxious to impress again on the British that this was not so. He wrote to the Governor of Natal offering his services in organising an Indian ambulance corps (though Gandhi's home was in Johannesburg, he considered himself a citizen of Natal, and that was where Phoenix was). The Governor accepted, and within a short time Gandhi had given up the house in Johannesburg, settled Polak there in a smaller one, sent his wife and children to Phoenix and had left for Durban to recruit men for his new enterprise. He was not to live with his wife and children again for the next four years.

When Gandhi and his twenty-three men arrived in the field it was obvious there was no rebellion to deal with – he was attached to a punitive force. His main work would be to nurse Zulus wounded in the government's operations – some were suspected enemies who had been flogged and whose unattended sores had festered, while others were 'friendly' Zulus who had been shot by mistake. When Gandhi's group followed a column into the field, they encountered more of these latter casualties, as the British soldiers moved into Zulu areas. 'This was no war but a man-hunt,' he wrote.[23] He had witnessed the efficient brutality of an imperial power. After six weeks the mission was deemed completed and Gandhi returned to Phoenix. He does not say so explicitly, but his experiences in the Boer War and the Zulu rebellion must have taught him the futility of venturing a frontal military attack on the dominant nation.

During his long marches in the sparsely populated land he had fallen again to thinking about what he should do to bring himself closer to spiritual self-realisation. He came to the decision, he later recorded, that 'he must accept poverty as a constant companion through life' and that without celibacy he could not serve humanity with his whole soul: 'I should have more and more occasions for service of the kind I was rendering, and . . . I should find myself unequal to the task if I were engaged in the pleasures of family life and in the propagation and rearing of children.'[24] This is presented as a renunciation of sex and the embracing of chastity – hardly a novel concept, since it was part of Hindu and Buddhist thought, had been a Christian concept at least since the time of St Jerome and had significant influence in the Catholic and Greek Orthodox traditions. 'It is celibacy that has kept Catholicism green up to the present day,' Gandhi said.[25] In the Hindu and Jain traditions chastity was normally reserved for older men who had already had families; it has no place in Judaism or Islam. In Gandhi's formulation, it seems less a renunciation of sexual desire than a rejection of wife and family. When Tolstoy similarly renounced his sexual nature when he was writing his novella of sexual disgust *The Kreutzer Sonata* in 1889–1890, his wife interpreted it as a rejection of her.

Gandhi discussed with his cousins Chaganlal, Maganlal and others whether he should stop having sex with his wife. He had been attempting to rein in his powerful sexual urges at least since 1900, when the long marches during the Boer War had given him similar time for reflection; but he considered that he had failed in the past because his motive was not pure – he had simply wanted to have no more children. Now in mid-1906 he made a decision and announced it, 'consulting' with Kasturba only when he was about to take the vow. As usual, Gandhi was seized with enthusiasm for his new idea and encouraged others to follow suit. In December 1907 he was telling readers of *Indian Opinion*: 'Adultery does not consist merely in sexual intercourse with another man's wife. We are taught by every religion that there can be adultery even in intercourse with one's own wife. Sexual intercourse is justified only when it is the result of a desire for offspring . . . it is the duty of every thoughtful Indian not to marry. In case he is helpless in regard to marriage, he should abstain from sexual intercourse with his wife.'[26]

Gandhi's ambition had been thwarted previously, he felt, because he had not made the brahmacharya vow: 'Up to this time I had not met with success because the will had been lacking, because I had no faith in myself, no faith in the grace of God, and therefore my mind had been tossed in the boisterous sea of doubt.'[27] Once he made the vow, his sex life would no longer be a matter of self-control, but of spiritual purity, a contact with the eternal.

Now he had declared his intention, how could he control his passions? He aimed at a fully integrated physical and spiritual state so again took to experimenting with his diet, introducing fasting along with exclusive diets – of fruit only or grains only. He had found, though, that changing his diet increased the 'relish' with which his body greeted the new food. Still worse, fasting increased the appetite. Over time he continued experimenting, deciding on such restraints as not taking tea or finishing the last meal of the day before sunset in an attempt to reduce reliance on physical sensation and to eat only precisely what the body needed. 'All restraint, whatever prompts it, is wholesome for men,' he said.[28] The ideal meal should be limited, simple, spiceless and, if possible, uncooked.

Now he was extending his dietary experiments not merely from the point of view of vegetarianism, but in order to maintain his chastity. Years of dietary experiments 'showed me that the brahmachari's ideal food is fresh fruit and nuts. The immunity from passion that I enjoyed when I lived on this food was unknown to me after I changed the diet.'[29] But such diets took their toll, he wrote to a doctor friend: 'I think it was when I was carrying on a fruit-and-nut diet experiment that I damaged my teeth. I believed that I had permanently damaged two molars.'[30]

Gandhi's ideas about diet and sex seem idiosyncratic to the point of mania, but there may have been a physiological reason why different diets worked to lower his sexual urge. He had serious constipation. His later secretary Pyarelal remarked: 'before he took to naturopathy, the Mahatma was virtually a slave to Eno's Fruit Salts. Every morning he put a spoonful of it at the bottom of a tumbler, poured in water and gulped down the fizzing liquid that gave him relief.'[31] If the reference to naturopathy – the method of Gandhi's London friend Dr Thomas Allinson – is accurate, it applies to Gandhi's condition as a young man, but Pyarelal may be referring to a later adoption of naturopathic methods. While in prison in South Africa Gandhi remarked that he 'had the bad habit of taking a long time for evacuation' and was unhappy when the warden or other prisoners tried to rush him at this business.[32] He was, as usual, by no means coy about sharing his physical state with this friends: he wrote in 1909 that one should aim at a diet and eating habits (length of mastication, for example) that would produce faeces that were 'consistent, free from odour and which should leave the seat [anus] without soiling it'.[33] When Gandhi was tormented by sexual thoughts, perhaps his impacted colon was pressing on his prostate gland and stimulating him sexually. This would explain why some diets, by reducing his constipation, would help him feel less sexual.

However the physiology worked, it was thus that in 1907, armed with a newspaper, a spiritual community, a strict vegetarian diet and chastity, Gandhi felt equipped to take on what was soon to be the united South African state.

5

The Army of the Poor

Boer laws that discriminated against the British were rescinded in the wake of the Boer War, but laws discriminating against Indians were imposed. These were the fruit of the labours of a bright young administrator called Lionel Curtis, who was concerned about the apparent ascendancy of Natal Indians whose industry and accumulation of wealth were putting them within reach of equality with whites; to maintain the racial balance they had to be brought under control. Curtis had met Gandhi in 1903 when the latter had tried to convince the colonialist of the industry, frugality and patience of his countrymen. Curtis replied: 'Mr Gandhi, you are preaching to the converted. It is not the vices of Indians that Europeans in this country fear but their virtues.'[1]

Curtis was the imperial nemesis of Gandhi, a man whose ideas were to shadow him for the rest of his life. Characteristic of Gandhi's best imperial opponents, Curtis was not a man without morality or vision but his version of these qualities was entirely different from that of the Indian. Just three years younger than Gandhi, he was brought up in an evangelical Christian family and was imbued with the conviction that the distinctions between religion and politics were false: public life must reflect spiritual truth. He was to write that he saw the British Commonwealth of Nations as 'simply the sermon on the mount translated into political terms'.[2] As an Oxford undergraduate he had taken to trudging the roads in the guise of a tramp to learn the workings of the Poor Law, and later worked with the poor in the East End of London. He studied for the Bar at Gandhi's Inner Temple and volunteered for service in the Boer War. After the war he determined to play a part in reconstructing the war-torn colonies and became one of 'Milner's kinder-garten', the bright young men surrounding the outstanding colonial administrator Alfred Milner. Curtis moved rapidly through the ranks until in October 1905 he was given responsibility for Asiatic affairs. He had already submitted a lengthy report on the Transvaal Indians that was the basis of a draft of amendments to the Asiatic laws of the province in September 1906.

Curtis believed that unlimited Indian immigration would mean the end of a white South Africa, and his ideas of the moral ascendancy of Britain in the world were tied up with notions of the superiority of European civilisation. If there were too much Indian or any other kind of civilisation in the mix, the Empire could not work its moral magic. He had already proposed registration as an administrative measure, but without the force of law, and the Indians had accepted voluntary registration. Now, with the objective of tightly controlling immigration, he drafted a law that would require every Indian aged eight and older to obtain a new certificate of registration, to provide finger and thumb prints and other identifying features. The police could demand these documents at any time and could even enter private homes to inspect them.

The proposed law's terms were offensive, and if unresisted they would be a major step on the road to complete segregation, even to segregated bazaars and the end of mercantile success in the Transvaal. The problem, as represented crudely by Jan Smuts's son in his biography of his father, was that 'The Indian people were breeding like rabbits and the country was fast becoming swamped by them' – so drastic action was needed, he said without irony, 'to ensure that the country should remain white'.[3]

Gandhi studied the draft law, translated it into Gujarati and published it in *Indian Opinion*. His view was that the law was not merely oppressive in its conception but was 'the first step towards hounding Indians out of the country, designed to strike at the very root of our existence in South Africa'.[4] Gandhi discussed the ordinance with leading members of the Indian community, who shared his anxiety about it. They hired the Empire Theatre in Johannesburg to alert all Indians in the Transvaal to their plight.

The registration issue dealt a blow at the heart of the Transvaal's elite

Indian community, *raison d'être* – the right to trade freely. By drawing their families into licensing, it additionally offended against their deepest principles. An assault on wives was beyond the limits of acceptable despotism. Gandhi had asked merchants, petty traders and hawkers to close their businesses hours before the meeting was going to start so that the streets would be testimony to a dramatic event taking place. The meeting had the backing of the Transvaal British Indian Association and all the main Indian commercial interests.

Two community leaders, Haji Habib and Haji Ojer Ally, were the main attractions at the meeting on 11 September 1906. The theatre was packed with more than three thousand Indians who had come from all over the Transvaal. Habib, one of the leading Muslim residents in Johannesburg, called on God to witness that he would never bow to the projected new law and asked the audience to swear the same oath – that they would rather go to jail than submit to registration. 'There is no disgrace in going to jail,' he said. 'Rather, it is an honour. Only a few people knew of Mr Tilak before he went to jail, today the whole world knows him.'[5] Gandhi was put on the alert: making political resolutions was one thing, but if they brought God into the issue he must explain the meaning of their actions. He stood and addressed the meeting: 'We all believe in one and the same God, the difference in nomenclature in Hinduism and Islam notwithstanding. To pledge ourselves or to take an oath in the name of that God or with him as a witness is not something to be trifled with . . . I hold that a man, who deliberately and intelligently takes a pledge and then breaks it, forfeits his manhood.'[6] He set the oath in the context of personal sacrifice, saying that no majority at a meeting could bind people, that they must act as individuals and be prepared for the worst – for insult, jail, extremes of heat and cold and hard labour. He was appealing to the taste for martyrdom that he hoped would be in the breasts of his listeners, reformulating a political standpoint into a spiritual one – though Gandhi was not the first to introduce spiritual values into a political movement: the question of religious fealty had already been raised by the leaders of the Muslim merchants.

Reinvigorated by Gandhi's statements, others spoke of the seriousness of the situation, and the audience stood with hands upraised and swore before God not to submit to the Transvaal Asiatic Ordinance if it became law. The seriousness of the pledge was emphasised in *Indian Opinion*: the Indian who submits to the law 'will have forsaken his God. Secondly his honour will have been lost. Thirdly he will have incurred the curse of all India.'[7]

Gandhi had discussed passive resistance in the pages of *Indian Opinion* as early as December 1904. He had argued that if there were prosecutions for trading without a licence, the person prosecuted should refuse to pay any fines and, if necessary, go to jail: 'There is no disgrace in going to jail for such a cause.'[8] The issue of trading licences was not, however, the gut issue that could lead to heroic acts of personal sacrifice. The government was to hear the strength of the community's feeling when a deputation saw the Colonial Secretary Patrick Duncan, and Haji Habib told him: 'I cannot possibly restrain myself if any officer comes and proceeds to take my wife's finger prints. I will kill him there and then and die myself.'[9] The minister responded that the government was reconsidering its position on women, then said the clauses relating to women would be deleted.

This was seen by the community as its first victory. Although the government declared it had already decided to exempt women, this is unconvincing. Curtis was a man who tended to get carried away with his own ideas: probably the truth was that as soon as his ordinance was printed, more sober counsel prevailed, knowing that the registration of women would be inflammatory.

In keeping with the principle of making political representations at the highest level, Gandhi and Haji Ojer Ally went to London to put their case. They were aided there by Sir Mancherji Bhownaggree (who had just lost his seat in the House of Commons in the Liberal landslide of 1906), by Dadabhai Naoroji and the British Committee of the Indian National Congress with whom Gandhi had previously established links. They met Lord Elgin, Secretary of State for the Colonies and Lord (then Mr) Morley, Secretary of State for India. They were given a polite audience and on their return journey received a telegram from Elgin saying he would not advise the imperial government's consent to the Transvaal Asiatic Ordinance becoming law. This was the occasion of great rejoicing, but the victory was short-lived, as Elgin knew it would be. As part of the postwar settlement a large measure of self-government was to be conferred on the Transvaal on 1 January 1907, under which the powers of veto of the imperial power were severely limited. The Transvaal government's second piece of legislation, after the budget, was the Asiatic Registration Act of March 1907.

Indians were supposed to register before 31 July, and on that day a mass meeting was held in the grounds of Pretoria's mosque. Gandhi translated a speech in English from the government pleading with the Indians to see the administration's side of the matter: the European community had asked for the measure, it had been passed according to due process; further opposition would be futile but General Smuts (who was chief parliamentary spokesman in the now self-governing state) would look into representations regarding minor changes in the law. The meeting again affirmed their determined opposition.

The emphasis that Gandhi placed on character and spiritual strength was specific to his approach, but he had as yet no name for this new philosophy. He writes about the principle of satyagraha coming into existence before the word existed to define it. In early 1908 he held a competition among *Indian Opinion* readers to find a word to describe what they were doing – exerting moral force to oblige an opponent to comply. His favourite cousin (often referred to as his nephew) Maganlal won the competition with a combination of Gujarati words to make *sadagraha* – firmness in a good cause. Gandhi amended this, using the words for truth and firmness – *sat* and *agraha*, 'firmness in the truth'. The development of the philosophy of satyagraha in South Africa was his most important contribution to political thought. Though it is sometimes translated as 'passive resistance', that is not what Gandhi wanted to convey. He felt there was nothing passive about what they were doing; moreover, a suggestion of passivity fed into notions of Indian indolence. Satyagraha was explicitly, in Gandhi's eyes, a movement not about self-determination or racial equality but about 'truth' as defined by him.

It was interpreted by one of Gandhi's most devoted followers thus:

There is a spark of divinity on every human breast. A satyagrahi tries to make this spark burn bright in the opponent's breast by first making it do so in his or her own case. Satyagraha must therefore be based on truth and love. Suffering is undergone by the satyagrahi in order to make the opponent think and is never inflicted upon the opponent. Non-cooperation and civil disobedience in various forms, with readiness to cheerfully suffer the consequences of such action and as a last resort fasting, are the only tools that a satyagrahi has and can use. By inviting self-suffering the satyagrahi tries to make the opponent think and understand the satyagrahi's point of view.[10]

Gandhi's chief means of propagating this view was *Indian Opinion*. He was delighted that it had 3,500 subscribers at the height of the struggle, with a readership of many more, given that a single subscriber would read his copy out to a group of his compatriots. The success of the newspaper's sales meant they could stop taking advertisements and the press could stop doing jobbing work; the spare capacity was used in the publication of books of moral worth. The paper was edited, after the sudden death early in 1906 of Nazar, by Europeans: Herbert Kitchin, Henry Polak and a Baptist minister, the Revd Joseph Doke. Doke was also to write the first biography of Gandhi, in 1909. Europeans, of course, could not be imprisoned under the Asiatic Registration Act and so the essential supply of information to the nation and to the world would not be broken by the victimisation of the paper's staff.

Many of Gandhi's supporters were Europeans: he singles them out for special praise in a chapter of his book *Satyagraha in South Africa*, perhaps because their support was inspired by anything but self-interest. As Gandhi was now without a home in Johannesburg he stayed with a German architect, Hermann Kallenbach, beginning a long process of introducing him to the path of renunciation. During the course of their friendship Gandhi persuaded Kallenbach to give up milk with him and to go on a pure fruit diet. Kallenbach became one of Gandhi's best friends: they were in contact until Kallenbach's death two years before Gandhi's. He wrote to Kallenbach that he did not understand the German's 'extraordinary love' for him – 'I hope I deserve it all' – later referring to it as 'love which is almost superhuman'.[11] He believed it to be proof of their having lived before in other bodies at a previous time and loved each other then. Kallenbach was later to sign an agreement drawn up with Gandhi that when visiting family in Europe he would travel third-class, spend no more money than would a simple farmer and not look lustfully at a woman. The agreement was ratified by 'more love and yet more love' between them, 'such love as I hope, the world has not yet seen'.[12]

Kallenbach's letters may have been even more affectionate; Gandhi described them as 'charming love notes'. He destroyed them as he knew Kallenbach would not want them read by anyone else – 'everyone considers that your love for me is excessive,' he wrote.[13] Kallenbach's was the only portrait he kept on the mantelpiece in his bedroom when he was in London lobbying for the recognition of Indian rights by the imminent South African Union. There has to be a suspicion of a homoerotic attachment on the part of Kallenbach, who was two years younger than Gandhi and never married, but there is no evidence that his affection for Gandhi ever approached the physical.

Kallenbach introduced Gandhi to sixteen-year-old Sonja Schlesin as a potential secretary. 'She is clever and honest, but she is very mischievous and impetuous,' he told him. Gandhi remarked: 'In a month's time she had achieved the conquest of my heart. She was ready to work at all times whether by day or at night. There was nothing difficult or impossible for her.'[14] Like Polak, Kallenbach and another early supporter, Herbert Kitchin, Schlesin was Jewish (though none of them, apparently, was observant, Polak was notable as a theosophist). Scrupulously principled, Schlesin took over the satyagraha movement's finances when its leaders were in jail, and even controlled the direction of the campaign in those challenging times. Gandhi said she had 'a character as clear as crystal and courage that would shame a warrior'.[15] Office life did not always run smoothly. Gandhi once recorded: 'Miss Schlesin in her folly started smoking a cigarette in my presence. I slapped her and threw away the cigarette . . . [She] wrote to me afterwards saying that she would never do such a thing again and that she recognised my love.'[16]

Schlesin had bobbed hair, wore a collar and tie and had a fiercely independent spirit – she went on to take an MA and made an attempt, with Gandhi's help, to become the first woman to enter the legal profession in South Africa; he applied for her to become an articled clerk but, as a woman, she was refused. Schlesin also took courage from the suffragettes, saying in a speech to the satyagrahis: 'Let me remind you of a similar crusade now being waged by my sisters in England. I refer to the suffragettes ... Many have already suffered imprisonment, more are ready, nay eager, to do so. If delicately nurtured women can do this, will hardy men, inured to toil, do less?'[17]

The procedure of taunting the law and going to jail as a matter of political protest, followed by a celebration for the released martyr, had been tried and tested in Britain from October 1905 with the arrest of the first suffragettes. A large number of 'prison volunteers' had been arrested in London in February 1907 amid considerable publicity. The previous year Gandhi wrote with unstinting praise of the suffragettes: 'Today the whole country is laughing at them, and they have only a few people on their side. But undaunted, these women work on steadfast in their cause. They are bound to succeed and gain the franchise, for the simple reason that deeds are better than words.'[18] He covered their activities with enthusiasm in *Indian Opinion*. 'Will Indian men be effeminate? Or will they emulate the manliness shown by English women and wake up?'[19]

The technique of obliging a foe to use superior strength in order to shame him, to gain a political end, was not specifically Gandhian. He had also taken wisdom from Henry David Thoreau's work, finding himself entirely in agreement with the American's standpoint that the best government is that which governs least; he also believed, with Thoreau, in the citizen's duty of civil disobedience to unjust laws, in the value of non-violent resistance and of the simple life, thoughtfully lived. He repeatedly referred to Thoreau on civil disobedience and quoted approvingly in *Indian Opinion* such sentiments as 'Under a government which imprisons any unjustly, the true place for a just man is also a prison .. . In a slave state prison is the only house in which a free man can abide with honour.'[20]

In taking action against the Asiatic Registration Act permit offices were picketed to deter those who intended to take out permits, and some bullying ensued, though this was deplored by Gandhi. When it proved impossible for the government to register more than five hundred Indians, they made the mistake of arresting a leader in order to coerce the others into submission: a man called Ram Sundara, who had been a moving force in the erection of a Hindu temple in Johannesburg, was arrested and tried in a courtroom filled with spectators. He was sentenced to a month's imprisonment, which was greeted by the community with rejoicing and a declaration of their own willingness to go to jail. Gandhi published a picture of him and a biographical sketch in *Indian Opinion*. While in prison he was sent in unaccustomed luxuries from outside and was fêted when he was released. It was of particular importance to Gandhi that this was a Hindu martyr, applauded by the mainly Muslim traders.

Ram Sundara was not, though, Gandhi lamented, of good character and he later left the Transvaal rather than be re-arrested. Gandhi's anger was untypically unrestrained: 'Now the hypocrite has been unmasked, we have no hesitation in exposing him to our readers . . . Ram Sundara is dead as from today. He lives to no purpose. He poisoned himself by his own hand. Physical death is to be preferred to such social death.'[21] Haji Ojer Ally was also to leave the Transvaal rather than be imprisoned. In a manifestation of those divisions in Indian society that were to torment Gandhi to his death, Ally reasoned that Gandhi's co-religionists, the Hindu hawkers, would suffer less from the campaign than his own brethren the Muslim traders, who would be ruined. 'Mr Ally could not continue to trust me fully because I was a Hindu,' Gandhi commented bleakly.[22]

Gandhi himself and other leaders were ordered to appear before the court at the end of December 1907, accused of non-registration, and called upon to demonstrate why they should not be removed. All were ordered to leave the country, all refused to do so by the prescribed time, and on 10 January 1908 appeared for sentence in a crowded court – a court in which Gandhi had previously appeared as counsel. He had heard of comrades having been sentenced to three months' imprisonment with hard labour, and when he was allowed to address the court he pleaded that if men who had been so sentenced had committed an offence, he had committed a greater offence by calling on others to disobey the law and should therefore receive a greater punishment. The magistrate did not comply with this plea and gave him two months' simple imprisonment.

Gandhi was ordered to put on dirty prison clothes and placed in a large cell where he cheerfully met other protesters; now he was in his element, surrounded by suffering satyagrahis. 'Every one of us was firm in his resolution of passing his term in jail in perfect happiness and peace', he said.[23] From the second or third day after the imprisonment of the leaders, other prisoners arrived in large numbers: Indian hawkers had, as arranged, courted arrest by refusing to show their licences, in order to fill the jails. By the end of January some two thousand Asians had been jailed, mostly Indians, though the Chinese also resisted the Act under their own leadership.

In a *Rand Daily Mail* cartoon General Jan Smuts was portrayed as a desperado with a gun labelled 'Asiatic Ordinance:' threatening the saintly Gandhi who challenged him to do his worst, Smuts found that his gun would not work.[24]

Gandhi used his time in prison to catch up on his reading: as well as the old favourites Ruskin and Tolstoy he read Plato on Socrates. For religious succour he followed a regime, perhaps somewhat self-consciously: the *Bhagavad Gita* in the morning and the Koran in English translation in the afternoon. In the evening he read the Bible to a Chinese Christian fellow prisoner.

After he had been in jail about two weeks he was visited by Albert Cartwright, editor of the daily *Transvaal Leader* and a man who had behaved fairly over the Indian cause and who had the ear of General Smuts. Cartwright came bearing the terms of a settlement from Smuts, the essence of which was that Indians should register voluntarily, then once the majority did so, the government would repeal the Asiatic Registration Act and take steps to legalise the voluntary registration. The draft was not, Gandhi was told, open to negotiation, though he wanted to make clear the condition that required the government to repeal the Act. The facts behind this compromise were that the movement was failing, some of its major leaders such as Ally and Haji Habib had left the colony, and hawkers had stopped working for fear of further persecution. By the end of December 1907 Gandhi had conceded that 511 Indians 'have applied for registration as slaves' – this was not the stuff of which victories are made.[25]

A few days later he was taken to see Smuts. Almost the same age as Gandhi and, like him, a British-educated barrister and a man of firm convictions, he had been Attorney General in the Transvaal, a general in the Boer War and had then returned to political life, still devoted to

Boer rights. He received the prisoner well, reminding Gandhi that he too was a barrister and that he had known Indian students (this was as close as the austere Smuts came to small-talk). Gandhi said that Smuts assured him the Act would be repealed as soon as most had voluntarily registered and there was no further disturbance. Smuts later denied conceding this. As one commentator said, 'Both Gandhi and Smuts manoeuvred well in muddy waters, and the compromise bought time for each.'[26] Smuts himself, showing genuine regard for Gandhi, later commented: 'If Gandhi was right to consider his people, I had to consider mine.'[27] When they had finished talking it was seven in the evening, and there was Gandhi in Pretoria with not a single coin in his pocket; Smuts's secretary gave him the fare to Johannesburg and he took the last train.

Arriving at Johannesburg, Gandhi went to the chairman of the Transvaal British Indian Association and called a meeting for late that night. Most Indians lived in the same area and a meeting was held in the grounds of the mosque, to which more than a thousand came. Gandhi explained the terms of the settlement and the community reacted with scepticism: they might not have been sophisticated in the political arts but they were knowledgeable about business dealings. They felt that if they registered voluntarily they would be surrendering their most powerful weapon with no gain – the right order of business was for the Act to be repealed, then for voluntary registration to take place.

Gandhi argued that they were not against some kind of registration, but against the stigma of non-voluntary registration. In the spirit of 'the new and powerful force which has sprung up in the community', he urged, 'a satyagrahi bids good-bye to fear. He is therefore never afraid of trusting his opponent. Even if the opponent plays him false twenty times, the satyagrahi is prepared to trust him for the twenty-first time, for an implicit trust in human nature is the very essence of his creed.'[28]

These were fine sentiments, but a Pathan who had always been true to the cause reminded Gandhi of his previous words, that the struggle centred on the obligation of giving fingerprints, an obligation only on criminals – so how did this fit with what Gandhi said today? Gandhi explained that the circumstances had changed: 'What would have been a crime against the people yesterday is in the altered circumstances of today the hallmark of a gentleman.'[29] It is easy to see how the community might consider Gandhi had sold them out. Indeed, one challenged that Gandhi had been bribed by Smuts with £15,000 and declared he would never give his fingerprints or allow others to do so. Furthermore, he would kill the man who took the lead in applying for registration. Gandhi responded that he was free of thoughts of anger or hatred against any assailant. Finally, after hours of discussion, the meeting over-whelmingly endorsed the settlement. But this was not the last time Gandhi would raise the expectations of the community, broker a deal, then find them angry and feeling that he had let them down.

On the morning of 10 February 1908 Gandhi prepared to take out a certificate of registration, as it had been agreed that the leaders would be the first to register. As they left the association's office one of the Pathans, Mir Alam, joined them. A few minutes from the Asiatic Regis-tration office the powerfully built Mir Alam accosted Gandhi and one of his companions aimed a blow at him from behind. Gandhi fell to the ground exclaiming: 'He Rama!' (Oh God!) and was kicked by Mir's com-panions in the face and ribs. When the other leaders around Gandhi tried to ward off the Pathans, they too were attacked until some Euro-pean passers-by approached, at which point Mir Alam and his com-panions ran off but were caught by the Europeans and taken into custody by the police.

Gandhi was taken to a nearby office and a doctor stitched his wounds. He sustained injuries to his ribs, his upper lip, his left eye and forehead; he had been assaulted with an iron pipe and a stick as well as having been kicked. He called for the assailants to be released and asked the Registrar of Asiatics who had just arrived on the scene to bring the papers to him, as he had sworn to be the first to register – 'if I am alive and it is acceptable to God'.[30] He was taken to the home of Joseph Doke, who with his wife took him in and commanded him to rest. When they asked if Gandhi wanted anything, he asked for their little daughter to sing the hymn 'Lead, Kindly Light'. For the next ten days while Gandhi recovered, Doke's house became a centre of pilgrimage for the Indian community ranging from hawkers to the chairman of the Transvaal British Indian Association.

When sufficiently recovered, Gandhi went back to Natal, where the terms of the Asiatic Registration Act did not apply. But here too Indians watched the progress of the movement, as it was feared that the repression in the Transvaal would soon be duplicated all over South Africa. Gandhi spoke at a meeting in Durban to explain the settlement, was again attacked, and again had to be rescued by Superintendent Alexander.

Gandhi's supporters accompanied him to Phoenix, where he once more explained the settlement in the pages of *Indian Opinion* and contemplated the meaning of his satyagraha ideas when put into practice. Now the Indians had voluntarily registered, the government must repeal the Registration Act – but it did not. General Smuts left the Act on the statute book and introduced a measure validating the voluntary registrations, at the same time making further provisions for the registration of Asiatics that put them in a worse position than under the pre-war Boer regime.

Shocked, Gandhi called a meeting of his committee. They reminded him they had accused him before of being too credulous, of believing everything he was told, and now the community must suffer for his gullibility. He responded that his 'credulity' was in fact his trust in people, a test of his faith in satyagraha.

The community now set about resurrecting its protest movement. Gandhi wrote to Smuts, charging him with his breach of promise, but Smuts did not reply. Gandhi then met Albert Cartwright, the mediator, who perfectly well remembered that Smuts had promised to repeal the Act; but the most he could do – writing newspaper articles denouncing him – was as nothing to the politician. The European community who were Smuts's constituency had no interest in calling him to account. Doubtless the general was also deferring to a higher truth, but one of different interpretation: his greater truth was the value of European dominance over the world, and in particular over 'savage' Africa, which was all part of God's plan as well as being in the interests of human progress.

The Indians now had to divest themselves of the certificates of registration, which had been treacherously obtained, and they determined to do it in the most public way possible. A large cauldron was set up in the grounds of the Hamidia Mosque in Johannesburg on 16 August 1908, the day the new Asiatic Bill was to be carried through the legislature. The cauldron was to burn the certificates if the government did not relent. As thousands of Indians crowded around a telegram arrived from the government announcing their refusal to change their course of action. A cheer went up from the crowd and they proceeded to set fire to their certificates. It was a dramatic gesture that reached as far as the British press – a coup for Gandhi, as such colonial news was rarely covered in British newspapers.

Smuts continued the assault on the Indian community with such measures as the Transvaal Immigrants Restriction Act, which banned the entry of all who did not understand a European language, and proposals for a new consolidated immigration bill for the whole Union. Gandhi signed a provisional settlement with Smuts who promised to address Indians' concerns in the next parliament; but he was not able to deliver, coming up against opposition particularly from the Orange Free State representatives who refused to tolerate any Indian immigration at all. Gandhi declined to include all South African anti-Indian legislation in his campaign, feeling such an approach would dull the edge of satyagraha.

The struggle was in danger of failing, however, because the government now declined to prosecute anyone over the Registration Act, so satyagraha was not producing the required element of suffering. The Immigrants Restriction Act gave an opportunity for Indians to challenge the law by declaring their intention to enter the Transvaal, then doing so and defying the government to prosecute. Of course, they had to be outside the Transvaal to start with, so Gandhi called on his Natal contacts. A group of Indians from Natal therefore entered the Transvaal, were arrested, ordered to leave, refused to do so and were duly imprisoned. Other Indians courted imprisonment by trading without a licence.

Gandhi suffered several periods of imprisonment during the campaign, including solitary confinement. The latter was more attractive to him than to some of the company he was obliged to keep, who were 'wild, murderous and given to immoral ways'. During a night in a crowded cell in Johannesburg two men threatened to rape Gandhi: they stared at the slight lawyer and mocked him, 'exchanged obscene jokes, uncovering each other's genitals'. Gandhi stayed awake most of the night on guard.[31] He elsewhere wrote that 'many of the native prisoners are only one degree removed from the animal'.[32] His passive resisters he said, took particular objection to being given garments stamped with N for 'native': 'We could understand not being classed with the whites, but to be placed on the same level as the Natives seemed too much to put up with.'[33] He successfully lobbied for separate lavatories for Indians, and that Indians should never be 'lodged with kaffirs', though some apparently preferred it as they could trade for tobacco and other items.[34] At this time *Indian Opinion* was running a series called 'Story of a Soldier of Truth', which was Gandhi's Gujarati translation of Plato's *Last Days of Socrates*. He had started to publish a free translation of Washington Irving's life of Mohammed in 1907 but had to stop because, however reverential he was, it gave offence to Muslims for Mohammed to be referred to in factual terms. Gandhi was still, after all his years of working with Muslims, failing to reconcile their world view with his own.

During his imprisonment from October to December 1908, Gandhi received a letter informing him that Kasturba was seriously ill: she was suffering frequent haemorrhages and losing so much blood that her life was in danger. But Gandhi declined to pay his fine, which would have permitted him to leave prison. He wrote saying he loved her, and begging her understanding:

> Even if you die, for me you will be eternally alive. Your soul is death-less. On my part, I would assure you I have no intentions of marrying another woman after your death. I have told you this a number of times. You must have faith in God and set your soul free. Your death will be another great sacrifice for the cause of Satyagraha. My struggle is not merely against the authorities but against nature itself. I hope you will understand this and not feel offended.[35]

In fact she pulled through and when he was released Gandhi travelled with her to Durban, where she underwent a curettage procedure. In her post-operative weakness the hospital doctor advised beef tea to redress her anaemia. Gandhi was against this and so, unremarkably for a traditional Hindu, was Kasturba. The doctor no longer wished to treat her if his regime was not going to be followed, so Gandhi took her back to Phoenix, where she was carried in a hammock the two miles from the station by men from the settlement.

Kasturba consented to be treated by Gandhi's hydropathic methods, though she had no faith in his remedies. As usual, she also received the dubious benefit of her husband's food fads. They argued about his proposal that she should give up salt and pulses in the interest's of health; he believed that the weak-bodied should avoid pulses (he also believed chastity was promoted by saltlessness – it is not clear why he recommended this for Kasturba). He explained: 'I suggested to her that she should give up vegetables and salt altogether. She should live on wheat and fruits only.'[36] Kasturba resisted this further restriction on her already limited diet, so Gandhi put moral pressure on her by vowing to renounce salt and pulses himself for a year; she begged him to change his mind but he felt he had achieved something by his vow and refused. She acquiesced, giving up salt and pulses (which at least did her no harm – she did recover). Gandhi considered this a triumph of satyagraha: he thus connected resistance and stubbornness in a domestic situation, for the achievement of a questionable goal, with political activism using the same techniques.

Kasturba may not have been the best patient, but neither did Gandhi have the tact of a born physician. 'I again gently but rebukingly remarked,' he confided to Kallenbach, 'that she was sinful in her thoughts and that her disease was largely due to her sins. Immediately she began to howl. I had made her leave all the good food in order to kill her, I was tired of her, I wished her to die, I was a hooded snake.' Reflecting on this scene, he remarked how she taught him the need for patience and self-sacrifice, but finally drew the moral: 'You cannot attach yourself to a particular woman and yet live for humanity. The two do not harmonise.'[37]

Fines and imprisonment having failed, the government resorted to deportations, first to other parts of Africa and then back to India. Some Indians lost land and property in these deportations, but many were former indentured labourers with no family or connections in their native land. Gandhi arranged for one of his co-workers to travel with the first batch of deportees and saw to it that sympathetic Indians received them on their arrival in India. They also managed to confound the government in cases questioning the legality of deportation, and the practice was stopped.

The cause was supported by donations from such benefactors as Ratanji Jamshedji Tata, who founded the Tata Iron and Steel Works, but needs were great and the destitution of the satyagrahis left the movement in a quandary. The families of those arrested had to be cared for. Gandhi decided the solution was to move the families to an ideal community such as Phoenix, the one he had established in Natal: in this way 'public funds would be largely saved and the families of satyagrahis would be trained to live a new and simple life in harmony with one another.'[38] The new settlement needed to be near Johannesburg. In May 1910 Hermann Kallenbach bought a farm of more than 1,000 acres near the city and gave Gandhi the use of it, rent-free. It had a huge orchard, two wells, a spring and some existing accommodation.

Gandhi decided to call it Tolstoy Farm, so his new community was not only built on land owned by a European and based on principles propounded by Ruskin, another European, it was also named after a European. He had been corresponding with Tolstoy, calling the writer 'the Titan of Russia' and signing himself 'a humble follower of your doctrine'. Tolstoy replied asking Gandhi to convey his fellow feeling to his 'beloved brothers, the Indian workers of the Transvaal'.[39]

Tolstoy Farm was less forbidding than Phoenix because of Kallenbach's influence: Kallenbach could accept a degree of renunciation, but had no passion for mortifying the flesh in the search for the spiritual. Gandhi also found his experience here rewarding: 'My faith and courage were at their highest in Tolstoy Farm.'[40]

There were no servants: every job from fetching water to building accommodation had to be done by the settlers wherever possible. 'The work on the farm was certainly harder than in jail,' Gandhi remarked.[41] He described his principles to a largely white audience at the Johannesburg Socialist Society, in 1910 comparing the 'selfish, godless and hypocritical' modern civilisation with that of the past. 'In the days of ancient civilization,' he paraphrased for *Indian Opinion*, 'men were kind, God-fearing and simple and looked upon the body as a means of spiritual uplift. It is necessary to revert to the ancient way of life and for that purpose to adopt simplicity and village life.'[42] Gandhi's reading – unlike, for example, that of Nehru – encompassed little history. His notion of the past related not to a reality but to the Rama Raj (rule of Rama) of Hindu myth.

On Tolstoy Farm men and women were housed separately, and drinking and smoking were prohibited. Gandhi prevailed upon Christian and other women whose husbands were imprisoned to change to a vegetarian diet (though he assured them they might eat meat if they wished). The food was the simplest possible with a staple of rice, dal, vegetables and porridge. Mealtimes were fixed and all dined together in a row. After meals there were prayers with readings from the Hindu epic the *Ramayana* or Islamic texts. They dressed in labourers' clothes – but the clothes of European labourers, not Indians – working men's blue trousers and shirts that were imitated from the uniforms of prisoners. When they needed to go to Johannesburg they walked the twenty-one miles to save on rail fares, and learned how to make sandals so they did not have to buy shoes.

As usual with Gandhi's experiments in ideal living, the education of the farm's children was neglected and they were expected to take part in all the work around the farm. What semi-formal schooling the children did receive was after the morning's labour and the midday meal, when even Gandhi said he found it hard to stay awake. Gandhi's insistence on the importance of native tongue meant Hindi, Tamil, Gujarati and Urdu were taught, as was English, and the Hindus learned Sanskrit. Gandhi undertook to teach his limited Tamil and Urdu, and to pass on his high-school Sanskrit.

Gandhi had them pay little attention even to the textbooks they did have, self-confidently proclaiming: 'I did not find it at all necessary to load the boys with quantities of books. I have always felt that the true textbook for the pupil is his teacher.'[43] He freely admits his own academic deficiencies, which were evident to others in his public life. Even speaking in Hindi his grammar was poor – an observer noted that Gandhi often got the genders of nouns wrong. When he offered to translate for Gopal Krishna Gokhale, the latter replied that Gandhi's linguistic abilities were 'an accomplishment on which you cannot exactly be congratulated'.[44]

Gandhi liked to 'experiment' not only with his own self-restraint, but with that of others. 'I sent the boys reputed to be mischievous and the innocent young girls to bathe in the same spot at the same time,' he once said, having fully explained the duty of self-restraint to them. They bathed at a fixed time, and Gandhi would generally be present. He also had them sleep together on an open veranda, the boys, the girls and himself, with a distance of only three feet between their beds: 'I made the experiment from a belief that boys and girls could thus live together without harm.'[45]

Inevitably nature would assert itself and on this particular occasion there was some sexual banter between the boys and two of the girls, who were presumably developing physically. When it was reported to Gandhi he remonstrated with the young men, but was troubled about what to do with the girls. He wished to give them some physical sign as a lesson to them and a warning to the boys. 'What mark should the girls bear?' he wondered. He was awake all night worrying about it, then suggested they let him cut off their long hair. The girls refused, but Gandhi worked on the elderly women on the farm and got their support and finally the girls came round and he cut off their hair himself.

Gandhi's eldest son Harilal had joined his parents in South Africa, in the company of his wife; he and his brother Manilal had thrown themselves into the cause and had been repeatedly imprisoned. Their enduring resentment at their lack of education was intensified when Gandhi accepted the offer of a scholarship to study in England from his old friend Pranjivan Mehta who had helped him during his first days in London, and instead of giving it to one of his own children (as Mehta had intended) gave it to his nephew Chaganlal. He chided Manilal: 'Why does the idea of study haunt you again and again? If you think of study for earning your livelihood, it is not proper; for God gives food to all. You can get enough to eat even by doing manual labour.'[46] He wrote to Harilal: 'I must advise you to shake off this craze for examinations. If you pass, it won't impress me much. If you fail, you will feel very unhappy.'[47] He even refused funds for Harilal to go back to India when his wife and child had returned there. Harilal endured six periods of imprisonment between 1908 and 1911 in his father's campaign.

When Chaganlal fell ill and failed to complete his studies, Gandhi was again in a position to choose a scholar to send to train as a lawyer. Harilal was again eager, but Gandhi again passed him over in favour of another young man. Gandhi understandably did not want to be accused of nepotism, but this seemed to be active discrimination against his own family. A flavour of the exchange between father and son can be gleaned from a letter to Harilal in March 1911:

There is nothing to be ashamed of in your being weak in mathematics and general literary education. You could have learnt them had I given you the necessary opportunity. The practical knowledge boys in India possess is not due to the education they receive in schools, but is due to the unique Indian way of life. It is due to the meritorious deeds of our ancestors that we find healthy standards of behaviour, thrift etc., around us, in spite of the repeated inroads of modern education, the immorality that we see among the people and their growing selfishness.[48]

Harilal left the settlement to seek a future in India in May 1911, saying to his mother: 'He just does not care for us, any of us.'[49] Gandhi noted his son's accusation: 'Unlike other fathers, I have not admired my sons or done anything specially for them, but always put them and Ba [Kasturba] last, such was the charge.'[50]

In 1915 Harilal wrote a 'half-open' letter for limited distribution, charging his now fêted father with neglect of his family, and particularly with keeping his sons 'ignorant' by denying them education. Of himself and his brothers Harilal said: 'You have treated us as a ringmaster would treat the beasts of the circus . . . You have spoken to us never with love, always with anger. In argument you have always used us with humiliating language: "You are ignorant . . . you lack understanding, you think you have reached the last frontier of knowledge." Walking and moving, sleeping and sitting, reading and writing, you have kept us in constant fear of you. You have a heart of stone.' The lot of Kasturba he felt, was worse.[51]

Another incident, near the end of the campaign when negotiations with the South African government were at a crucial stage, showed how seriously Gandhi treated matters of personal morality. His son Manilal and a woman at Phoenix called Jeki, the daughter of Pranjivan Mehta were found to have 'fallen' twice while Jeki's husband was away in Fiji. Presumably they had sex. His reaction, as usual over sexual matters, was extreme: he imposed a seven-day fast on himself and vowed to have only one meal a day for the following four and a half months. Thus, he said, 'Everyone came to realise what a terrible thing it was to be sinful.'[52]

Manilal fasted with him. 'He will, I hope, be able to bear the seven days' fast,' Gandhi said, 'but if he dies in the process, it will not be a matter for regret.'[53] He further ordered Manilal to swear to a lifetime of celibacy and relented only in 1927, under pressure from Kasturba, when Manilal was thirty-five. Jeki he had fast, have her hair cropped, take off her jewellery and wear mourning as a sign of remorse. He wrote: 'Never before have I spent such days of agony as I am doing now . . . The heart seems to have gone dry. The agony I am going through is unspeakable. I have often wanted to take out the knife from my pocket and put it through the stomach.'[54] Later he had Jeki sent away to her husband as she was 'without pity, without remorse'.[55] There may be another element in his anguish over this affair: perhaps he was involving her in the experiments in sexual control that were later to dominate his life. He once wrote of the sleeping arrangements at Phoenix: 'We were most of us here on the veranda sleeping side by side, Jeki was next to me.'[56] In one way he found the experience with Manilal and Jeki helpful in that he was able to perfect the technique of the long fast: he learned the necessity of drinking water even if it were distasteful, and the spiritual focus he gained by having the *Ramayana* read to him.

Gandhi's troubled relationship with his family is one of the most difficult aspects of his already complex character. He once remarked of his sons: 'They have better character than other boys. It is only when I judge them by a standard of my own that I find them lacking.'[57] Harilal had charged his father with preferring his nephews (second cousins, to be precise) to his sons; as the eldest son he felt he had a greater right to his father's love than any other person. In fact it was precisely this relationship that ensured Gandhi would reject him. His disgust with sex sprang from his belief that he must control his strong sex drive or he could not accomplish spiritual greatness. His anger at his own father for his early marriage has to be seen in the context of his wish to be free from the things of the flesh. Thanks to that early marriage, Gandhi had become tainted by carnality before he knew his own mind. Before he could reject it, he was burdened by those things of this world – his wife and children. Later he developed an indifference to the product of

sex, his children, as if they tied him to the earthly world as living symbols of his carnal nature, and were of no import. When they became
sexual beings themselves, his revulsion was almost palpable.

The union of the four South African nations was the pressing national
issue after the Boer War, promoted by such idealistic imperialists as the
administrator Lionel Curtis. The union was to take place in 1910, and
as the moment approached Gandhi again travelled to London to lobby
politicians on behalf of the Indians, this time accompanied by Haji Habib
(who had returned to South Africa). He was able to call on the services of a friendly peer, Lord Ampthill, a former acting Viceroy of India.
The Transvaal premier Louis Botha informed the delegation he would
compromise on the practical operation of the law but would not repeal
the Asiatic Registration or Immigration Acts. He maintained his determination to have the new Union of South Africa a racial state, with the
immigration door wide open to whites but opened only sporadically
and under specific conditions to Asians. Lord Crewe, the current Secretary of State for the Colonies, faced with negotiating with Gandhi,
declared he was 'a quite astonishingly hopeless and impracticable person
for any kind of deal, but with a sort of ardent, though restrained, honesty which becomes the most pigheaded obstinacy at the critical
moment'.[58] Gandhi was still at this time using the language of assimila-
tion and so would dress in a silk hat, a morning suit, a tie, smart shoes
and socks.

When he wrote home from London he included a picture of some
suffragettes with the approving message, 'Many of the ladies in the picture have been to jail.'[59] He lost sympathy with them when they took to
greater 'militancy' including attacks on property, but he gained from
observing them, mentioning their exploits in almost every report he
sent to *Indian Opinion*. The publicity value of sending women to jail
may have occurred to him here, and he wanted to prepare his followers
for the next stage.

Gokhale visited South Africa in October–November 1912, with some
encouragement from the imperial government and a welcome by the
South African authorities for this Indian moderate. The campaigner
found the experience of Tolstoy Farm less than congenial, resenting their

display of poverty which he thought of as 'extremism', and he did not enjoy Gandhi's and Kallenbach's attempts to make him more comfortable by giving him a cot and a commode and bringing him food. 'You all seem to think that you have been born to suffer hardships and discomforts, and people like myself have been born to be pampered by you,' he said. 'I will bear any amount of hardship but I will humble your pride.' He talked pointedly of the 'avalanche of half-baked ideas' threatening to overwhelm India.[60] He had great admiration for Gandhi, however, telling an Indian audience: 'Gandhi has in him the marvellous spiritual power to turn ordinary men around him into heroes and martyrs.'[61]

After a thorough briefing from Gandhi, Gokhale met with Smuts and Botha. He returned and gave Gandhi the result of the meeting: 'You must return to India in a year. Everything has been settled. The Black [Asiatic Registration] Act will be repealed. The racial bar will be removed from emigration law. The £3 tax will be abolished.'[62] Gandhi did not this time believe the assurances of the South African government – it was Gokhale's turn to be gulled. Gandhi thanked him for his efforts. When he saw his 'political guru' off on 1 December 1912, he wore Indian dress for the first time since he was a child.

The state was now stepping up its attacks. The South African racial state was lumbering towards its apotheosis in the complete racial discrimination of apartheid (finally to be written into law in 1950). As part of this process the machinery of state in all its manifestations moved towards the creation of a racial dimension in every part of life. Thus the Supreme Court ruled in March 1913 that only Christian marriages were legal in South Africa; Hindu, Muslim and Zoroastrian (Parsi) marriages were void – an unconscionable insult to Indians. Now the women supporters of Gandhi, who had not previously courted jail, started joining the struggle actively – entering the Transvaal illegally, hawking without a licence and committing other offences, but the government declined to imprison them. A new immigration bill, published in April 1913, intended to erode existing rights even further.

Gandhi's satyagraha campaign had not included the £3 tax to be paid by freed indentured labourers, which was a bitter imposition on the poorest class of Indians in Natal. Now that the government had promised Gokhale they would repeal the tax (a promise on which, true to form, it later reneged), he felt justified in including it in his demands. This would, for the first time, bring the vast mass of indentured labourers into the struggle – a not inconsequential matter at a time when Gandhi's forces were not strong: – he wrote to Gokhale of a maximum of sixty-five or sixty-six and a minimum of sixteen on whom he could rely. This was hardly a mass movement. In keeping with this change in focus he closed Tolstoy Farm and concentrated his followers on Phoenix, as it was more sensible to engage over indentured labourers where they lived in Natal.

Underlying this change of direction were challenges to Gandhi's leadership, following his failure to deliver on any of the issues favoured by his elite merchant backers: registration, the location of bazaars and free movement within South Africa. Gandhi was facing such accusations of failure that he refused to attend a meeting of the Natal Indian Congress as long as the secretaries who rejected his policies remained in office. At one public meeting he was actually blamed for the erosion of merchant rights over the years he had been active. With more justice, he was criticised for his increasing assumption of the mantle of leadership, his unwillingness to adopt alternative policies to those he had personally worked out, and his reliance on European lieutenants while passing over able Indians. A motion of no confidence was later passed on Gandhi by the Congress, but by that time he had already outflanked his opponents with dynamic action.

Declining in personal influence, with his back against the wall and a dwindling band of followers, opposed by his own movement and with the trading community unwilling to further sacrifice their livelihoods, Gandhi determined on 'my final offering to the God of Truth'.[63] He decided to sacrifice all the settlers at Phoenix, men and women, excepting only a few needed to run *Indian Opinion*, and children under sixteen. As the campaign rolled on, in fact, one issue of the newspaper was published by the children, working alone. The satyagrahis were to court arrest in the most direct way possible.

He did not confide in Kasturba as he felt that merely to ask her was to command her, and she should court jail of her own volition. She was offended at his apparent lack of confidence, and insisted on joining the women's 'invading party'. She and three other women were arrested for illegal entry to the Transvaal and imprisoned for three months. The effect on public opinion in India of women being imprisoned was electric. Other insults to the Indian community had been accepted as the lot of those who went abroad to find a new life. The insult to women implicit in the new interpretation of marriage and their imprisonment was more than the nation could bear. Channelled by Gokhale, numerous meetings rained outrage on the South African government.

The movement had its martyrs. Gandhi writes of Valliamma Munusamy, a sixteen-year-old girl who caught a fever in jail and died emaciated soon after release. In true martyr's fashion she insisted, even knowing it would cause her death, that she was 'ready to go to jail again'. 'Who would not love to die for one's motherland?' Gandhi reports her as saying – which, if the translation of her words is accurate, opens up the question of what she thought the struggle was about.[64] Did the poor of South Africa believe their sacrifices were for India?

Other women, mainly Tamils, went to the coal-mining centre of Newcastle and called on the indentured labourers in the mines to go on strike over the £3 tax. The strike was preceded by a public meeting addressed by a veteran satyagrahi, Thambi Naidoo, also a Tamil, who was able to play on the bitter resentment over the tax. The tax on former indentured labourers who wished to stay in Natal after their indenture was hated for what it was: a means to get rid of Indians who had come as labourers and intended after their period of indenture to make a life for themselves in South Africa; many were forced back to work again under contract. With these labourers, Gandhi had finally hit on a force that could be mobilised and tapped – much of his energy in this last campaign was engaged not in motivating the labourers but in restraining them.

Gandhi travelled to northern Natal and toured the striking mines where the labourers lived in compounds, their accommodation provided by the mine owners who had now cut off their electricity and water supplies. He decided to lead them out of the compounds, but his problem became how to feed and accommodate the hundreds of strikers. They had been living on the breadline so they had no savings.

The Indian traders gave food, though they did not want to support Gandhi publicly because they had trading relations with the mine owners.

A Tamil Christian called Lazarus gave space on his small plot of land for the labourers to sleep. In one of his astonishing displays of confidence, Gandhi told the strikers to come to him with nothing except their clothes and blankets – he promised to supply food for them as long as the strike lasted. As word spread, hundreds of labourers with their wives and children carrying bundles of clothes on their heads flocked to Gandhi to sleep on the ground and receive meals from communal pots. Gandhi explained that his intention was to 'march them to the Transvaal border to court arrest. We should be arrested on the way. This avoids the difficulties of lodgings, etc., and keeps the men going.'[65] So the machinery of the state was to be used to feed and house the strikers, thereby prolonging the strike.

The coal owners asked to see Gandhi and put to him their very reasonable argument: that the £3 tax was imposed by the government but the miners were striking against *them*. The strike was the only weapon the labourers had, Gandhi replied; he advised the owners to put pressure on the government to repeal the tax – which was, in fact, what they were already doing. Smuts's policy was to wait and see, knowing that the need to look after the strikers was placing an enormous strain on Gandhi's finances.

Gandhi now had upwards of four thousand strikers and dependants. He told them he could supply them with a pound and a half of bread and an ounce of sugar each per day; they must bear abuse and violence from the authorities, if arrested they must go quietly and bear the hardships of jail willingly. The labourers explained they were used to hardship, and from 28 October 1913 they marched with Gandhi at their head. Gandhi himself took part in all the necessary operations of the 'army': overseeing the sanitary arrangements, cooking and serving food. As a leader he was not only always visible to his followers, he was there taking part in the same activities that were expected of them. Such empathy was one of his finest leadership qualities. A journalist described the marchers as 'an exceedingly picturesque crew. To the eye they appear most meagre, indeed emaciated; their legs are mere sticks but the way they are marching on starvation rations shows them to be particularly hardy . . . Mr Gandhi is looked upon with absolute veneration and is habitually addressed as *Bapu* [father].'[66]

Gandhi wrote to assure the government that he and his labourers did not intend to settle in the Transvaal, but wanted to protest against the government's breach of its pledge to repeal the £3 tax and 'as a pure demonstration of our distress at the loss of our self-respect'.[67] The government was welcome to arrest them where they were, he added helpfully.

Gandhi had his seasoned satyagrahis posted on the route in advance to organise the food – people such as Hermann Kallenbach and Sonja Schlesin who as Europeans had some, but not complete, protection from arrest. In the town of Volksrust just inside the Transvaal border the local Europeans held a meeting at which some threatened to meet the Indians with bullets if they crossed over. Kallenbach bravely attended, despite the risk of personal violence, and put the Indians' case. The procession passed through Volksrust in peace.

The police did not arrest the marchers but twice arrested Gandhi, though the march proceeded as planned and Gandhi each time received bail and rejoined the march, now closing in on Johannesburg. They were aiming to stop at Tolstoy Farm, but were arrested en masse at Balfour and placed on three special trains which took them back to Natal.

Finally Gandhi was arrested again, tried and sentenced to nine months with hard labour for inducing indentured labourers to leave Natal. In Volksrust jail he met Kallenbach and Polak, who had also been arrested. New satyagrahis were arriving in prison every day for crossing into the Transvaal. In Natal, where the trainloads of marchers had been taken, they were summarily tried and sent to jail. Now the government had a problem: imprisoning the strikers meant they could not go back to work even if they wanted to. The coal mines would have to close down, which would cripple the nation's industry. The government now did the worst thing it could in the eyes of the world: it declared the mines to be prison outposts, their European staff to be warders, and forced the labourers underground. This was not, therefore, even indentured labour – it was slave labour. Gandhi's strategy had forced the government to use its utmost power, to behave with extreme brutality to defend an unjust law with yet further injustice. Ideally, from Gandhi's point of view, the suffering of the labourers was being played out on a world stage.

Following the lead of the miners, now labourers in other industries struck, starting with the workers on the sugar plantations in southern Natal. This led to further violence: mounted military police charged, armed police opened fire on the strikers. At one point in November 1913 the majority of Natal's sixty thousand Indian workers were out on strike. There was no law against striking and the government's actions were completely illegal. The Viceroy of India, Lord Hardinge, criticised the South African government for its handling of the protesters and so, more diplomatically, did the Colonial Office in London. Finally Smuts ordered the release of Gandhi, Polak and Kallenbach, then the rest of the satyagraha prisoners, and as a fig leaf for his embarrassed climbdown, set up a commission of inquiry that was guaranteed to find for the Indians while whitewashing the government's behaviour.

Gandhi now adopted another costume, for the first time following the example of his hero Tolstoy who had decided not only to live but to dress like a peasant. Instead of appearing as the Western-educated Indian lawyer in a combination of European and Parsi dress, Gandhi now wore a plain, knee-length white cotton tunic and the skirt-like lungi worn by labourers. He was barefoot and his head was almost completely shaven excepting for a patch on top, as a sign of mourning for the ten Indians who had been killed in confrontation with the police and for whose deaths he took responsibility. He was thus dressed when he waited outside Pietermaritzburg prison on 22 December 1913 to meet the women prisoners, including Kasturba, who had been visibly enfeebled by her ordeal. In all some 2,500 Indians, or nearly one-fifth of the resident Indian population of the Transvaal, went to jail, many of them several times.[68]

Gandhi did not contribute to the fatuous process of the 'commission of inquiry' but was prepared to meet with Smuts and other members of the Union government. Smuts was by now preoccupied with a white railway workers' strike over which he declared martial law. The European strikers made no pretensions to peaceful protest – they were willing to overturn the government if they did not get their way. Not wanting to gain from his opponent's discomfort, Gandhi called off a march that was to be held to criticise the partisan composition of the commission of inquiry.

Gandhi seemed to enjoy his relationship with the European administrators, even when he was arguing against them. When he was in

Pretoria Central Jail he spent some of his time making Smuts a pair of leather sandals, to show his lack of rancour. The general prized them; but when Gandhi left, Smuts remarked: 'The saint has left our shores, I hope for ever.'[69]

The commission did its job of whitewashing the government's actions and proposing an acceptable climb-down. The Indian Relief Bill of 1914 abolished the £3 tax and cancelled arrears; non-Christian marriages were recognised. However, free movement across borders within South Africa was still restricted, registration was still required, and no more just administration of Indian commerce was introduced. Still, by 1914 Gandhi considered the satyagraha struggle that had begun in 1906 was completed, even though he was subject to severe criticism from former supporters who pointed out the differences between the objectives of the campaign and its achievements. On the positive side, over these years Indians had fostered a sense of community and pride in their background and were now a force to be reckoned with.

The white administrators and demonstrators who opposed the Indians were, of course, also expressing their rights in the context of the racial state, which Gandhi and his supporters showed no sign of opposing in its entirety. The Indian traders' argument was that their race and financial status should guarantee rights to them, not that every Indian (or African) should have civic rights. Gandhi was pushing the racial state towards the form it was ultimately to take anyway: that of a buffer racial group of Indians and 'coloureds', with intermediate rights, between the whites at the top and the blacks at the bottom.

The lack of concern in the campaign for the rights of the African natives was understandable in the circumstances, but unattractive. Gandhi showed sympathy for the rights of the Africans, but any more concrete alliance would have outraged the Europeans and would not have pleased Gandhi's merchant constituency. His campaign had done some good for the Africans, however, in that it had shown not only that struggle against the South African regime was possible, but that, if the struggle were waged as a campaign against injustice, it would attract a fair amount of European support – a message that Nelson Mandela and the African National Congress would be able to put to devastating effect. This was

Gandhi's most important gift to the people of South Africa: the shaping of the racial struggle into a form that would attract maximum moral support.

It is hardly too much to say that, in common with many people who have to go abroad to seek their fortune, not least the merchants and labourers who formed his constituency, South Africa made Gandhi. In practical terms, his work for the Natal Indian Congress and the Transvaal Indian Association taught him how to run a political organisation; *Indian Opinion* taught him how to run a newspaper and Phoenix and Tolstoy Farm how to run a self-sufficient community. Financially, Gandhi made a good income from the law: he paid back the money he had spent on his London education nearly five times over from his successful South African law practice, so he felt himself free from family obligations.

In the eyes of others he had gained an international reputation, and his political techniques and skills were attracting comment. In India, he was to be given access to the higher levels of nationalist politics, something he had not achieved in 1902, before the South African campaign had raised his profile. In 1910 Gokhale even proposed him as president for that year's session of the Indian National Congress.

But Gandhi would not have considered these his most important achievement: his spiritual progress was what mattered most to him. The speculative young man in London conducting experiments with food had found his own path and felt moved to instruct others. He had formulated the basic principles of satyagraha: of non-violence and of suffering for a cause. He had begun not only to practise but to promote celibacy; he had developed the ability to motivate large groups of people. In South Africa, Gandhi had found his constituency; many of his closest disciples were and would continue to be Christians and Jews. The people he got on well with were Western seekers after spiritual truth, who approved of the vision he was enunciating on his spiritual journey. Muslims were more resistant to his message, wanting to weigh the advantages of his approach against others; one assumes the Muslim traders were spiritually satisfied with the message of Islam and saw no benefit in further searching. Gandhi's attitudes were grossly at variance with theirs: it was hardly possible not to notice that he was attempting to live as cheaply as possible, whereas the merchants' objective was material prosperity.

Educated Hindus could respect him, but they did not want to follow him. He might receive support from wealthy Indians of either religion, but it was by motivating the poor that he would set the political world alight. His greatest success had come with the impoverished Tamil Hindu workers: almost by chance, the labourers of Natal had shown him the way.

On 18 July 1914, aged almost forty-five Gandhi gathered up his closest supporters and left South Africa for India after more than twenty years. He was now a mature man with a purpose.

6

Village Activist

Gandhi had devoted his practical efforts to the rights of Indians in the new Union of South Africa, but he had simultaneously pursued a parallel track in developing a theory of Indian independence. His eye was always on the horizon of emancipation for his home nation. In the first years of the twentieth century he diligently prepared for leadership in the Indian independence movement. He determined that the next time he mounted the political stage in the subcontinent he was not going to be patronised and allotted a minor role as he had been in 1901 at the Calcutta session of the Indian National Congress.

While in London in 1909 Gandhi had made a point of contacting and getting to understand the Indian expatriate community which, in its youthful manifestation, tended towards violence. He said he had come in contact with 'every known Indian anarchist in London', whose bravery had impressed him but whom he thought misguided.[1]

Gandhi had arrived in London in the July; at the beginning of that month Sir Curzon Wyllie, an official at the office of the Secretary of State for India, had been shot by a student, Madanlal Dhingra, at a reception of the National Indian Association. A Parsi doctor who had tried to prevent the assassination was also killed. Dhingra insisted he had acted alone, and was hanged for his crime. In fact he was inspired by a coterie of nationalist revolutionaries gathered around Vinayak Savarkar, an incendiary who ran India House, a hostel for Indian students in Highgate, North London. Savarkar had trained Dhingra for the killing; an initial assassination attempt on Lord Curzon, who was responsible for the deeply resented partition of Bengal, had been unsuccessful.

Gandhi condemned the violence unequivocally: 'No act of treachery can ever profit a nation. Even should the British leave in consequence of such murderous acts, who will then rule in their place? The only answer is: the murderers.' He was thus intolerant both of violent acts in themselves and of their spiritual effect on those who committed them. Freedom could not result from evil deeds: 'India can gain nothing from the rule of murderers.'² The later ascendancy of Gandhi's attitude via the Congress Party has obscured the fact that the violence of the likes of Savarkar was vying with passive resistance as a technique of the nationalists. Violence was also, significantly for the British, an ever present probability for the independence movement if a non-violent approach failed.

Gandhi made a point of meeting extremists. Dressed in a starched shirt and a swallow-tail coat, he gave a speech at a dinner organised by some of them. He explained to Lord Ampthill:

I have endeavoured specially to come into contact with the so-called extremists who may be better described as the party of violence. This I have done in order if possible to convince them of the error of their ways. I have noticed that some of the members of this party are earnest spirits, possessing a high degree of morality, great intellectual ability and lofty self-sacrifice. They wield an undoubted influence on the young Indians here.³

This was the background against which, on the voyage back to South Africa in late autumn 1909 aboard the *Kildonan Castle*, Gandhi wrote *Hind Swaraj* ('Indian Home Rule') in Gujarati on the ship's stationery. The original manuscript shows few deletions. This work, the most important of his life, came direct from the heart. It was written in just over a week, literally with both hands: when he developed writer's cramp in his right hand, he switched to his left. In the foreword he said: 'I have written because I could not restrain myself.'⁴

It has been called 'a rather incendiary manifesto for a man of peace'.⁵ Its thirty thousand words resist forms of Western struggle, including terrorism. Gandhi stated that he wrote it 'in answer to the Indian school of violence'.⁶ He gives a brief history of the home rule movement, the partition of Bengal that caused an 'awakening' of Indian political life, and the swadeshi movement inaugurated by the leading nationalist Bal Gangadar Tilak that urged the boycott of foreign goods and the promotion of home produce.

Hind Swaraj contains everything that Gandhi had gathered from Ruskin, Tolstoy and Thoreau on the simple life well lived, with additions from Edward Carpenter. The book is a strong condemnation of what stood for progress in the West: 'I feel that if India would discard "modern civilisation" she would only gain by doing so,' he wrote, in describing its message. 'I am not aiming at destroying railways or hospitals, though I would certainly welcome their natural destruction. Neither railways nor hospitals are a test of a high and pure civilisation. At best they are a necessary evil. Neither one adds one inch to the moral stature of a nation.'[7] The destruction of these, along with the law courts, machinery and cloth mills, would take place in due course as the nation's moral integrity was refined. Gandhi wanted a return to conditions before the industrial revolution that had made economic prosperity the main object of politics.

'If India adopted the doctrine of love as an active part of her religion and introduced it in her politics, Swaraj would descend upon India from heaven . . . I bear no enmity towards the English but I do towards their civilisation.'[8] He lauded the culture of India before the advent of the great cities and railway networks, the village India that still existed 'where this cursed modern civilisation had not reached'. He saw the spiritual legacy of India as having been corrupted by Western ideas and technology: 'What you and I have hitherto considered beneficial for India no longer appears to me to be so . . . railways, lawyers and doctors have impoverished the country so much that if we do not wake up in time, we shall be ruined.'[9] Railways spread the plague; lawyers were lazy and over-remunerated for questionable services; doctors encouraged illness by effectively treating conditions which would not arise were people's lifestyles better. 'I have indulged in vice, I contract a disease, a doctor cures me, the odds are that I shall repeat the vice.'[10] Gandhi had once, he said, wished to be a doctor, an ambition he had no more. He wrote elsewhere: 'I was entirely off track when I considered that I should receive a medical training. It would be sinful for me in any way whatsoever to take part in the abominations that go on in hospitals.'[11] He also attacked factories, air transport and publishing.

The way to return to this blessed pre-industrial state was by 'passive resistance', which was defined as 'a method of securing rights by personal suffering; it is the reverse of resistance by arms . . . Those who want to become passive resisters for the service of the country have to observe perfect chastity, adopt poverty, follow truth and cultivate fearlessness.' Gandhi warned: 'A man who is unchaste loses stamina, becomes emasculated and cowardly. He whose mind is given over to animal passion is not capable of any great effort.'[12]

The immediate surprise of *Hind Swaraj* is the form in which the book is written – that of a Socratic dialogue, with which Gandhi had familiarised himself by reading Plato while in prison. The 'Editor' represents Gandhi, the 'Reader' his opponents who prefer more violent means of direct action. The authorities he cites are almost all Western: six books by Tolstoy, two each by Ruskin and Thoreau but also *The White Slaves of England*, R.H. Sherard's book (1897) on the distress of industrial workers, and the homosexual utopian socialist Edward Carpenter's *Civilisation: Its Cause and Cure* which described civilisation as a disease of the communities of men. Carpenter was a vegetarian who ran his own small community near Sheffield. Gandhi's use of him is particularly noteworthy, because Carpenter urged gender equality and greater openness about sex, a recognition of the decency and beauty of sexual relations as part of a general 'liberation' from civilisation's yoke. Gandhi, selective as always, simply did not engage with this discourse.

Hind Swaraj was revolutionary in its rejection of modernity; other liberation movements had rejected their masters on the basis of Western liberalism in a call for national self-determination and the rights of man. Gandhi rejected everything for a purely Indian model with its elevation of farming and the village economy as ideals to be pursued, while the nation would turn its back on modernity. Gandhi did not want 'English rule without the Englishmen'. It was not British strength but Indian weakness and blind self-interest that kept the British in India, he argued.

He had previously read Annie Besant's nationalist work and reprinted her essay 'How to Build a Nation' in *Indian Opinion* in 1907; he was also influenced by the conservative Catholic G.K. Chesterton's reflections that Indian nationalism was not very Indian if it merely hankered after Western institutions. This was a time of revolutionary manifestos for the new century. Just a few years earlier, in 1902, Lenin had written his pamphlet *What Is To Be Done?* which adumbrated the way forward for communism, asserting that the working class could not be expected to carry forward the revolution spontaneously – that would produce only a trade-union consciousness. What they needed was a cadre of dedicated professional revolutionaries to lead and inspire them. Gandhi, with his ashram-trained satyagrahis and centralised theoretical base, was not so far from this ideal. He was remarkable, but he was also a man of his time: the influences that had acted on him had acted on others who also wished to remodel the world.

Unlike the communists, who embraced modernity and material progress (their underlying philosophy was dialectical *materialism*, after all), Gandhi thought a state of perfect harmony could only be reached by spiritual means. He was not blind to the achievements of other revolutionaries, however, and said of Bolshevism that 'an ideal that is sanctified by the sacrifices of such master spirits as Lenin cannot go in vain.'[13] And like the communists, Gandhi was mistrustful of what the Marxists would call 'bourgeois democracy'. He was uncomfortable with the swings of voters' opinions and with control by political parties over the political process, which left little room for the Gandhian ascendancy of individual conscience. Though he always worked within organisations with a declared democratic aim, Gandhi did not want to commit himself as a fighter for democracy. When asked to define what sort of government he was fighting for in India he said: 'I am not interested in words, and I never worry myself about the form of government.'[14] There has to be a suspicion that a benevolent king presiding over a nation of villages would have suited Gandhi very well. He also believed in cooperation, not conflict, between labour and capital. He had no difficulty in accepting support from Ghanshyam Das Birla, a leading industrialist with interests in almost every industry, who was a benefactor and follower of Gandhi for thirty-two years, from soon after Gandhi's return to India until his death.

Astute Indian observers noted the roots of Christian thinking in the redemption through suffering promoted in *Hind Swaraj*. Shyamji Krishnavarma, in his monthly journal *The Indian Sociologist* ('an organ of freedom, and of political, social and religious reform'), described Gandhi as 'an admirer of Jesus Christ' and argued that he was trying to put into practice 'the extreme Christian theory'. He satirised the imperialists' belief in Christianity: 'They seem to think that Jesus Christ meant the Englishman to do all the smiting and his Indian victims all the turning of the cheek.'[15] Krishnavarma, another English-educated barrister nationalist, criticised Gandhi's 'doctrine of self-sacrifice or voluntary surrender'. He was right in his belief that Gandhi approved of the elevation of suffering in Christianity: he had his Indian followers learn the words of the hymn 'When I Survey the Wondrous Cross'; he was always moved to tears by such lines as 'See from His head, His hands, His feet/ Sorrow and love flow mingling down.'[16]

Hind Swaraj was published serially in South Africa in *Indian Opinion*, then as a book in Gujarati. The Bombay government in March 1910 seized as seditious copies of *Hind Swaraj*, but also Gandhi's Gujarati translations of Plato's *Defence of Socrates* and of Ruskin's *Unto This Last*. As Gandhi said: 'They are in a state of panic and, wishing to do something, they intend to stop the circulation of literature that shows the slightest independence of spirit.' He went on to offer a lesson to the Indian government in now to stop the spread of violence: 'The only way we know to eradicate the disease is to popularise passive resistance of the right stamp. Any other way, especially repression, must fail in the long run.'[17] Gandhi's very Gandhian response to such repression was to repeat the offence: to publish his own English translation of *Hind Swaraj*.

After the completion of the South African campaign, Gandhi could take up the threads of his work on Indian independence. He left for London in July 1914, Kasturba and Kallenbach with him. Kallenbach took his prized pair of binoculars, which Gandhi threw out of a porthole to emphasise to his friend the necessity of divesting himself of worldly goods. It was probably just as well, since a German arriving in an English port in August 1914 with a powerful pair of binoculars would have been considered a spy. While the Gandhis and Kallenbach were at sea, Europe was moving towards war.

Gandhi again volunteered to serve in the ambulance corps, which was a less rewarding experience for him than such service had been previously as he became involved in challenging the discipline that the instructors, mere raw recruits, attempted to impose on the rest of them – he called it a 'mini satyagraha'. Gandhi contracted pleurisy and was not, in the event, engaged for nursing duties. His general health and his resistance to disease had been undermined by his fast over the 'fall' of Manilal and Jeki and by his excessive diets: he was at this time eating peanuts, bananas, lemons, olive oil, tomatoes and grapes, but no milk, cereals or pulses. He took a solemn vow not to take milk or ghee (clarified butter) again.

In London he was visited by the Under-Secretary of State for India Charles Roberts and his wife Lady Cecilia. Lady Cecilia was solicitous for his health and urged him to drink milk, even finding a substitute milk preparation for him, but Gandhi discerned it was in fact powdered milk and discarded it. To treat his illness with more sensitivity to his wishes, he called in his old colleague from the Vegetarian Society, Dr Allinson, who reassured him he need not drink milk and furthermore prescribed a fat-free diet, with a regime of fresh air and warm baths. But medical opinion was that Gandhi would never improve in the English climate and that he had better return to India, which had been his planned objective. Kallenbach had been going to accompany him, but as an enemy alien he could not be given free access to India, so he returned to South Africa.

Gandhi had been expecting to meet Gokhale in London to discuss his future political career, but his mentor had gone to France for a cure for his diabetes and was stranded there because of the war. Gokhale asked his friend the nationalist poet Sarojini Naidu to visit Gandhi, an encounter that started a long and affectionate relationship which was without the fawning on Gandhi that characterised his relations with many others who were close to him. Naidu, an educated and independent woman, always tempered her respect for him with humour aimed at his spiritual pride. When Naidu first met him he was 'a living picture of a little man with a shaven head, seated on the floor on a black prison blanket and eating a messy meal of squashed tomatoes and olive oil out of a wooden prison bowl'. She burst into laughter at this improbable vision of the great leader. Gandhi invited her to share his meal: '"No thanks," I replied, sniffing. "What an abominable mess it is."'[18]

A reception was held in his honour by British and Indian admirers at the Hotel Cecil. Among those present were Sarojini Naidu and Mohammad Ali Jinnah, who was heading a Congress delegation that was in London lobbying parliament. Gandhi told the audience his impoverished labourers were 'the salt of India; on them will be built the Indian nation that is to be'.[19] This was news: the independent India of previous aspirations was going to be constructed by the lawyers and administrators of the Indian middle class – the introduction of the ignorant masses was Gandhi's contribution.

As noted earlier, what to wear on different occasions was always a preoccupation with Gandhi. He had lately been defining dress as appropriate to climate rather than to anything else, decrying the popular notion 'that it is best for us to put on European dress, that it is more impressive and wins us greater respect from people'. He conceded that 'the European costume is suitable for the cold countries of Europe, the Indian costume suits both Hindus and Muslims in India'.[20] On the way to India on the *Arabia* at the end of 1914 Gandhi switched back from European dress to the clothes of an indentured labourer, thereby identifying himself with his greatest triumph, though he decided that in future he would wear the 'customary dress' of his class in Gujarat – a turban, shirt, dhoti, cloak and scarf. Not for the first time he was on the one hand pondering a challenge to empire, and on the other fussing about his wardrobe. When he and his family arrived in Bombay on 9 January 1915 it was obvious his concern for his appearance was justified: a vast crowd was waiting to see the great leader return to his homeland. He was fêted at receptions given in his honour, including one hosted by the Gujarati community and chaired by Jinnah, one of its leading politicians. Gandhi surprised his hosts with his simple Indian costume and his insistence on speaking in his native Gujarati rather than in English.

His response to Jinnah's urbane welcoming speech was that he was 'glad to find a Mahomedan not only belonging to his own region's sabha [assembly] but chairing it'.[21] He meant the remark positively, but it was the first time, though not by any means the last, that he completely failed to understand Jinnah, for whom his religion was a fact like his height or hair colour, not a path by which he should live his life, and certainly not a matter he wanted singled out for mention.

Raihana Tyabji, daughter of a wealthy family in Bombay, testified to Gandhi's attractiveness despite his deliberately ordinary appearance: 'I was in my teens. I caught a glimpse of him in the midst of silks and brocades, frills and sparkling jewels. He was dressed in a coarse khadi (hand-spun) dhoti and looked like a small-time tailor who'd wandered in by mistake. I lost my heart to him. He became my father, my mother, my girlfriend, my boyfriend, my daughter, my son, my teacher, my guru.'[22]

His achievements had impressed the imperialists also: the Governor of Bombay Lord Willingdon wished to meet him. The Governor asked his guest to tell him if he intended any action against the government, a request to which Gandhi willingly consented. Willingdon continued: 'You may come to me whenever you like, and you will see that my government does not wilfully do anything wrong.'[23] He was later, in 1915, honoured by the government of India with the Kaiser-i-Hind gold medal for services to Indians in South Africa. The British thus tempered their political suspicion of Gandhi with praise for his undoubted qualities of leadership, in the hope that they could ease him into the role of a reformer like Gopal Krishna Gokhale rather than a firebrand such as Bal Gangadhar Tilak who had been released from jail the previous year.

Workers had approached Gandhi about an oppressive customs cordon at Viramgam station (between princely Kathiawar and British India); Gandhi spoke to Willingdon, who sympathised but said it was a matter for the national government. When Gandhi had occasion to meet the Viceroy in 1917 (by which time the position was held by Lord Chelmsford) he raised the matter and the cordon was removed. Gandhi represented it as a success for satyagraha – though objectively, it looked more like routine diplomacy forestalling civil disobedience over an unjustifiable procedure.

Laxmidas had died in March 1914, and his middle brother Karsandas the previous year, leaving Gandhi head of the family. He travelled to Rajkot and Porbandar to see his bereaved relatives; then, that business over with, he was eager to see his Phoenix family. The travelling community of Gandhi's supporters had already arrived at Shantiniketan, an educational centre near Calcutta, founded by the poet and Bengali nationalist Rabindranath Tagore who in 1913 had been awarded the Nobel Prize for literature. There they were assisted by Charles Freer Andrews, a teacher at Shantiniketan. A former Anglican clergyman, Andrews had met Gandhi in South Africa during the final campaign when Gokhale had sent him from India to observe and assist. He became one of Gandhi's keenest (though not uncritical) supporters, writing several books promoting his message to Western audiences.

The Phoenix party had been assigned separate quarters with Gandhi's cousin Maganlal in charge, and he made it his business to see that all Gandhi's rules were scrupulously observed. When he arrived, Gandhi attempted to extend his self-help message to the pupils at Shantiniketan, having them sack the cooks and take on all the kitchen duties themselves. This was not universally welcomed – they were at the centre to be educated, not to work in the kitchens. 'There used to be daily discussions,' he remarked laconically. The 'experiment' was dropped. Although Gandhi was eager to apply his satyagraha principles to India, Gokhale had advised him not to dive straight into activism but to observe and learn for a year. Gokhale had found *Hind Swaraj* so crude and hastily conceived that he thought Gandhi would destroy the book after spending a year in India. In fact, in 1921 Gandhi would commend it: 'It teaches the gospel of love in place of that of hate. It replaces violence with self-sacrifice, it pits soul-force against brute-force.'[24]

When Gokhale died in Poona on 19 February 1915, Gandhi went there immediately. He thought it a good death: 'He died in harness. He was in full possession of all his faculties to the last and he was working away.'[25] Of Gokhale's personal message for him he wrote: '[He] used to tell me that I was so harsh that people felt terrified of me and allowed themselves to be dragged against their will out of sheer fear or in the attempt to please me, and that those who found themselves too weak assumed an artificial pose in the end. I put far too heavy a burden on people.'[26]

Gandhi had never joined Gokhale's Servants of India Society, feeling that merely to do Gokhale's bidding was sufficient, without the constraint of an organisation. With Gokhale gone, Gandhi now applied for membership of the society, which meant that, given his experience and national standing, he would be in a position to take over the now leaderless organisation. Some members of the society, meeting at Poona, favoured his admission while others were strongly against it, doubtless fearing that within a short time of his joining, the society would be just a vehicle for Gandhi's ideas. He withdrew his application for membership before it caused more dissent.

He attended the Kumbha Mela, a religious festival held once every twelve years, where he was introduced to the kind of life he could expect when he appeared in public: his entire time was taken up with sitting in a tent having religious discussions with pilgrims who called on him and being treated as an object of 'darshan' – religious merit gained by observers gazing on an exalted person. Now that Gandhi was one such, he was never, for the rest of his life, to be left alone. He complained at the festival: 'I was followed even to the bathing ghat by these darshan-seekers, nor did they leave me alone whilst I was having my meals.' He wrote of their 'blind love' making him angry and 'sore at heart'.[27] Offended by the impiety of greedy holy men and by the hypocrisy and slovenliness of many of the pilgrims, Gandhi decided to impose an act of self-denial 'in atonement for the iniquity prevailing there and [to] purify myself'.[28] He therefore took a vow in April 1915 to eat only five articles of food a day, counting such items of flavouring as cardamoms as separate articles, and never to eat after dark.

In May 1915 Gandhi set up the Satyagraha Ashram at Kochrab near Ahmedabad where the Phoenix ashramites formed the core in a house on land rented to them by a local barrister. Gandhi had wanted to settle in Gujarat as his home province (and that of many of the ashramites), but also wanted to be close to Ahmedabad as it had long been a centre of hand-loom weaving and he had determined that weaving was going to be important in the independence movement. He also felt, unashamedly, that the necessary funds would be best obtained from well-wishers in such a wealthy city. It was important, too, to be in a British area not (like Rajkot) a princely one, as it was British power in India that Gandhi would challenge.

Whereas the first ashram, Phoenix, was set up to save money in order to ensure the success of *Indian Opinion*, and the second, Tolstoy Farm, to give a home to imprisoned passive resisters, now Gandhi declared to the *Madras Mail* that his objective was the 'training [of] young men, and also women and children, for long service to the Motherland'. Everyone should perform some work of manual labour; for the first time it was 'proposed also to introduce hand weaving' and, inevitably, vows of both poverty and chastity would be 'strictly observed at the institution.'[29]

The discipline that Gandhi imposed was even more severe than that in the South African ashrams. He elaborated on his already stringent rules of conduct: 'If I need only one shirt to cover myself with but use two, I am guilty of stealing one from another. For, a shirt which could have been of use to someone else does not belong to me. If five bananas are enough to keep me going, my eating a sixth one is a form of theft.'[30] He compiled lists of tools and kitchen utensils for the ashram, to be paid for by the Servants of India Society, as pledged by Gokhale. This time the rules were written down well in advance. The inhabitants were divided into three classes: controllers, novitiates and students. The controllers were sworn to truthfulness, refusing to lie even for the good of the country; to non-violence; to celibacy, to 'control of the palate'; to non-stealing (meaning both the obvious and not taking more from the community than one's absolutely basic needs) and non-possession. They were also expected to use swadeshi (Indian-made produce), to be fearless, to use Indian languages rather than English, to do manual work and to weave cloth on hand-looms. The two lesser grades aspired to similar standards.

The rules were later refined to demand that the ashram inhabitants renounce Hindu beliefs on untouchability and that they act as though they were outside the caste system – though without undermining caste discipline. Gandhi maintained a delicate balance between the wholesale renunciation of Hindu beliefs, which would have alienated his vast potential constituency, and a rejection of such practices as untouchability which were incompatible with common decency.

One of Gandhi's associates wisely suggested a vow of humility for the ashram, perhaps because he had observed the spiritual arrogance of the ashramites; but Gandhi rejected the suggestion, fearing 'humility would cease to be humility the moment it became a matter of vow.'[31] Charles Andrews also had qualms about the rules – he recalled: 'I wrote out for him a long statement very earnestly asking him to withdraw the vow of celibacy, which appeared to me one of those short cuts, foreign to the Hindu religion, bringing inevitable evil in its train.' Gandhi replied at length, stating amongst other things: 'Those who want to perform national service, or those who want to have a glimpse of the real religious life, must lead a celibate life, no matter if married or unmarried.'[32] His supporters, like his opponents, were to become familiar with this approach of his to criticism, which simply reiterated the initial proposition with greater emphasis. Andrews remained with Tagore's settlement and did not join Gandhi's group.

Gandhi had long been refining his proscription of sex to include married couples, and it was no longer obvious that he felt sex was permissible even for the purpose of procreation. He wrote that sexual indulgence 'and the resultant loss do much physical harm. The vitality of both mind and body developed through many years is so much impaired by even one such occasion that it takes a long time to regain it and, even so, the original state is never restored wholly . . . I have vivid memories of the exalted state of mind before a lapse and the pitiable condition after it.' His advice was that husbands should not be alone with their wives, that they should sleep in separate rooms, remain fully occupied with useful activity and pure thoughts, and when they felt passion they should take a cold bath.[33]

As time passed, even more severe discipline was imposed, so that by the late 1920s three infringements of the rules meant expulsion; frequent infringements included lateness at prayer meetings and not spinning the required daily quota of yarn. The many rules and the fixed regime may be said to have had a function in terms of discipline, much as army life involves many rules that independently have no great value but which encourage the habit of obedience. Celibacy had a function in addition to its contribution to blind discipline: the manipulation of sex by a cult leader such as Gandhi serves to increase devotion to himself, weakening bonds between couples and increasing attachment to the guru.[34]

The ashram day was to begin at 4 a.m. with prayers at 5, then breakfast and manual work from 7 to 8.30. School work followed for the children, then a midday meal, then more school work between 12 and 3, then manual work. The evening meal was between 5 and 6 with prayers at 6.30. From 7 p.m. the ashramites were free to study and receive visitors. No paid teachers were employed, but five people among the thirty-five ashramites were teachers and able to take on the task of educating the children, so at least this aspect of life was not as neglected as it had been in previous communities of Gandhi's.

With plague raging in Kochrab in summer 1917, the ashram moved to a new site some four miles north of Ahmedabad. Gandhi was pleased with its proximity to Sabarmati Central Jail, the place of incarceration where satyagrahis expected to end up. Many were disappointed at the lack of political engagement in the ashram where time was taken up with tedious chores and prayers, but there was never any doubt that Gandhi was preparing his followers for a holy war in which some might die. One evening after prayers, when he was explaining the importance of ashram discipline and the role he envisaged for it in the national struggle for freedom, he said that

> he looked forward to the day when he would call out all the inmates of the Ashram, who had been trained in those disciplines, to immolate themselves at the altar of non-violence. Unmoved, he would watch them fall one after another before a shower of bullets, without a trace of fear or hatred, but only love in their hearts. And then, when the last one of them had fallen, he would himself follow.[35]

Gandhi did not in the end command his followers to commit suicide, but in the light of the late-twentieth-century cults of Jim Jones at Jonestown, David Koresh at Waco and Marshall Applewhite at Rancho Santa Fe, Gandhi's exhortations have an uncomfortably modern ring.

One challenging reform that Gandhi had to put into effect was to ban from the ashram 'this miserable, wretched, enslaving spirit of "untouchableness" . . . an ineffaceable blot that Hinduism today carries with it'.[36] The ashramites were sworn to oppose discrimination against untouchables, but this was an easy pledge to make when there were no untouchables in sight. This despised class were not expected ever to want to enter the ashram – they had internalised the disgust others felt towards them, and rarely even attempted to mix with the other castes. Then, a few months after the ashram was established in September 1915, Gandhi received a request via a trusted supporter for an untouchable family to join them. He had not expected that the pledge to oppose untouchability would be challenged so soon, but he welcomed Dud-abhai, a Bombay teacher, his wife and daughter into the fold, so long as they kept to the rules as others did.

Now that the ashram was 'contaminated', all financial support stopped. The man in charge of the well, which the ashram shared with other locals, considered that drops of water from buckets pulled up by Dud-abhai would contaminate him and so he took to swearing at the ashramites and molesting Dudabhai. They were threatened with a social boycott – they would be ostracised and denied community facilities as a way of forcing them all to leave. Gandhi told Dudabhai to put up with the abuse and continue drawing water at any cost. This had a benefi-cial result: his bullying having no effect, the abusive well-keeper 'became ashamed and ceased to bother us'.[37]

Gandhi reacted to the critics with characteristic courage: if they were forced out of the area, he would move the entire community to Ahmed-abad's untouchable quarter and set up there. He would not compromise with injustice. He soon discovered that the ashram was out of funds and that they had nothing for the next month. A short time afterwards, a car pulled up outside the ashram and a messenger sent for Gandhi. The car's owner was Ambalal Sarabhai, who ran one of the biggest tex-tile mills in Ahmedabad. He gave Gandhi enough money to secure the future of the ashram for a year – financially, they could now weather the storm.

However, there was also hostility within the ashram: the women were particularly offended by the presence of untouchables. Dudabhai's wife and daughter were not allowed into the kitchen, and anything the child touched was washed. Kasturba and Maganlal's wife Santokben were the worst offenders, scrupulously avoiding any contact with the untouch-able family.

For the fledgling ashram this was a challenge of greater magnitude than its financial troubles. At the regular evening prayer meeting one day, Gandhi delivered an ultimatum: Dudabhai and his family must be completely accepted – anyone who did not want to accept them must leave. He had put it to Kasturba in person: 'I have told Mrs Gandhi she could leave me and we should part good friends.'[38] Kasturba stayed, moved by Gandhi's paradoxical appeal to orthodoxy: 'The argument that a woman in following in her husband's footsteps incurs no sin appealed to her and she quieted down.'³⁹ Several residents went to Gandhi's room and begged his forgiveness, and some approached the untouchable family to apologise. Maganlal, however, Gandhi's most trusted disciple, fasted in protest against the admission of untouchables. Gandhi fasted in response, and Maganlal left with his wife.

Gandhi's position was thus borne out: his supporters were put on notice that opposition to untouchability was not a pious sentiment, but a fact. He was later to note that it was the most orthodox Hindus who went on to fund the ashram's growing expenditure; his steadfastness on this point of principle had not driven them away.

Gandhi was actively seeking out people of ability who would be both useful to him, and obedient. This was a key combination. The problem was that the ashramites were dutiful but lacked the capacity for independent action, while the Congress activists had the opposite qualities – too much independence and not enough obedience to Gandhian thought.

One new disciple who would leave a lasting record was Mahadev Desai, a lawyer and member of Annie Besant's Home Rule League. About a visit in August 1917 he wrote that Gandhi 'created in me mixed feelings of love, dismay and joy'. The twenty-five-year-old idealist had been told by Gandhi: 'It is not without reason that I have asked you to visit my place every day. I want you to come and stay with me. I have seen your capacity during the last three days. I have found in you just the type of young man for whom I have been searching for the last two years.' He said he had spoken in this way to only three persons before – Polak, Schlesin and Maganlal – but of the latter he said: 'Let us, however, leave aside Maganlal. The intelligence I have found in you I did not see in him.'⁴⁰ Desai became 'my man', in Gandhi's words. He and his wife joined him in Champaran on the forthcoming indigo campaign, and Desai was Gandhi's constant companion and amanuensis till his death at Gandhi's side twenty-five years later.

Gandhi's dictatorial behaviour with his children continued at the ashram. In 1916 he cast Manilal out because he helped his destitute brother Harilal. Harilal needed assistance because he had lost money speculating with his employer's funds and so had lost his job. 'This letter will make you sick,' Gandhi wrote to Kallenbach. 'Yet I must give you the information. Manilal has deceived me again. He gave some money to Harilal and disowned all knowledge of it when I questioned him.'[41] Manilal was sent from the ashram to Madras, where he was to rely on his own resources; he could return only after he had earned the sum he had given Harilal plus the cost of the journey. Gandhi went on a fast. He seemed unable to conceive that giving Manilal the choice of disobeying his father or abandoning his brother was putting an impossible moral burden on the young man. For Gandhi an action was right or wrong. He did, however, later send a letter to a publisher in Madras, recommending Manilal for a job in a printing company.

It may have been Kasturba's silent reproaches that led Gandhi to have pity on Manilal; she would not criticise his decisions outright, but her displeasure was known. He said: 'I learned the lessons of non-violence from my wife. Her determined resistance to my will on the one hand, and her quiet submission to the suffering my stupidity involved on the other hand, ultimately made me ashamed of myself and cured me of my stupidity.'[42] Later Gandhi was to complain that Manilal was 'finding out ways of ease and luxury. The life of discipline is gone for him. That of indulgence has begun.'[43] Harilal was unable to support his wife Gulab and she had to go back to her parents; she also visited the ashram, where Gandhi found it easier to enjoy the presence of his grandchildren than that of his children.

Gandhi now marked out his constituency. His great success in South Africa had been with the poor, and now he increasingly identified with them by his dress, his living standards in the ashram, his use of the vernacular rather than English, and his tireless travelling in vile third-class train compartments. Congress had ignored the masses, never claiming to be speaking for the poor and illiterate millions of India. The British had encouraged the restive middle class: their electoral rights were based on taxable income or education. Gandhi campaigned for self-improvement: he wanted his countrymen to pay more attention to personal cleanliness and sanitation, and he argued with the authorities for improved conditions for rail and boat passengers.

He also argued for a common language, originally promoting Hindi but then, feeling it was not sufficiently inclusive, he called for Hindustani to be adopted. Hindustani, a mixture of Hindi and Urdu, would as a national language in its written form replace written Urdu (a modified Arabic script) with Devanagari script (with the distinctive line running along the tops of the letters linking them together). This was therefore not a straightforward matter and was another potential source of disunity between Hindus, who wanted a pure form of Hindi to be the national language, and Muslims, who wanted to stay with Urdu. Gandhi eventually suggested that all pupils should learn forms of Hindustani written in both scripts. He was taken to task by those who charged him with insincerity over the language question because of the liberal use he made of English himself. He was also criticised by those who felt the charm and purity of Hindi were being sacrificed to please Muslims. One severe critic (and Hindu militant), Nathuram Godse, remarked: 'Everybody in India knows that there is no language called Hindustani; it has no grammar, it has no vocabulary. It is a mere dialect, it is spoken, but not written. It is a bastard tongue and a cross-breed between Hindi and Urdu, and not even the Mahatma's sophistry could make it popular.'[44]

At the opening of Benares Hindu University in February 1916 in what has been called one of the most incendiary speeches he would ever make, Gandhi's address followed Annie Besant's, who had argued for the constitutional development of India's status within the British Empire. Gandhi, now having served more than the year of political silence demanded of him by Gokhale, was more radical. In the uneasy atmosphere following a recent bomb attempt on the life of the Viceroy Lord Hardinge (who, incidentally, was sympathetic to Gandhi and had acted to end the indentured labour system), he spoke against violence in the nationalist cause. His fine distinctions may have been lost, for he was talking about political violence and applauding the spirit, though not the actions, of the 'anarchists'. 'Please stop it,' said Annie Besant, and the princes who were on the platform got up and left in a body, perhaps under the misapprehension that he was condoning attacks on the political ruling class.

To applause, Gandhi continued: 'I compare the richly bedecked noblemen with the millions of the poor. And I feel like saying to these noblemen: "There is no solution for India unless you strip yourselves

of this jewellery and hold it in trust for our countrymen in India . . .
Our salvation can only come through the farmer. Neither the lawyers,
nor the doctors, nor the rich landlords are going to secure it."[45] What
seemed so inflammatory, akin to communism, even, was not quite that:
he was not calling on the peasantry to overthrow their masters, but on
the masters to realise their moral responsibilities to the poor.

In 1916 advances were being made in nationalist politics in India,
with Gandhi playing no more than a minor role, if any. Since the moderates Pherozeshah Mehta and Gokhale had both died in 1915, the way
was open for the radicals to make progress: Tilak and Besant both started
Home Rule Leagues in 1916, in Poona and Madras respectively, and
Jinnah later became chairman of a Home Rule League in Bombay. 'Home
rule' at this time meant dominion status within the Empire as enjoyed
by Australia, New Zealand, Canada, Newfoundland and South Africa.

All nationalists were concerned about the unity of India after independence; great efforts were made to bring Muslims over to home rule.
The Muslims, who constituted a fifth of the population of India, feared
they would be swamped by the 'Hinduisation' of the nation if the British
left. This was by no means without justification. The Muslims had con-
quered India in the sixteenth century, to be displaced in their turn by
the British; for many Hindus home rule meant the restoration of a Hindu
nation, and Gandhi's profound Hinduism did nothing to dispel this
notion. Such Western-looking secularists as Jinnah and the Nehru family
were a better bet for a state in which citizenship would be more important than religion, but such a state would be anathema to Gandhi's way
of thinking.

Though Jinnah was known as the ambassador of Hindu–Muslim unity,
he was far from being a conventional Muslim. He was a sophisticated,
westernised, secular Muslim who drank, ate pork, and had married a
Parsi, the daughter of a friend, having fallen in love with her at first
sight when she was sixteen. He felt no shame about enjoying the culture of the West as well as that of the East, and the good things of life.
He was, therefore, as far removed from Gandhi as it was possible for a
man to be while still sharing the same platform – at the Bombay Provincial Conference held in Ahmedabad in October 1916 Gandhi proposed
– successfully – that Mohammad Ali Jinnah should preside.

Jinnah had not been a member of the Muslim League at its foundation in 1906, as the League had then been dedicated to loyalty to the
concept of British government in India. In 1913, however, the League
changed its platform to one of Indian independence. Jinnah then joined
and became a leading figure of both the Muslim League and the Indian
National Congress. It was his view that in an independent India Muslim
safety would be guaranteed by their holding one-third of parliamentary
seats.

Jinnah had become a member of the Imperial Legislative Council in
1910. Another member was Motilal Nehru, an immensely successful
lawyer who was defiantly secular in his behaviour: he insisted on English being spoken in his lavish home, drank the finest wines, paid scant
regard to religion and, as a gesture of his contempt for Hindu bigotry,
though he was a Brahmin kept an 'untouchable' as his personal servant.

The Lucknow Pact was an agreement drawn up between the Indian
National Congress and the Muslim League. At a meeting at the home
of the Nehru family in Allahabad in the United Provinces, the Congress
and the League, convening at the same time in Lucknow in December
1916, agreed to work together for early self-government on the basis of
arrangements that would provide a constitutional system, with direct
elections and separate electorates for religious minorities. Gandhi had
no great role to play in these political manoeuvres. Indeed, the secular
mind that conceived of India as having separate electorates to protect
the interests of religious minorities was remote indeed from his notion
of an India of self-sufficient villages out of the *Ramayana*, their peoples
united by spiritual striving.

In 1916 Gandhi for the first time met Vallabhbhai Patel, a man from
a farming background but by his own efforts a London-trained barrister; he was from Gujarat, as were Gandhi and Jinnah. Destined to
become home minister and deputy prime minister in the first Indian
government, Patel had regarded Gandhi with suspicion for his cranky
ideas, once suggesting he would 'ask you if you know how to sift peb-
bles from wheat. And that is supposed to bring independence.'[46] When
they renewed their acquaintance later that year in Lucknow when Congress and the Muslim League met, he fell under Gandhi's spell. Gandhi
later had Patel take command of a satyagraha of peasants who were

resisting unjust tax demands in the Kheda district of Gujarat; it was here that Patel earned the right to be considered Gandhi's first lieutenant in the campaign field.

Gandhi's modus operandi, as usual, was via religion, not electoral machinery. He formed a relationship with the Ali brothers, two educated Muslims who had approached him after a speech he made to students in Calcutta. In common with many Muslims, the brothers were disturbed that India's position in the British Empire meant they found themselves set against the Ottoman Empire in the war that had begun in 1914. Since the sixteenth century every Ottoman emperor declared himself Caliph, or head of the community of believers, thus bestowing on himself a religious as well as a state authority. As Turkey dominated Arabia, where the holy shrines of Islam were located, supporters of the Ottomans could claim an attack on their Empire was in fact an attack on their religion and on the heirs of the Prophet. This was the Caliphate, referred to as Khilafat in India. Mohammad Ali and Shaukat Ali had been imprisoned under the Defence of India Act for preaching opposition to the British war effort and support for the Khilafat.

Gandhi saw the Khilafat issue as one near to his heart, combining religion with anti-British feeling; he felt it was an issue about which he could unite Hindus and Muslims. He had felt it improper to benefit from Britain's difficulties in the First World War, however, and at that time had moderated his anti-Britishness. Annie Besant, on the other hand, believed 'England's need is India's opportunity' and had set out to exploit the hard-pushed Empire. Incensed by the British reaction to the Easter Rising in Dublin in 1916, Besant rose to new heights of denunciation of the Empire. The new Viceroy Lord Chelmsford bowed to demands to have her silenced, and she was interned in 1917. Gandhi had considered mounting a satyagraha campaign over the issue but did not receive Congress support and thought better of it. Besant was released in September that year. Gandhi was prepared to promote local heroes, but it was not until he felt confident enough to back Jawaharlal Nehru that his campaigns backed any national figures. He also considered a satyagraha for the Ali brothers, but by the time he was able to proceed with it there were other more pressing demands on his time.

Gandhi made no great attempts to woo Congress leaders, as he had done on his previous attempts to enter national politics. His great achievement in his first years back in India was to mobilise industrial and farm workers. He had been pestered by a farmer called Rajkumar Shukla, who turned up first at Lucknow where he and Gandhi were both attending the Congress of December 1916. Shukla wanted Gandhi to turn his attention to the distress of the indigo planters in Champaran. Gandhi was ignorant of indigo and did not even know where Champaran was; and when he did, he was not inclined to travel to the Himalayan foothills in the province of Bihar. Shukla pursued him to another city, then returned to the ashram where he waited for Gandhi in order to repeat his request. When Gandhi went to Calcutta on an engagement, Shukla was there too. Finally Gandhi consented to visit Champaran, and travelled to Bihar on the train with Shukla, who was able to explain further.

In the indigo plantations subsistence farmers were obliged to cultivate three out of every twenty parts of their best land with the plant that produced the precious dye, to be delivered at fixed prices to their landlords. This was an unfair imposition, but the farmers had been further exploited and their rents manipulated by the greedy landlords as the world price of indigo changed. The farmers had become embroiled in legal battles in which their lawyers had impoverished them further without solving their problems. Shukla was a relatively well-off small farmer who had been involved in agitating against the landlords and briefly imprisoned because of his campaign. Realising he was out of his depth and making no progress, he turned to the inspirational abilities of Gandhi.

When they arrived at their destination, just before midnight, a crowd of students were waiting for the great man, but were at first disappointed they could not find him in either the first or the second-class carriages. They had ignored Shukla, an ill-educated peasant, until he revealed that Gandhi was with him. Shukla took them to him, saying: 'Here is the Mahatma.' This was perhaps the first time the honorific 'great soul', commonly used in India of people who have attained a level of spiritual enlightenment, was used of Gandhi.[47] The students were so overwhelmed by his presence that they uncoupled the beasts from the carriage that had been sent for him and pulled it themselves.

Gandhi's first act of organisation was to call the lawyers who had been representing the farmers and tell them they must forget about the court cases – this situation had to be handled politically. They must take depositions from the farmers to demonstrate how bad the situation had become, and they must expect no fees for this work. Gandhi could not understand two of the local languages and had difficulty with the Hindi dialect spoken regionally, so he needed translators. Six lawyers agreed to work with him, perhaps startled by the novelty and audacity of Gandhi's suggestion and by the sheer force of his personality. One of the helpers, a vakil (court pleader) and translator, was Rajendra Prasad, later to be India's first president.

Gandhi called on the British Planters' Association in April 1917 to inform them of what he was doing, and set off on a tour of the countryside to see the conditions for himself. He raised funds from wealthy Biharis and made public announcements in the newspapers so the nation knew what was happening in this remote corner of the subcontinent. He sent out volunteers to gather information around the villages, travelling on foot and by elephant to outlying areas. Among the villagers, who knew nothing of Congress or national politics, Gandhi assumed mythical status. He was seen as the fearless avenger of their woes, inheritor of the mantle of the heroes of the *Ramayana*. He was ordered to leave by the local government, which was in the pockets of the planters. Refusing to go, he was put on trial.

The Bihari government attempted to have the case against Gandhi postponed, but he was determined both to plead guilty of refusing on order to leave the province and to make a statement. He explained that he had come to study the problems between the farmers and the indigo planters 'with the assistance, if possible, of the administration and the planters', whom he had contacted for their observations.[48] Gandhi had also already written details of the situation to the Viceroy and other dignitaries. After a short delay, the case against him was withdrawn and he was assured of official assistance in his inquiry.

Gandhi set up with his helpers in a house to which the peasants came and told their stories, or just came to 'have darshan' of Gandhi. His commission tolerated government detectives being present when the statements were recorded, treating these uninvited guests with courtesy so that, far from intimidating the interviewees, they lent an official seal of approval to the proceedings. Some eight thousand statements were taken from 850 villages over a six-month period.

There was another story being played out in Bihar. The planters controlled the government there, but the more sophisticated officials of the national government knew Bihar was a benighted province and that its fraudulent behaviour would not stand up to the sort of international scrutiny that Gandhi could attract. Gandhi's satyagraha was backed by the government of India – they would not allow the administration in Bihar to persecute his supporters for the sake of the planters' corrupt gains.

Consequently, the Lieutenant Governor Sir Edward Gait asked to see Gandhi and told him he was willing to convene a government inquiry. Gandhi sat on the resulting committee, which produced a report unanimously in favour of the farmers, recommended the planters return some money to them and called on the government to forbid by law compulsory planting. Eventually the Champaran Agrarian Act of 1917 abolished the forced cultivation of indigo and reduced the rent increases imposed on the farmer. It did not end unrest in the region between the farmers and their landlords, but Gandhi's organisational skills were widely praised.

With the Ahmedabad mill-hands' dispute, a conflict on the ashram's doorstep, Gandhi branched out into far more controversial territory. The mill owners were represented by Ambalal Sarabhai, who was a Gandhi sympathiser, as he had shown by his earlier donation of funds to the ailing ashram. He entertained at his home such associates of Gandhi as Rabindranath Tagore, Motilal Nehru, Harry and Millie Polak and C.F. Andrews He was unconventional in other ways too: he treated his wife on terms of equality and she had been *his* choice of bride, not his parents'. He later said his friendship with Gandhi was based on a common passion for abolishing caste and other inequalities within Indian society, and a joint interest in ending British domination.[49] Gandhi had backed the swadeshi movement to promote home-produced textiles, which had given a tremendous boost to Indian textile mills like that of Sarabhai; but Gandhi had now turned against factory methods and was

Gandhi the trainee barrister in London in 1888–91, with his slicked-down hair and clear parting, wearing a three-piece suit with wing collar and bow tie. (Photo by Henry Guttmann/Getty Images)

Gandhi as a radical lawyer in South Africa with his secretary Sonja Schlesin and his friend Hermann Kallenbach. (Dinodia/Topfoto)

Gandhi and Kasturba in 1913, Gandhi wearing the knee-length white cotton tunic and the skirt-like lungi of the indentured labourers whom he is leading to victory. (Ullsteinbild/TopFoto)

Annie Besant, radical precursor of Gandhi as a mystic and nationalist leader. (The Granger Collection/TopFoto)

Madeleine Slade, known as Mirabehn in Gandhi's ashrams, an English gentlewoman who became one of his disciples. (Photo by Wallace Kirkland/Time Life Pictures/Getty Images)

Gandhi wearing the coarse, homespun cloth called khadi that became a uniform of nationalist defiance and an encouragement to local industry. (Picturepoint/TopFoto)

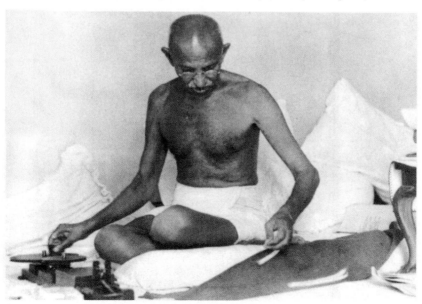

The transformation from English gentleman to ascetic is complete: Gandhi spinning cloth, posing for a picture wearing only a loincloth. (Ullsteinbild/TopFoto)

Gandhi and Sarojini Naidu, preparing to defy the Salt Act at Dandi in 1930.
(Press Association Images)

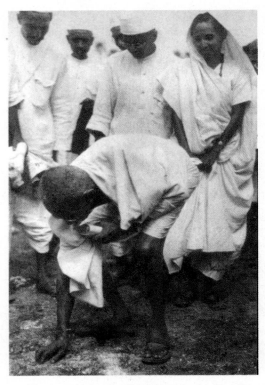

The picture widely represented as Gandhi picking up salt at Dandi on 6 April 1930.
In fact it was taken at Bhimrad three days later. (Picturepoint/TopFoto)

Gandhi finding his dress not entirely appropriate for the British climate as he arrives for the round-table conference on Indian constitutional reform in 1931.
(AP/AP/Press Association Images)

Lancashire textile workers cheer Gandhi, September 1931. (Ullsteinbild/TopFoto)

Gandhi in characteristic pose, leaning on two women, his 'walking sticks'– here, his doctor and biographer Sushila Nayar to his left, and his grandniece (by marriage) Abha Gandhi to his right. (AP/AP Press Association Images)

Gandhi's assassin, Hindu extremist Nathuram Godse, in a Delhi court-room to hear his arraignment. (AP/AP/Press Association Images)

The loincloth versus the sharp suit: Gandhi with Mohammad Ali Jinnah, leader of the Muslim League. (Ullsteinbild/TopFoto)

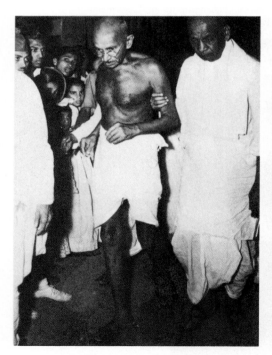

Gandhi with loyal follower Vallabhbhai Patel, later home minister and deputy prime minister of independent India. (Max Desfor/AP/Press Association Images)

Gandhi with future Indian prime minister Indira, daughter of Jawa-harlal Nehru, later Indira Gandhi. (Picturepoint/TopFoto)

Gandhi with Lord and Lady Mountbatten, the last Viceroy and Vicereine of British India. (AP/AP/Press Association Images)

Gandhi sharing a joke with Jawaharlal Nehru, who became the first prime minister of independent India. (Max Desfor/AP/Press Association Images)

Gandhi with Abha, to his left, and his grandniece (sometimes referred to as his granddaughter) Manu to his right. They were beside him when he was shot dead. (Ullsteinbild/TopFoto)

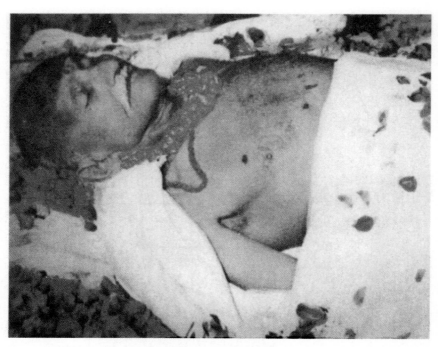

Gandhi on his bier, strewn with flowers, after his assassination on 30 January 1948.
(Ann Ronan Picture Library/HIP/TopFoto)

soon to be promoting hand-spinning – though it had not yet become the obsession it was later to be.

The mill-hands were represented by Ambalal's sister Anasuya. She had been married early but had renounced married life and went to England to study medicine, then social work. Back in India, she dedicated herself to social issues affecting industrial workers, earning the soubriquet Mother of the Labour Union. She campaigned for the rights of women workers and set up schools for factory children.

The present dispute had begun after a plague in Ahmedabad had led the factory owners to pay a 'plague bonus', aimed at keeping the workers at their machines when many were fleeing the city. This could be up to 70 per cent of their basic pay. When the plague subsided, so did the bonus, and the workers called for an increase in their rates. Anasuya asked Gandhi to speak to them. Gandhi was pleased to enter labour relations – it was where he had made his only real success in South Africa, after all. He made a speech calling on the workers to put forward only just demands and to be clean, to rid themselves of their addictions and to ensure their children got an education.

In the face of agitation, the mill owners decided to pre-empt any industrial action by taking the initiative, and imposed a lock-out starting on 22 February 1918. As the representative of the mill owners, Ambalal Sarabhai now found himself opposing not only his sister but Gandhi too, the spiritual leader whose work he was funding. Under the terms of the lock-out, only those workers who were prepared to accept an unnegotiable 20 per cent increase on their basic pay would be allowed to work. The workers agreed amongst themselves to settle on a demand for 35 per cent.

Gandhi offered to arbitrate, and spent mornings and evenings in the workers' districts in the company of Anasuya and some of his supporters, advising, giving them medical help and distributing leaflets which the few literate workers read to the others. Gandhi would sit under a babul tree and teach about the necessity of suffering and the fear of God. They would then drive back to Ambalal's home for tea, where Ambalal would often join them and talk over the day's events; or he would come to Gandhi's and eat unappetising ashram food with the workers' representatives and discuss the dispute.

The lock-out ended and a strike began on 11 March. The strikers' conditions worsened and they became restive when Gandhi forbade them to picket the mills; this was clearly not an industrial dispute as they understood it. As the strike wore on the workers' attendance at the large daily meetings was declining, and those who did attend were despondent. On 15 March, when Gandhi's nephew and lieutenant Chaganlal went to call them to a meeting, he was rebuffed. Anasuya and Gandhi 'come and go in their car, they eat sumptuous food, but we are suffering death-agonies; attending meetings does not prevent starvation,'[50] they protested.

At the next meeting Gandhi was pained, but his response was unequivocal: 'Unbidden and all by themselves the words came to my lips: "Unless the strikers rally and continue the strike till a settlement is reached, or till they leave the mills altogether, I will not touch food."' The workers were immediately struck by his sincerity and begged him to desist, but once he had made a pledge Gandhi was determined to keep to it. He explained later: 'My pledge is directed to making the mill-hands honour theirs and teaching them what value to attach to a pledge . . . I saw that it was necessary to show them by example how, for the sake of one's pledge, one had to undergo suffering.'[51]

Gandhi's followers wanted to join him in the enterprise but he forbade them with: 'Leave this to me, fasting is *my* business.'[52] It was not the last time that he would use his own body in a struggle with which he was identified, but to resort to such a moral weapon for a mere industrial dispute centring on a pay rise was extreme. He had previously fasted for personal spiritual reasons, or (arguably) to punish those who disobeyed him. Now fasting had evolved from being a response to the behaviour of his family or ashram members into an attempt to influence outside events. He was using it to put pressure on the industrialists, though he explicitly rejected this obvious conclusion and focused on the fast as a means to compel the strikers to keep their word.

It would bode ill for Gandhi's national prestige if he failed in this dispute on his own doorstep. He wanted the workers to stick to the 35 per cent that they had pledged, but the mill owners had also pledged not to give more than 20 per cent: why should one pledge be worth something and another nothing? Ambalal offered to accept the 35 per cent wage increase if Gandhi would promise to stay out of all labour disputes in Ahmedabad for ever. The psychologist Erik Erikson who studied this event in Gandhi's life in detail and spoke to many of the people involved considers that at this time Gandhi underwent extreme mood swings, at one moment seeing the fast as a necessary step towards all-Indian leadership, at another as a betrayal of the principles of satyagraha. 'In trying to use his homeland as a platform from which to ascend to national leadership, he suspected he might have slipped into the muck of Bania [merchants'] bickering.'[53]

The strike ended after three days of fasting, on 18 March, when the mill owners accepted arbitration and there was a compromise – 35 per cent for the first day, then 20 per cent and a complicated formula for the interim thereafter until the arbitrator had come to a decision. Gandhi considered this satisfied the pledge that the mill workers would not return to work without securing a 35 per cent increase, though he acknowledged that such an increase for only one day fulfilled the letter rather than the spirit of the pledge. The mill owners and the strikers had accepted a compromise because neither wanted to have Gandhi's death on their hands. This was the first of seventeen public fasts.

Notwithstanding the ongoing war, the British were continuing with proposals for the reform of Indian government that had begun with the Morley–Minto reforms introducing the direct election of Indians to legislative councils in 1909. The new Secretary of State for India Edwin Montagu, a true lover of India, began his tenure at the India Office with a declaration that, though no longer the clear endorsement of self-government at first intended, nevertheless enshrined the principles of a continuing move towards independence: 'The policy of His Majesty's Government, with which the Government of India are in complete accord, is that of the increasing association of Indians in every branch of the administration, and the gradual development of self-governing institutions, with a view to the progressive realisation of responsible government in India as an integral part of the British Empire.'[54]

Montagu travelled to India in 1917 to investigate with the new Viceroy Lord Chelmsford means by which Indians could be given more political opportunities. Among others he met Gandhi, Annie Besant, now released from jail, and Jinnah. It was widely believed (and perhaps by Jinnah himself) that when the septuagenarians Besant and Tilak were dead or at least infirm, Jinnah was the one Indian with the experience and ability to become the nationalist leader. Montagu noted that Gandhi 'dresses like a coolie' and 'lives practically on the air'.[55]

With the fair wind of a sympathetic Viceroy and an equally sympathetic Secretary of State, Gandhi felt they were sufficiently on the way to Indian independence for him to put into effect his radical beliefs about national reform. His goal was the change in society that could be brought about after independence; national self-rule was not for Gandhi, as it was for most politicians, in itself the goal.

The Secretary of State and the Viceroy produced the Montagu–Chelmsford Report in July 1918 proposing 'nationhood within the Empire', in which elected representatives would take over all matters in India except those involving foreign relations, finance and law and order. Congress held a special session in Bombay at the end of August to discuss the proposals, which culminated in the Government of India Act of 1919: this extended the franchise and increased the powers of both the central and provincial legislative councils. It introduced the concept of 'dyarchy', dual government, with power supposedly shared between the British imperial and the Indian democratic authorities. The concept had originally been proposed by Gandhi's old nemesis from South Africa, Lionel Curtis, and his round-table group of political thinkers. These advanced imperialists felt that the Empire could only be preserved as a federation of self-governing parts.

Gandhi's attitude to the British these days was cordial. He accepted an invitation to attend a war conference in April 1918 at which he again affirmed his support for the Empire. He wrote to the Viceroy that if it were within his power 'I would make India offer all her able-bodied sons as a sacrifice to the Empire at its critical moment; and I know that India, by this very act, would become the most favoured partner in the Empire and racial distinctions would become a thing of the past.'[56] He argued with his Indian friends that it was their duty to assist the British, that Indians could not preserve the country so long as they had no military tradition, and that to receive military training was a stepping-stone to home rule. If they demanded a status with the British akin to that of

Australia and Canada, they must 'render all possible help to the government at the present juncture . . . Our hope lies in the survival of the Empire . . . Besides, we shall learn military discipline as we help the Empire, gain military experience and acquire the strength to defend ourselves.'[57]

He produced and widely circulated an enlistment leaflet: 'We are regarded as a cowardly people. If we want to become free from that reproach, we should learn the use of arms.'[58] In answer to a query from Andrews that this was a long way from his proclaimed non-violence, Gandhi remarked that you could not teach non-violence to someone who could not kill – they might just be a coward. It was an argument he was later to use about sex – that there was no virtue in an impotent man refraining from intercourse. Reverting to his long-standing admiration for the English, he said: 'It is because every Englishman can stand on his legs and can defend his home and his village against any invader that the English village appears so incomparably superior to ours.'[59]

Recruiting was frustrating and lonely and he was without the support of many of his erstwhile admirers. Congress was against both unconditional support for the war and unconditional support for the Montagu–Chelmsford reforms which they felt did not go far enough; Gandhi was isolated except for his recent convert Vallabhbhai Patel, who walked as much as twenty miles a day with him in the Kheda region of Gujarat, where they had been campaigning against unfair taxes. Only a few recruits ever responded to their recruiting drive, however: many felt that the government had done little for them, and they failed to follow Gandhi's complex spiritual logic and considered his requesting them to bear arms was a frank contradiction of his exhortation to non-violence.

His current limited diet had already been giving him difficulties, he wrote: 'The skin has become too tender and delicate. A knife would tear it, much more easily than anybody else's. Although I invariably walk barefoot, the soles of my feet refuse to become tough and hard, as would anybody else's. My gums have become flabby and the few teeth I have left are more ornamental than useful.'[60] Now on the recruiting campaign, receiving little practical support from the peasants in terms of transport or even food, and his gruelling days sustained only on peanut butter and lemons, Gandhi fell ill. Inevitably, he responded to his sickness by fasting. He returned to the ashram where Kasturba, seeing his weakened state, decided to feed him up, giving him favourite foods. He believed he then committed the sin of over-eating: 'The devil had only been waiting for an opportunity. Instead of eating very little I had my fill of the meal. This was sufficient invitation to the angel of death. Within an hour the dysentery appeared in an acute form.'[61] He went on to his next appointment but had to ask for a commode, and again succumbed to the illness. 'I thought all along that I had an iron frame,' he said, 'but I found that my body had now become a lump of clay.' He refused medical help, so his hosts called Ambalal Sarabhai who took him to his home and insisted on calling a doctor, whose diagnosis was that Gandhi was suffering from a nervous breakdown exacerbated by weakness because of his poor diet.

After nearly a month of illness he returned to the ashram, still believing he was going to die. He wrote valedictory letters to his children: 'I feel that I am now going. It is only a question of a few days.' He commended them to cherish the gift of character he had given them.[62] He could speak only with difficulty, and would spend his time listening to members of the ashram reading aloud from the *Bhagavad Gita*. His friends and supporters begged him to take more nourishment, particularly milk. He was nursed by his wife but, he wrote to Maganlal, 'I simply cannot bear to look at Ba's face. The expression is often like that on a meek cow and gives one the feeling, as a cow occasionally does, that in her own dumb manner she is saying something . . . her gentleness overpowers me.'[63] Kasturba knew his ways and she pointed out to him in January 1919, after he had been ill for months, that his vow of abstinence related only to cow's milk, so he could take goat's. Thus the ethical dilemma was solved and the milk of a different ungulate brought him back to health – coupled with rest and relief from his onerous recruiting responsibilities when Germany and her allies were finally defeated in November 1918.

The influenza pandemic hit the ashram in 1918, killing Harilal's third son and his wife Gulab who were staying there, and some of the ashramites. Gandhi's words of comfort to his son were in his own curious style: 'I fully realise that your state at present is like that of a man dreaming. Your responsibilities have increased, your trials have increased and your temptations will increase likewise. To a man with a family, the check of being such, that is, having a wife, is a great check. That check over you has now disappeared. Two paths branch out from where you stand now. You have to decide which you will take.'[64] Harilal, now twenty-eight, rapidly declined into alcoholism.

Politically, Gandhi had been sidelined by the constitutionalists Motilal Nehru and Jinnah, who had turned religion into a matter of voting percentages and had spoken in language understandable to the imperial power. An attitude of progressive reform on the part of the British government underlined an intention to progress slowly towards an independent, democratic nation within the British Empire. This might have been the end of the story for Gandhi as a major political figure, had the British not now made the monumental error of judgement enshrined in the Rowlatt Act of March 1919.

7

Arousing India

India could be justifiably proud of her contribution to victory in the Great War: more than 1,400,000 Indians had volunteered for service – one of the reasons for Gandhi's lack of success in recruiting was that those who were able and willing to go to war for the Empire had already done so. Their contribution had been impressive, the more so because, unlike military service in Britain after 1916, it had been voluntary, not conscripted. If Britain were true to her word, Indians could expect rewards for their loyalty.

British legislators, however, brought up on an old-fashioned view of rulers and ruled and suspicious of democracy, were unwilling to relinquish the powers they had adopted during the war under the Defence of India Act. The government of India appointed a Sedition Committee in 1917 with Justice Sidney Rowlatt as president, to investigate revolutionary activity in India. The committee sat in camera, so the details of its deliberations were not known or subject to day-to-day scrutiny. Reporting in April 1918, it presented India's political problems as the result of nationalists who were all seen as violent and anarchistic. The only solution the report had to offer was to create new laws to curtail political freedoms, to extend wartime restrictions to a nation that had contributed so much to the war effort.

The Rowlatt Bills were informed by principles exactly the opposite of those enshrined in the Montagu–Chelmsford Report, which stressed citizenship not subjecthood. A stronger Secretary of State than Montagu or a more courageous Viceroy than Chelmsford would have noted the Rowlatt Committee's findings and moved on. The Rowlatt report gave ammunition to hawkish enemies of political reform in India, and its authors were more determined than Montagu and Chelmsford.

The Rowlatt legislation was the greatest mistake the British made in regard to India in the whole period of their rule: the repression of their opponents marked the beginning of the end of the British administration. The proposals, introduced on 6 February 1919, had been roundly denounced by the Indian National Congress and the Home Rule League and were attacked by all the Indian members of the Imperial Legislative Council, including Vithalbhai Patel, brother of Gandhi's supporter Vallabhbhai.

Gandhi attended the proceedings of the government's legislative chamber for the only time in his life to hear the debate on the Bills (his general non-attendance demonstrating something of a lack of interest in the functioning of democracy). He was impressed by the Liberal Srinivasa Sastri's eloquence, but not so the Viceroy. Sastri and Jinnah resigned from the Legislative Council in protest at the government's intransigence.

Gandhi was still unwell. He wrote to Sastri that he could:

> no longer watch the progress of the Bills lying in bed. To me the Bills are aggravated symptoms of the deep-seated disease. They are a striking demonstration of the determination of the civil service to retain its grip of our necks ... I consider the Bills to be an open challenge to us. If we succumb we are done for ... If the Bills were but a stray example of lapse of righteousness and justice, I should not mind them but when they are clearly an evidence of a determined policy of repression, civil disobedience seems to be a duty imposed upon every lover of personal and public liberty.[1]

He determined he must be active, despite the advice of his doctors. On 24 February he summoned to the ashram some of the home rule leaders from Bombay–Sarojini Naidu, the *Bombay Chronicle* editor B.G. Horniman, Vallabhbhai Patel and Anasuya Sarabhai. Then he drafted a satyagraha pledge that if the Bills became law, and until they were withdrawn, 'we shall refuse civilly to obey these laws and such other laws as a committee to be hereafter appointed may think fit'. So if the government could make all-inclusive laws, Gandhi could equally offer all-inclusive opposition to them. He considered those making the pledge to be 'Indian covenanters' who for the first time were openly defying the British.

The Indian members of the Imperial Legislative Council, though unanimously against the proposed Acts, refused to support civil disobedience. Congress leaders did not want to see a mass movement. Nor did either Annie Besant or Jinnah think satyagraha was a viable option. Besant felt that to urge the indiscriminate disobedience of laws was a dangerous thing; Jinnah believed that it was suave politicians who made the weather – he did not consider mobilising the masses. Undaunted, Gandhi set up the Satyagraha Sabha (the Satyagraha Society) on 7 March 1919 despite the disdain of those he called the 'intelligentsia', who questioned his methods of working and his insistence on the use of Gujarati in the Sabha (which, as it was spoken by a regional minority of Indians, was indeed a peculiar choice for a national movement).

Gandhi was uncertain how to start the agitation until, he said, he fell asleep thinking about it and the answer came to him. He rushed to explain: 'The idea came to me last night in a dream that we should call upon the country to observe a general hartal [strike]. Satyagraha is a process of self-purification, and ours is a sacred fight, and it seems to me in the fitness of things that it should be commenced with an act of self-purification. Let all the people of India, therefore, suspend their business on that day and observe the day as one of fasting and prayer.'[2]

Gandhi had had an operation for piles in January 1919 and was addressing meetings sitting down in May, still too weak to stand. He was cheered to find the middle ranks of the home rulers avidly supporting him, and his protest developed into a nationwide campaign with fasting, prayer, strikes and mass meetings. Many more came forward to sign the satyagraha pledge. He later told supporters that this was one of the occasions when he saw God: 'He ascribed the success in getting people's response to God's intervention.' [3] He suggested laws that could be non-violently disobeyed by, for example, distributing his proscribed books, *Hind Swaraj* and his translation of Ruskin's *Unto This Last*, but the government declined to prosecute. He sent a letter to the police commissioner in Bombay: 'Dear Mr Griffith, May I send you a copy of the unregistered newspaper issued today by me as its editor? Yours sincerely M.K. Gandhi', but even this provocation failed to result in an arrest for sedition.[4]

The date for the national strike was fixed for 30 March, then changed to 6 April, though in some places, notably Delhi, the earlier date prevailed because of confusion in the messages. Cities stopped work as people swarmed into the streets shouting: 'Mahatma Gandhi ki jai!' (Victory to Mahatma Gandhi). It seemed that all India had only been waiting for the word. Hindus and Muslims, with their separate grievances, joined in the protest. There were parades and speeches in mosques and temples, but the protests quickly descended into violence, starting with a riot in Delhi when the satyagrahis confronted the Indians tea-sellers outside the railway station who were unwilling to join the hartal, presumably because they could not afford the loss of a day's earnings. Lahore and Amritsar experienced violence, too. Telegraph wires were cut and railway bridges sabotaged, shops and homes were plundered, government buildings destroyed.

Gandhi was arrested when he tried to get to Delhi, was then released and returned to Bombay, where he witnessed mounted police charging a crowd. He returned to Ahmedabad, which was under martial law after violence from mill-hands. He then held a meeting, promised a three-day fast, called on those responsible for the violence to confess their guilt, and temporarily suspended the campaign – his supply of volunteers had dwindled, and those who did volunteer were undisciplined and would accept no systematic training. This was not Gandhi's vision of satyagraha. He was quickly realising that the protests were getting out of hand and had already, before he knew of the events in Amritsar, confessed that the call for civil disobedience in an untrained population was a 'Himalayan miscalculation'.

The authorities in Amritsar, concerned at the political implications of Hindu–Muslim amity, arrested two Congress leaders, one from each religious community. Protests in response to this led to troops firing on the crowds, and rioting. Buildings were set on fire, British officials were killed and a woman missionary brutally attacked. Brigadier General Reginald Dyer took military control and forbade all public meetings. When a meeting was called in Jallianwala Bagh (Garden) on 13 April 1919 about ten thousand people gathered there. General Dyer stationed his

Gurkha and Baluchi troops on high ground and had them fire into the crowd until their ammunition was exhausted: 379 were killed and 1,137 injured. Dyer went on to issue a series of orders aimed at humiliating the Amritsar population, such as ordering Indians to walk on all fours when they passed down the lane where the English missionary had been assaulted. The 'crawling order' may never have been put into effect, but there were floggings for petty offences such as disregarding the curfew order and refusing to salaam to British officers.

The censorship that was in force meant it was some time before the news was out. India, the Empire and then the rest of the world reacted with predictable disgust. It was as if in ten minutes of precisely orchestrated butchery the British had relinquished all pretence of moral authority. Gandhi, true to form, was not as disgusted by the deaths (for death could always be conceived of as heroism in the cause) as he was by the abnegation of the rule of law in the arbitrary punishments meted out, in the 'lawless repression' under martial law: 'These tribunals were not courts of justice but instruments for carrying out the arbitrary will of an autocrat. Sentences were passed unwarranted by the evidence and in flagrant violation of justice.'5

Among the outrages was the arrest and deportation of B.G. Horniman, the editor of the *Bombay Chronicle* and a supporter of Gandhi, along with the suppression of the newspaper. The nationalists who controlled the *Chronicle* also owned an English weekly, *Young India*, which they now suggested should be published more frequently to replace the *Chronicle*, and with Gandhi editing it. Thus he was supplied with what he had previously lacked in India – the mouthpiece of a regular national publication which he had not enjoyed since the days of *Indian Opinion* in South Africa. He also took editorial control of *Navajivan*, a Gujarati newspaper. Though he did not remain as editor of *Young India*, citing pressure of other business, he continued to use it to voice his opinions.

Public opinion in Britain was also stirred, and an official commission was eventually set up by the government of India which censured General Dyer and he was relieved of his command. The Secretary of State Edwin Montagu criticised Dyer's behaviour but came under attack from Conservative back-benchers: Dyer had enthusiastic supporters in Britain. A combination of factors that had nothing to do with India had weakened Montagu: his friends were few, his political alliances weak, and the anti-Semitism of some fellow MPs had undermined him.

The most striking effect of the Rowlatt Acts and of the massacre at Amritsar was to wipe out moderate opinion among Indian nationalists. Any belief in gradual progress, even among such westernised members of the middle class as the Nehrus, was gone. Motilal Nehru's son Jawaharlal had been to Harrow and Cambridge and had been called to the Bar at the Middle Temple. Back home in Allahabad in 1916, he had undergone an arranged marriage to a conventional Kashmiri Brahmin girl, and the following year their daughter Indira, the future prime minister, was born. Annie Besant was a Nehru family friend and Jawaharlal Nehru became secretary of the local branch of the Home Rule League. On his return from education in England, Jawaharlal had entered the legal profession and taken an interest in nationalist politics. He had met Gandhi at the 1916 Lucknow Congress, having admired him from afar because of his work in South Africa, 'but he seemed very distant and different and apolitical to many of us young men'.[6]

Nehru had read about Gandhi's satyagraha pledge against the Rowlatt Acts and wanted to join in the campaign, but Motilal, a leading lawyer and constitutional politician, could not countenance his son's breaking the law and going to jail. Out of respect for his father, Jawaharlal restricted himself to provocative gestures like eating his dinner, which he insisted should be only bread and milk, from a steel bowl which sat incongruously with the family's silver and crystal. Motilal practised sleeping on the floor, so that he would experience some of the hardship his beloved son would undergo if he went to jail.

Divisions within the Nehru family reached such a pitch that to defuse the tension Motilal invited Gandhi to stay in his opulent house, which now became a home for him when he was in Allahabad. Motilal once commented: 'I do not agree with anything that Gandhiji says, and he knows it, but he still has more respect for me than for those half-witted disciples of his.'[7] Gandhi wisely advised Jawaharlal to be patient and not to upset his father. When he left, he took with him Motilal's daughter Sarup, who had taken Hindu–Muslim unity a little too far and fallen in love with a Muslim employee of her father. He was encouraged to leave the country; she was sent to Gandhi's ashram, which she found 'austere beyond belief', the day starting at 4 a.m., dreadful food, no tea or coffee, and romantic attachments not encouraged.[8] Motilal quickly found a wealthy Brahmin husband for his eldest daughter, who now took the name Vijaya Lakshmi. The couple went to Gandhi for his blessing after the wedding and he gave them a lecture on sacrifice for the national cause and urged them to take a vow of chastity. Vijaya, a future Indian ambassador to the United Nations, was up to the challenge. 'Why did you give your permission to our marriage if you thought it was wrong for us to live together as husband and wife?' she demanded. 'I want a normal married life.'[9] Gandhi backed down.

Motilal was more affected by the Amritsar massacre than was Jawaharlal, as the older man had trusted to British decency, fair play and steady progress towards independence. Motilal Nehru had been active in Congress since 1888 and was president of the Congress in Amritsar during December 1919 to January 1920 at which the Government of India Act was grudgingly accepted but condemned as inadequate, and which called for further reforms and for the repeal of the Rowlatt Acts. The Rowlatt provisions were in fact never used, and the Acts were repealed in 1922. Never has an imperial power sacrificed so much for so little.

Jawaharlal described the Congress in Amritsar as 'the first Gandhi Congress . . . the majority of the delegates, and even more so the great crowds outside, looked to Gandhi for leadership.' Gandhi was asked to modernise the Congress constitution, which he did in a form that made the membership requirement so minimal that, it was open to everyone in India. Nehru later described Gandhi talking to a group of erstwhile supporters:

> He was humble, but also clear-cut and hard as a diamond, pleasant and soft-spoken but inflexible and terribly earnest. His eyes were mild and deep, yet out of them blazed a fierce energy and determination. This was going to be a great struggle, he said, with a very powerful adversary. If you want to take it up, you must be prepared to lose everything, and you must subject yourself to the strictest non-violence and discipline. When war is declared, martial law prevails, and in our non-violent

struggle there will also have to be dictatorship and martial law on our side, if we are to win.[10]

Jawaharlal Nehru vividly described the widespread excitement that he first witnessed at home in Allahabad, when a delegation of peasants came looking for Gandhi. Jawaharlal went out to see them, then on to their villages where they were complaining of the oppression of vicious landlordism. The visit to the places where most Indians lived was a revelation to Nehru: he found the whole countryside afire with enthusiasm, enormous gatherings would form by word of mouth, 'people would come streaming out or even running as fast as they could. They were in miserable rags, men and women, but their faces were full of excitement and their eyes glistened and they seemed to expect strange happenings which would, as if by a miracle, put an end to their long misery.'[11] Nehru thus grasped the reality of India, as had Gandhi: the masses were ready to be mobilised.

By mid-1919 they were well on the way at the ashram not only to weaving cloth (as they long since had, using mill yarn) but to spinning their own yarn. Gandhi first emphasised the use of spinning and weaving for economic reasons: villages could be self-sufficient in cloth, and India would not have to import it from other countries – notably from Britain, where India had been a strong market for the Lancashire cotton mills. Gandhi was later to expound on the spiritual benefits of spinning, and urge a vow of swadeshi: that people should swear to confine themselves to cloth manufactured in India and to destroy foreign cloth. He described the 'tiny wheels of God' that 'spin slowly, but most effectively'.[12]

Curiously, Gandhi came to dominate the Muslim movement for the Khilafat. After the Ali brothers were released from jail, they joined the Congress and Gandhi joined the Khilafat committee. This was a problem for Gandhi's more sober supporters, who wondered why he was so keen to defend the rights of the Ottoman Empire while attacking the British Empire, when he had always claimed to be against imperialism, not against the British. He wrote condescendingly to Harry Polak: 'You cannot understand the religious viewpoint which guides me in this matter.'[13] Even the loyal Maganlal suggested he was backing the Khilafat out of expediency, to which charge he responded explicitly, if cynically, using the image of churning a spiritual sea into butter: 'Khilafat is the great churning process of the ocean that India is. Why should we worry as to what will come out (poison or nectar) from the movement? It is enough that we are certain that the activity is pure and righteous.'[14]

There was in fact no religious core to this matter – the people of Arabia, who had been fighting to throw off Turkish rule, were perfectly capable of caring for the holy sites of Islam. The Khilafat movement was an opportunistic means of stirring up Muslim opinion in India; the rest of the Muslim world, preoccupied with their own problems, had little interest in the sultan of Turkey. Gandhi's support for the Khilafat meant he had to exaggerate the ability of the Turks to maintain their Empire, and minimise their misrule. Among recent incidents was the genocide of perhaps one and a quarter million Armenians during the 1914–18 War, an atrocity far in excess of anything perpetrated by the British Empire. Gandhi refused to acknowledge the massacre: 'I distrust the Armenian case,' he said.[15] It was an instance of moral neglect that would be mirrored by his later failure to appreciate the enormity of the Holocaust. He was blinded by his spiritual light into thinking that the only important thing was individual experience of God, ignoring the bigger picture.

Jawaharlal Nehru found in his peregrinations in the Indian countryside that peasants in most rural areas thought the word 'khilafat' came from *khilaf*, an Urdu word meaning 'against', and just took it to mean opposition to the government for the many woes they suffered at the hands of authority.

Nationalists attempted to encourage Hindu support for Muslims over the question of the Khilafat by attempting to overcome animosity between Hindus and Muslims over such issues as cow slaughter. Hindus were infuriated by the Muslim use of beef, and though Gandhi too was offended by cow slaughter he made a point of reminding them that the cruelty shown to bullocks who were kept in harness was an evil which it was in their power to address; and it was no contribution to righteousness to kill a Muslim for killing a cow. He was not fetishistic about cows, but he rationalised their position in Hinduism, telling Andrews: 'The worship of the cow is the Hindu's unique contribution to the evolution of humanitarianism. It is a practical application of the belief in the oneness, and therefore the sacredness, of all life. The great doctrine of trans-migration, or rebirth, is a direct consequence of that belief.'[16] He resisted an offer from the Muslims officially to link Hindu support for the Khilafat with their own refraining from the practice of cow slaughter, feeling they should do it as a matter of goodwill.

Gandhi decided, without the agreement of Congress, that non-cooperation with the government would start on 1 August 1920. By chance, this was the day Tilak died, so that Gandhi was now even more clearly identified as the major nationalist leader – the others were either dead or had been outmanoeuvred.

Non-cooperation entailed the refusal to attend government functions, withdrawal of children from government schools and colleges, the boy-cott of British courts, withdrawal from elections, the boycott of foreign goods and the adoption of swadeshi on a large scale. The strategy included the surrender of titles and honorary offices bestowed by the British; in keeping with this, Gandhi returned his Kaiser-i-Hind, Zulu War and Boer War medals to the Viceroy – 'not without a pang', he noted.[17]

In his appeal to pupils to leave their schools and colleges, Gandhi was addressing the young over the heads of their parents for the sake of national revolution, an appeal Mao Tse Tung was later to make in China. The radical nature of his call led to conflict with liberal educationalists who saw the promotion of education as a positive element of British rule. As evident in his attitude to his children's education (though not to his own), Gandhi mistrusted the influence of education. If he had convinced them of the disloyalty to India inherent in receiving education from the British Empire, he commanded the students of Benares Hindu University, 'Do not remain in the university for a moment longer, do not even breathe its air.'[18] Two hundred students took a pledge not to pursue their education. Many erstwhile supporters, notably Tagore, opposed Gandhi in this campaign.

A special session of Congress was held in Calcutta during 4–9 September 1920 to consider the issues of the Khilafat and of non-cooperation. Gandhi was opposed by Jinnah and by Annie Besant, but with the Ali brothers and Motilal Nehru on his side and the trainloads of Khilafat supporters packing the conference hall, he had a clear majority. In the end the vote was 1,855 for Gandhi's policies and 873 against.

Gandhi went on to a Home Rule League meeting in Bombay and insisted on changing its programme to that of complete home rule, while Jinnah argued that 'self-government within the British Commonwealth' was still the most realistic goal. Jinnah and others resigned; it was the beginning the bitter rivalry between them. Gandhi invited Jinnah back, but he responded that he was fully convinced that Gandhi's programme 'must lead to disaster'. He declared, 'Your methods have already caused split and division in almost every institution that you have approached hitherto, and in the public life of the country not only amongst Hindus and Muslims but between Hindus and Hindus and Muslims and Muslims and even between fathers and sons.' Gandhi's extreme programme had been successful because it had 'for the moment, struck the imagination mostly of the inexperienced youth and the ignorant and the illiterate'.[19]

At the annual session of Congress held in December that year at Nagpur, Jinnah appeared immaculately attired in Western fashion as usual. He stood before the Congress delegates who were dressed in khadi and opposed the non-cooperation programme, which he referred to as 'Mr Gandhi's'. The conference hall erupted with cries of 'Mahatma Gandhi!' Jinnah's speech was howled down with boos, hisses and catcalls until he was finally driven from the platform, humiliated in front of his pretty young wife. He later resigned from the Congress and devoted himself to his lucrative legal practice and an independent political career. Gandhi's acquiescence in this political humiliation was a major mistake that would yield bitter fruit twenty-five years later.

Outside the conference people were lighting bonfires of foreign cloth, picketing liquor shops and fraternising with untouchables – for the first time Congress included a campaign against untouchability as part of its programme. Within a year it had six million new members. Congress adopted a flag to represent free India: a tricolour with orange for the Hindus, green for the Muslims and white for the others (along the lines of the flag of Eire: green for the Catholics, orange for the Protestants and white for peace between them). Gandhi also proposed that the spinning-wheel (charkha) should appear in the centre of the flag.

The promotion of spinning was now a major preoccupation, fuelled by Gandhi's belief that before the British came all India used to be self-sufficient, with every family spinning its own yarn. This was not true: there were many places in India that did no spinning before the arrival of the British; but after Gandhi there was no such dearth of spinners. Spinning became an essential activity not only for the poor, giving them work when planting and harvesting were not possible, but for all nationalists. Rabindranath Tagore criticised the 'cult of the chakra[sic]' arguing that 'while creating man's mind, God did not have for his model the spider mentality doomed to a perpetual conformity in its production of web... it is an outrage upon human nature to force it through a mill and reduce it to some standardised commodity of uniform size and shape and purpose'.[20]

Gandhi said that when he first suggested hand-making cloth as a panacea for India in *Hind Swaraj*, he had not even seen a hand-loom or a spinning-wheel. Now he was promoting hand-spinning as not only economically desirable but as spiritually necessary. He began to devote an hour a day to spinning on a wheel, and the ashram residents had to overcome technical difficulties in order to spin and then weave their own cloth. Soon they were all dressed in rough white khadi. It was to become a symbol throughout India of the nation's call for independence and self-reliance. Gandhi's recognition of the importance of clothes had led him to dressing his army of national liberators in a way that signified unmistakeably his defiance of the Empire and its produce.

Making the coarse cloth was one thing – ensuring people wore it, another. His ally in this was Saraladevi Choudhurani, a Bengali nationalist activist who had married a nationalist from Lahore, Rambhuj Dutt Choudhuri. When Gandhi was finally, with the ending of restrictions relating to the Amritsar massacre, given official permission to visit the Punjab, Choudhuri was in prison and Saraladevi was his host. She was nationalist royalty, a niece of Rabindranath Tagore, and had long been active in Congress; in 1920 when Gandhi first stayed at her home she was forty-seven and he fifty. She represented all the intellectual ability, the female companionship that Kasturba had never supplied. 'I call her my spiritual wife', he wrote to Kallenbach. 'A friend has called it an intellectual wedding.'[21]

She could also do what his male followers could not – act as a khadi fashion model by wearing the homespun garments in rich colours, thus opening up the way for the adoption of khadi by women for whom nationalist passion was not enough to influence their clothing choices. Saraladevi accompanied Gandhi on his journeys round the Punjab, speaking at his meetings or singing nationalist songs, promoting the merits of homespun.

In March 1920 he was staying with her and writing in his usual affectionate terms: 'Saraladevi has been showering her love on me in every possible way.'[22] He wrote warmly to her when he felt unwell: 'I am no better today. I must confine myself to bed. You still continue to haunt me even in my sleep.'[23] When she visited the ashram there was jealous criticism from other residents of the amount of time he spent alone with her, and of the way he allowed her to escape chores – no emptying chamber pots for her. He chided her on her lack of ambition in the domestic sphere, however: 'Great and good though you are, you are not a complete woman without achieving the ability to do household work.' He signed it 'LG' for Law-Giver, a teasing name she used for him.[24]

He even discussed polygamy with Saraladevi, recounting the event later as

[an] argument I had with a woman with whom I almost fell. It is so personal that I did not put it in my autobiography. We have considered if there can be this spiritual companionship. The marriage relationship is a matter of contract. Your parents arrange it in your childhood and you have nothing to do with it. I come into contact with an illiterate woman. Then I meet a woman with a broad, cultural education. Could we not develop a close contact? I said to myself. This was a plausible argument, and I nearly slipped.[25]

At the end of 1920 when he was wanting the relationship to cool off, he emphasised the condescending nature of his affection for her in a way that could not but irritate a mature woman who had been active on the Congress stage for twenty years: 'So far as I can see our relationship, it is one of brother and sister. I must lay down the laws for you, and thus ruffle you. I must plead gently like a brother ever taking care to use the right word even as I do to my oldest sister.'[26] The end of the relationship was precipitated by other people, including his son Devdas and his amanuensis Mahadev Desai, who warned him of the danger he was in. It may have been that such warnings of his excessive closeness to her came when he was in a receptive mood as Saraladevi was becoming demanding and he felt he could do without her.

Despite his unprepossessing physique, Gandhi was always attractive to women and he enjoyed their attention. Saraladevi was just the most serious of his encounters. Normally these concerned single women who lived at the ashram, such as the pretty Danish missionary Esther Faering who was the recipient of many affectionate letters from him. Millie Polak gave her interpretation of Gandhi's attractiveness: 'Most women love men for such attributes as are usually considered masculine. Yet Mahatma Gandhi has been given the love of many women for his womanliness: for all those qualities that are associated with women – great faith, great fortitude, great devotion, great patience, great tenderness, and great sympathy.'[27]

The Gandhi magic also worked on men. Gandhi met Pyarelal, who was to be one of his most faithful disciples, his constant companion and biographer, in the aftermath of the Amritsar massacre. Pyarelal Nayar (who was always known by his first name alone) was then a student and part of a deputation that approached Gandhi when Congress was held in Amritsar at the end of 1919. The deputation had come to ask his advice on behalf of a person implicated in the trials concerning martial law then in progress. Could he recommend an amnesty? they wanted to know. Pyarelal described his first impression of Gandhi:

He had just had his bath and was on his way to midday dinner. Wrapped in a white Kashmir pashmina shawl, he sat bolt upright looking a picture of dignity and repose. There was majesty in his simplicity. The deep mellifluous voice held one spellbound. The eyes reflected an infinity of kindliness, compassion and peace. The body was thin to the point of emaciation but the prominent barrel chest gave a sense of tremendous power. The broad, smooth brow showed not a wrinkle. The countenance was radiant, the skin silken smooth and the complexion clear.[28]

The students asked him what hope they could have, in that atmosphere, for a person confessing to political murder? Gandhi said: 'I would not let even the worst murderer go to the gallows. In my Ashram there are several persons who were implicated in cases of political murder. They made a clean breast of it. Converted to non-violence, they are today among my most trusted workers.' Pyarelal, who had lost his father, an officer of the judiciary, when he was young, saw everything to admire in Gandhi:

> In his voice there was a calm assurance, and boundless compassion joined to an unearthly detachment that was strangely soothing; a quiet dignity and sense of kingliness, suggestive of an access to some hidden reservoir of power which recked [recognised] no obstacle, knew no defeat and could find a way, as it were, even through an impenetrable granite wall . . . One *felt* it. It was the deep calling unto the deep. Here was what I had been looking for – a glimpse of the power of the spirit which is its own seal and sanction, which no power on earth can subdue and that never fails.'[29]

In autumn 1920 Pyaralel gave up his studies in response to the call to non-cooperation and joined the ashram at Sabarmati. He was soon, with Mahadev Desai, devoting all this time to Gandhi. He described how Gandhi could go on day after day, week after week with only three or four hours' sleep, and how he expected others to maintain his own high levels of performance. 'One had to be ready for any emergency at a moment's notice. Difficulty of an assignment or lack of resources was never accepted as an excuse for non-performance.'[30] Gandhi insisted on doing everything, so far as possible, for himself. 'If he wanted a paper to be looked up or his spittoon to be brought to him, he went for it himself instead of ordering anyone; he even mended his own clothes. He preferred writing to dictating.' Pyarelal one day counted fifty letters written by Gandhi in his own hand at the end of which he was so exhausted that he pressed his temples between his hands and 'slumped on the floor just where he was sitting, without even spreading the bedding against which he was leaning. He simply pushed it aside.'[31]

He used a piece of red khadi as a satchel for keeping files and papers, he wrote with a steel nib and insisted on his desk always being clear:

'Woe to anyone of his staff who referred to him a letter more than forty-eight hours old.'[32] When others drafted letters for him, he liked short replies – more than five or ten lines he threw away. His diet now consisted of goat's milk, raisins and other fruit that were measured out with care. Pyarelal once increased his number of raisins from nineteen to twenty-three, but 'he detected it and gave me a discourse on the danger of "blind affection".'[33] The menu for each meal was adjusted carefully according to how his system had responded to the previous meal, the amount of sleep he had had or expected to have, and the physical and mental strain already undergone or in prospect.

By 1921 Gandhi had all the elements of his unique enterprise in place: a secure base in the ashram; a talented retinue of disciples, of whom Desai and Pyarelal were only the most accomplished; a national party obedient to his wishes in Congress; in khadi, a uniform for his army; an economic programme in spinning and self-sufficiency, a newspaper for his weekly pronouncements, and a philosophy in satyagraha to inspire and embolden his followers.

The new Viceroy, the lawyer Lord Reading (formerly Rufus Isaacs), met Gandhi six times in 1921 and found nothing striking about the appearance of this bare-legged man in white dhoti and cap:

I should have passed him in the street without a second look at him. When he talks the impression is different. He is direct and expresses himself well in English with a fine appreciation of the value of the words he uses. There is no hesitation about him and there is a ring of sincerity in all that he utters, save when discussing some political questions . . . his religious and moral views are admirable and indeed on a remarkably high altitude but I must confess that I find it difficult to understand his practice of them in politics.'[34]

Gandhi promised that home rule could be secured within a year, to be achieved by non-cooperation with the British and in the context of a constructive programme consisting of the abolition of untouchability, Hindu–Muslim unity, the promotion of hand-spinning and hand-weaving, and the prohibition of alcohol and drugs. He travelled relentlessly throughout India talking of non-cooperation and non-violence to vast crowds, many of whom could not hear him but were satisfied just to have sight of the living saint dressed in his white khadi.

He called for a complete boycott of foreign cloth by 1 August 1921, which led to huge bonfires on 31 July. The pile of doomed fabric in Bombay was about a mile in diameter. Gandhi himself applied a lighted match to it, thereby feeding into the notion of the symbolic value of destruction and renewal in Hindu mythology. Jewish, Christian and Muslim traditions would abhor the waste; Gandhi's supporter Charles Andrews protested at 'destroying in the fire the noble handiwork of one's fellow men and women abroad'.[35] Why not give the cloth to the poor, at home or in other countries? Gandhi was asked. He replied that for-eign cloth was 'sinful' – 'We should look upon foreign cloth as so much dirt and, just as we would not pass on to others the dirt on our person, so we should not pass on this dirt of foreign cloth to others.'[36] At the end of the piece in which he wrote this, however, he relented, noting that Muslims were sending foreign cloth to help Turkish refugees from Smyrna.

He continued with his spiritual disciplines, having decided in spring 1921 that he would have a silent day a week – he would not speak on Mondays except in an emergency – and it was a discipline he main-tained to the end of his life. Later in 1921 he took a vow to spin every day for half an hour. He also decided to further refine his clothes. He discarded the long dhoti, sleeveless jacket and cap he had been wearing and on 23 September that year he went clad only in a loincloth to a meeting of weavers. He represented this as an act of solidarity with the poor who could not afford enough khadi to replace the foreign cloth that he was insisting they burn. He also argued that there was currently too little khadi to go round, so 'if most of the men could do with as little cloth as he, then there would be enough khadi for the women' – though he never urged others to dress as skimpily as he did (and this argument was obviously valid only in the short term, if at all).[37] There was never any question of Muslims voluntarily wearing nothing but a loincloth – sharia law requires modesty in dress from men as well as from women – so amid the talk of unity here was another clear sign of difference.

In going almost naked he was imitating the clothing – or lack of it

– of the sadhus, the mendicant holy men who populate India begging for alms and offering such spiritual boons as the impregnation of barren women. In future he would go bare-chested, with naked legs and a loin-cloth, plus a shawl, or not, as the temperature dictated. It was as if, having got his Congress supporters to adopt his mode of khadi dress, he now had to go one better. Thirty years earlier in London he had been wearing a wing collar and a top-hat. When Sonja Schlesin wrote from South Africa that taking to this state of undress was just spectacle, all show and no spiritual substance, he countered that it was just a natural progression of the way his thinking had been taking him. 'Believe me there is nothing spectacular in the loin-cloth.'[38]

The next stage in the home rule (or swaraj) programme, if non-cooperation by the public were not successful, would be for Gandhi to call on government officials to leave their posts and soldiers to lay down their arms, and for a tax strike to start in a selected area. He had to achieve independence before the end of 1921 if the pledge of 'swaraj within a year' were to be fulfilled. His pronouncements became increasingly desperate: 'We must not drink or gamble', 'We should control our animal passions. If we do this, surely then we could have swaraj.'[39]

Now he was presenting British rule as satanic – Ravena Raj not Rama Raj, rule by a demon, not by a god – and as having to be ended. He presented his movement as one straddling 'religion and irreligion, powers of light and powers of darkness.' It was the Muslims and Hindus who had 'religion and honour as their motive' as against European civilisation representing 'the spirit of Satan'.[40]

The visit of the Prince of Wales, later Edward VIII (attended by the young Louis Mountbatten, among others) was boycotted and the royal retinue encountered empty streets. Violence broke out in Bombay on 21 November 1921 when the self-sacrificing element of non-cooperation showed its ugly side. The violence was not an attack on the British but the bullying of those Indians who did not maintain the boycott. Liquor shops were wrecked, trams stopped and passengers molested, their Western clothes forcibly removed: Parsis, Christians and Jews were attacked. Five police and fifty-three demonstrators were killed. Gandhi witnessed the violence of crowds looting shops and shouting: 'Victory to Mahatma Gandhi!' After the riots C.F. Andrews describes him as 'haggard and emaciated, as one who had just passed through the valley of the shadow of death'.[41] He declared he would fast until Hindus and Muslims made peace with the other communities whose members had been assaulted. He broke the fast after two days on assurances of good behaviour from the various groups.

Meetings were banned in response to the violence surrounding the prince's visit, and Gandhi reacted by calling on his troops to defy the bans, hold meetings and be prepared to be imprisoned. Many were, including Nehru father and son. Before the end of January 1922 thirty thousand had been arrested. Non-cooperation having taken the movement so far, on 1 February Gandhi wrote to the Viceroy to tell him that he proposed to launch a mass civil disobedience movement against the government. As a first step towards national civil disobedience he settled on the area of Bardoli in Gujarat, again picking the province he knew best for a trial run.

On 4 February his plans were to be disrupted: a procession shouting 'Victory to Mahatma Gandhi!' in the village of Chauri Chaura in the United Provinces broke into taunts and then scuffles with the police, who became frightened and opened fire. Their ammunition soon gave out and they took shelter in the police station, which the mob attacked then set fire to, burning or hacking to death twenty-two policemen. On 12 February Gandhi persuaded the Congress working committee to suspend the civil disobedience: non-cooperation was to be replaced by a programme of spinning, temperance, educational improvement and working with local untouchables to ameliorate their lot. He refused, he said, to lead a movement 'half-violent and half non-violent, even though it might result in the attainment of so-called swaraj'.[42] Thus he retained the moral high ground, refusing to excuse, or compromise with, violence.

Jawaharlal Nehru recalled that he and other prisoners learned of this latest development 'to our amazement and consternation . . . were a remote village and a mob of excited peasants in an out-of-the-way place going to put an end, for some time at least, to our national struggle for freedom?'[43] Nehru and others were released in March. He was later to reflect that Gandhi had acted almost by instinct, gradually developing a sense of how the masses were behaving: 'All organisation and discipline were disappearing; almost all our good men were in prison, and the masses had so far received little training to carry on by themselves.'[44]

The movement had been running out of steam, and what momentum there now was had been taken over by anarchistic elements. Impressive though Gandhi's rousing of the country was, its success was limited. Courts, schools and colleges continued to function, the police and the army remained loyal to the Empire. The Khilafat movement had already begun to be recognised as the absurdity it always was. Secular Turks in 1922 deposed the sultan, supposedly the great caliph for whom the Indians were agitating, and Islam was not shaken to its foundations. The Turks announced a secular republic and the Caliphate was declared defunct in 1924 by Kemal Ataturk, a very modern leader, more in the mould of Jawaharlal Nehru than Gandhi. Thus died the Khilafat, the last significant indicator of popular Hindu–Muslim unity in the Indian nationalist campaign.

On 10 March 1922 Gandhi was arrested at the ashram. When asked, he gave his age as fifty-three and his profession as 'farmer and weaver'. He was tried eight days later for inciting disaffection against His Majesty's Government via three articles in *Young India*. He pleaded guilty, declaring that he did not ask for mercy: 'I am here to invite and submit cheerfully to the highest penalty that can be inflicted upon me for what in law is a deliberate crime and what appears to me to be the highest duty of a citizen.'[45] He was sentenced to six years' imprisonment, but the judge showed such sympathy as to express the hope that the course of events in India would make it easier for the government to reduce the term and release him. The first great campaign for Indian independence was over.

8

The Salt March

To Yeravda jail in Poona Gandhi took a few books such as the *Bhagavad Gita*, a dictionary, a translation of the Koran and a Bible. He also took his spinning-wheel to which he had become increasingly attached, listening to its whirr as to a mantra, but it was taken away by his jailers. He said he would fast if he could not spin, and it was restored. On the first night in jail he said to Shankerlal Banker, the editor of *Young India* who had been imprisoned with him: 'Take God's name and go to sleep. The best way to overcome all difficulties is to recite Ramanama.'[1]

'At last I am having a quiet time,' he wrote to Charles Andrews from his ten-foot-square cell.[2] He would rise at 4 a.m. and go to bed at 10 p.m., filling the day with activity; he devoted six hours a day to reading history, biography, theology and even some of Kipling's verse. It was here that he wrote *Satyagraha in South Africa* and published it serially in *Young India*, dictating it to his devoted cousin and disciple Maganlal Gandhi. He would spin and do related tasks for four or more hours" and walk outside for an hour in the morning and half an hour in the evening; if it were raining he would walk around his cell. At dawn and at sunset he said prayers, recited texts and sang devotional songs. He devoted an hour a day to teaching Sanskrit to Shankerlal, who appointed himself Gandhi's servant; he massaged his master's head and feet in the evening before bed, cooked for him, cleaned his cell and washed his clothes. Gandhi later took to performing these last two tasks himself as he felt he could get the cell cleaner and use less soap when washing clothes than his friend. Shankerlal referred to other specifics of caring for Gandhi: his master would count the match-sticks in the match-box and work out how many should last for exactly seven days, and he insisted on exactly a hundred currants for breakfast and that the pieces of bread served to him should be of equal size.[3]

Intermittently Gandhi was suffering severe abdominal pains which intensified at the beginning of January 1924, and he was removed to Sassoon Hospital, Poona, under Colonel Maddock, the surgeon general of the area. On 12 January he was operated on for appendicitis. Although released unconditionally on 5 February, he stayed in hospital for another month, recovering his strength. In a typically Gandhian gesture he resolved not to attack the Empire until his six-year sentence was up in March 1928, thereby respecting the spirit of his term of imprisonment.

He used some of his time for literary activities: he resumed the editorship of *Young India* and *Navajivan* and published his two autobiographical pieces serially, first *Satyagraha in South Africa* and then, from 1925, *An Autobiography or The Story of my Experiments with Truth*. From 1926 he published his discourses on the *Bhagavad Gita*.

On the political front, Congress was in some disarray after Gandhi's departure. They had boycotted the 1920 elections, but many now argued that they should fight elections and represent the ideas of independence in the councils of India. Eventually Motilal Nehru, C.R. Das and Vithalbhai Patel formed the Swaraj Party. Via this vehicle they returned to national politics: they were elected to the national assembly in November 1923, where they found themselves again in the company of Jinnah, who had been elected as an independent Muslim candidate. Jinnah's expert political manoeuvring led to the creation of a pro-independence bloc consisting of his group of independents and the Swarajists, who outnumbered the imperial loyalists.

Gandhi was not happy that the Swarajists were cooperating with the legislature; he felt it diverted people's minds from the regeneration of national life that he thought of as the ideal path to independence. He tried to exclude Swarajists from taking leading positions in Congress, but after narrowly winning a vote against them he relented. He gave in to them if they supported him on khadi: so they could stay on the councils to which they had been elected as Congress representatives as long as they accepted that Congress membership was now open only to those who used a spinning-wheel. His engagement with wider society now centred on khadi, Hindu–Muslim unity and opposition to untouchability.

Gandhi was not the only enemy of the British to be released, and not the only one claiming to be representative of the true culture of India. Vinayak Savarkar who had been involved in the assassination of several British officials, was released in 1924. He took part in the formation of the Rashtriya Swayamsevak Sangh – the RSS, or National Volunteer Association – in 1925 'to protect Hindu culture'. They were a quasi-military body that practised drills and salutes and had their own flag; ideologically they were anti-Muslim and in favour of maintaining caste divisions and keeping the untouchables down. Some Hindus were clearly looking towards more martial interpretations of their faith. Gandhi had emphasised the spiritual, contemplative side of Arjuna's advice to Krishna on the battlefield, seeing the battle in the *Bhagavad Gita* as a spiritual one. For many, a literal interpretation was the correct one: the battle Arjuna was enjoined to fight was real.

India had been aroused by the idea of non-cooperation in the hope and belief that it would lead to religious amity and towards a self-sufficient and peaceful nation. It was the arousal of a sleeping beast, however, and there was no certainty that the beast, when stirred, would be docile. Sarojini Naidu wrote to him, Gandhi recorded, that 'speeches and homilies on peace would not do. I must find out an effective remedy. She was right in saddling the responsibility on me. Had I not been instrumental in bringing into being the vast energy of the people? I must find the remedy if the energy proved self-destructive.'⁴ He therefore in September 1924 took a fast for Hindu–Muslim unity in the North-West Frontier where there had been riots. He took the position that the fast was a personal penance for not being completely non-violent himself, a piece of reasoning whose logic evaded even his most devoted followers. Now experienced at this exercise, he fasted for twenty-one days, taking just water and having an enema twice daily. He undertook the fast at the home in Delhi of Muhammad Ali, who felt that he should at least have been consulted before his guest embarked on a procedure the requirements of which must have strained hospitality. Gandhi attracted both Hindu and Muslim leaders to his bedside and focused attention on Hindu–Muslim relations as a key national issue. Prayers were offered all over the country for his life; a unity conference for some two hundred national leaders of different interest groups was held in Delhi with Motilal Nehru presiding. They issued calls for the toleration of acknowledged differences while accepting, however, that nothing was going to stop Muslims slaughtering cows or Hindus playing music that might be heard from mosques – two of the most frequent triggers of communal unrest.

But Hindu–Muslim unity had its limits: Manilal Gandhi sent a message to his parents from South Africa in 1926 that he wanted to marry Fatima Gool, daughter of a Muslim merchant who was a long-term friend of the family. Gandhi senior responded, 'Your marriage will have a powerful impact on the Hindu–Muslim question. Intercommunal marriages are no solution to this problem. You cannot forget nor will society forget that you are my son.' Warnings were followed by threats – if he were to marry Fatima, 'I fear you may no more be the right person to run *Indian Opinion* – so he would lose his job. Manilal would also, Gandhi suggested, be cut off from his family: 'It will be impossible for you, I think, after this to come and settle in India.'⁵ Manilal backed down, as he always did, and as a concession to family harmony Gandhi so far compromised with the idea of matrimony as to find a Gujarati Bania girl for Manilal. He begged a solemn assurance from his son: 'that you shall treat her as your companion, never as a slave; that you shall take as much care of her person as of your own; that you shall not force her to surrender to your passion, but that you shall take your pleasure only with her consent. I would advise you to set certain limits on your enjoyment.'⁶

Respect for other cultures was, then, fine so far as the cultures kept their distance from one another. This was not unlike Gandhi's, attitude to caste: 'I have devoted much thought to the subject of the caste system and come to the conclusion that Hindu society cannot dispense with it, that it lives on because of the discipline of caste,' he said in 1916.⁷ He was now opposed to reform: 'The caste system is a perfectly natural institution . . . I am opposed to the movements which are being carried on for the destruction of the system . . . We do not associate with members of other communities for eating or enter into marriage relationships with them.'⁸ He thought the fewer women a man might legitimately feel lust for, the better; and if his lust were restricted only to members of his caste 'You are benefiting spiritually by curtailing the extent of your choice of women.'[9] As usual he failed to appreciate that sexual desire might equally originate with the woman.

A caste-based problem was presented when his son Devdas at twenty-seven wished to marry fifteen-year-old Lakshmi, daughter of a major political supporter of Gandhi's, Chakravarti Rajagopalachari (later to be Governor General of India). They were told to spend some years apart, to see if they still wanted to marry after not seeing or writing to each other. The reasons that have been given for withholding parental consent are that Lakshmi was a top Brahmin and the Gandhis lower-caste Banias; that Lakshmi was considered too young to know her own mind; and Rajagopalachari said that Gandhi and he 'both felt that our political association should not be cemented by a marriage alliance'.[10] The couple were married six years later.

A more congenial match for the families concerned was Gandhi's third son Ramdas's marriage to another Kathiawari Bania, Nirmala, an orphan who lived on Gandhi's ashram with her aunt (many of Gandhi's disciples were fatherless or orphans). Gandhi selected her as a wife for Ramdas when she was sixteen, but told them to wait; they married when she was eighteen and Ramdas thirty. Their early years of married life were spent working among the peasants in Bardoli, but Ramdas's lifestyle showed that his father's teaching could have the opposite effect to that desired. 'Ramdasji took a large house for us and filled it with expensive English things – spoons, china, clocks – and he was always giving me beautiful clothes,' Nirmala said. 'He was earning only forty rupees a month as a volunteer worker. I would say, "We should live within our means. Anyway, what is the point of all this finery and good living? You may be sent to jail at any time." And he would say, "This home may be our last home, so let's be jolly, eat well, and be carefree. Let tomorrow take care of itself." When he found her reading one of Gandhi's tracts on celibacy he said, 'What are you doing reading that stuff?'[11]

Romain Rolland, another admirer of Tolstoy, wrote a biography of Gandhi in 1924 that introduced him to a wide and sympathetic audience. The uncompromising title chosen by the 1915 Nobel laureate, *Mahatma Gandhi: The Man Who Became One with the Universal Being*, suggested a less than critical approach. The publication of this book was an important stage in the progress of Gandhi's reputation as a world figure. Rolland's first words give what was to become the universal image of Gandhi: 'Soft dark eyes, a small frail man, with a thin face and rather large protruding eyes, his head covered with a little white cap, his body clothed in coarse white cloth, barefooted. He lives on rice and fruit and drinks only water. He sleeps on the floor – sleeps very little, and works incessantly.'[12] Rolland introduced Gandhi's back-to-nature ideas infused with Eastern mysticism to a northern hemisphere that was used to polarising into choices of political right or left. Spiritual people could look to Gandhi and see an alternative solution in a world of materialism: 'If the spirit of India now surges forth from temples and forests, it is because it holds the message for which the world is sighing,' Rolland wrote.[13]

Madeleine Slade was one seeker after truth who was influenced by the book: she travelled to India after reading it and writing to Gandhi. The daughter of an admiral, Sir Edmond Slade, she had been a solitary child, devoted to nature and to music. A meeting with Rolland when he was writing about Gandhi led her to transfer her adulation from Beethoven to the Mahatma. When she read Rolland's book 'the dawn in my heart glowed brighter and brighter, and by the time I had finished, the Sun of Truth was pouring his rays into my soul.'[14] She was thirty-three when she first set eyes on Gandhi in 1925, and fell to her knees in front of him. 'You shall be my daughter,' said Gandhi, who had never had a daughter and seems to have nursed a longing for one. Madeleine, who insisted on cutting off her long dark hair as a sign of spiritual devotion (to the bewilderment of other women ashramites who saw no requirement to follow suit), was given the name Mira after a princess who had renounced everything for God, with the suffix -behn meaning sister, so was called Mirabehn – Sister Mira. She became invaluable as editor of Gandhi's English when he was writing letters to imperial functionaries or producing English translations of Gujarati works, including his *Autobiography*.

She therefore for a time formed part of a secretarial triumvirate, along with Mahadev Desai as primary assistant and Pyarelal as a third (and less practical) one. In December 1925 Gandhi was writing, 'You have been constantly in my thoughts. This three days' separation is good discipline' – which gives some idea of the amount of time they were normally spending together.[15] Back in England the concept of going to the East in search of spiritual knowledge was not foremost in the minds of the gossip columnists, and they considered it bizarre that an upper-class girl should forgo marriage prospects at home to consort with a half-naked Indian. There was also gossip in the ashram about their close-ness – for all its spiritual pretensions, the ashram was always a hotbed of gossip. Gandhi found it increasingly difficult to deal with the highly strung woman, and his letters betray his frustration with her: 'No one else would have felt like committing suicide over a simple innocent remark of mine . . . this disease is idolatry. If not, why hanker after my company! Why touch or kiss the feet that one day must be dead cold?'[16] Eventually he was to send her away to work in other ashrams, though he wrote plaintive letters to her: 'You are on the brain. I look about me and miss you . . . All the time you were squandering your love on me personally, I felt guilty of misappropriation. And I exploded on the slightest pretext. Now that you are not with me, my anger turns itself upon me for having given you all those terrible scoldings. But I was on a bed of hot ashes all the while I was accepting your service.'[17] He once confided to a friend: 'I have not made any man or woman weep as bit-terly as I have made her.'[18]

Gandhi was to attract more and more Westerners to his way of life. By the late twentieth century other spiritual leaders had emerged from India to present the spiritual mysteries of the East in English – Mahar-ishi Mahesh Yogi, Bhagwan Shree Rajneesh ('Osho') and Sathya Sai Baba – all with their ashrams and their unique message. Gandhi's ashram may have been the first at which a successful attempt was made by Indians to package Indian beliefs in an internationally attractive form. His immediate predecessors, Annie Besant and her mentor Madame Blavatsky, were Europeans who developed an active interest in Indian religious thinking; Gandhi was the home-grown article.

Westerners found much that was familiar in the ashram; Gandhi's prayer meetings incorporated Christian hymns and blessings, and evi-dence of Ruskin's and Tolstoy's thought was not difficult to detect. The value of divesting oneself of property and other material ties was rooted deep in the Indian notion of the spiritual life; but the work of one's own hands and the dignity of labour were an import from European socialist thinking.

In a wholesale and stinging assault on Gandhi's mode of operating his son Harilal attacked his insistence on petty regulations concerning salt or milk or any of the other things he would rule on – these had no bearing on character, Harilal said. There were other, more desirable, aspects of character to be encouraged: unselfishness, charity, courage. Instead of promoting these, Gandhi fostered acolytes who paid lip-service to the high principles of the ashram while in fact pleasing him merely by keeping to the minutiae of the dietary rule book and obeying his every word without question.[19] One of the ashramites later talked of the pettiness of their reliance on Gandhi: 'We became so dependent on him that we couldn't make any decision without consulting him: "Bapu how much hair oil should I use?" "Bapu, should I get my head shaved?" "Bapu, should I have one or two spoonfuls of soybean paste?"'[20]

Enemas were a persistent part of ashram life, and had apparently been so since South Africa. Gandhi used to tell a story of a European girl who was close to him in South Africa and who suffered from per-sistent headaches. He said to her: 'You must be constipated. I'll give you an enema.' As he was preparing the syringe she undressed and, pre-sumably unable to withhold herself from a man she loved who was about to penetrate her in his own way, came up to him and embraced him. Gandhi said: 'Do you take me to be your father or your paramour?' She backed away, embarrassed; he gave her the enema and, true to form, made her confess her transgression to friends and family.[21]

Gandhi aside (for he suffered from chronic constipation), the ques-tion has to be asked whether the inhabitants of the ashram, living on their vegetarian diet, were in fact constipated or was Gandhi projecting his symptoms on to them – or was the preoccupation with enemas just a neurotic obsession with cleanliness within and without? He had a daily enema and prescribed the treatment widely; he told Kasturba to give one to his future daughter-in-law Nirmala, who said: 'I felt very shy about taking an enema from my future mother-in-law, but Ba was gentle and motherly. After a couple of days, I learned to give myself an enema.'[22] While he prescribed enemas to the ashramites, it is not apparent that he often participated in administering them. To have done so (particularly to Indian women, for whom modesty was an important cultural requirement) would have been extreme behaviour, even for Gandhi.

One of the great personal events of the 'quiet years' was the death in April 1928 of his right-hand man Maganlal in Bihar after a brief illness. Gandhi, at fifty-eight, was distraught to lose the man 'whom I had singled out as heir to my all'. In his obituary remarks he was particularly keen to praise Maganlal for his celibacy: 'When I presented to my co-workers brahmacharya as a rule of life even for married men in search of Truth, he was the first to perceive the beauty and the necessity of the practice and, though it cost him to my knowledge a terrific struggle, he carried it through to success.'[23]

Failure, though, in whatever sphere, was punished by the withdrawal of the ashram's love. Chaganlal Gandhi had been guilty of petty larcenies involving trivial sums of money over a number of years: he left the ashram. The ashramites felt it would be fair to give Chaganlal some or all of the 10,000 rupees' worth of savings he had made over when joining the community, to help him and his family in life outside. Gandhi refused, to the disappointment of many ashramites who felt his principles could be better tempered with charity.

He also felt it necessary to expose the sins of Kasturba in an article in Gujarati in *Navajivan*: 'I believe hers to have been an immaculate life. It is true that her renunciation has not been based on an intelligent appreciation of the fundamentals of life, but from a blind wifely devotion ... But the white surface of these virtues is not without the glaringly dark spots.'[24] Although impelled by a sense of wifely devotion to eschew worldly possessions, the longing for them persisted to the extent that she laid up a couple of hundred rupees for her own use out of the money presented to her by various people. This became known when the small sum was stolen from her room and she was upset about it.

When a widow and a young unmarried man had an affair, Gandhi put the future of the ashram in the hands of God. He embarked on another experiment with 'vital foods' that 'had not been brought into contact with fire', meaning uncooked.[25] Twenty-two people joined him in the experiment in an attempt to rein in unruly passions, but they suffered intestinal problems, Gandhi went down with dysentery, and they discontinued the experiment.

Gandhi was elected president of Congress for 1925; he now devoted little time to Hindu–Muslim relations, saying: 'For the time being I have put away in my cupboard this Hindu–Muslim tangle. That does not mean that I have despaired of a solution . . . But I must confess to you today that I cannot present a workable solution that you will accept.' It was a sad premonition of the future.[26] Muslims such as Shaukat Ali were complaining that although they had subsidised the non-cooperation movement including Gandhi's travels and Motilal Nehru's *Independent* newspaper, their interests were not now being supported by Congress. Gandhi wrote a pained note saying that the Khilafat committee had paid for his expenses at their insistence, and he now felt inclined to return the whole sum, with interest.

During 1925–7 Gandhi travelled widely, taking a tour in eastern and northern India and then to southern India and Ceylon. In 1929 he visited the Himalayas, north India, Sind and Burma. A later follower of Gandhi, G. Ramachandran, explained how when he was seventeen he first saw his future leader: 'In Travancore the lowly, downtrodden untouchables suddenly started walking on roads that for centuries had been reserved for high-caste Hindus. The maharaja arrested hundreds of them. Bapu [Gandhi] arrived, and the untouchables organised a rally to hear him speak.' Ramachandran's parents would not allow him to attend but he slipped out of the house and watched Gandhi at a distance through a vast crowd, calling them to silence by merely raising his finger. He explained: 'The crowd expected Bapu to attack the maharaja, but practically the first thing he said was "I've come here on a pilgrimage to help the Harijans gain their self-respect, but I've also come here to pay my respects to your great maharaja."' Gandhi knew the maharaja's spies would carry this obeisance back to him. The crowd was beginning to turn hostile, but Gandhi controlled them with what Ramachandran called 'his magic finger'. Within a few days of the rally, Gandhi had persuaded the maharaja to allow the untouchables to walk on the roads.[27]

The British acted clumsily over Indian political reform, which proceeded along the lines of the 1919 Government of India Act. Stanley

Baldwin's conservative government set up a statutory commission led by Sir John Simon which was to tour India in 1928. They made the mistake of not appointing a single Indian to the seven-man commission, thus bringing about unity in the nationalist movement – all Indian politicians were equally offended. The previously quiescent country was now aroused, and the commission, which included future prime minister Clement Attlee, was met on its tour with demonstrations waving black flags calling 'Simon, go back!' The violence of anti-Simon Commission demonstrations led to serious injury and the death of a prominent leader, Lala Rajput Rai, which in turn led to bomb attacks by outraged Punjabi youth against the authorities. Gandhi was not actively involved in the boycott of Simon, fearing that that have would stimulated a national revolt, unprepared and with no clear goal except protest.

Congress politics was polarised around two camps: those calling for dominion status within the British Empire, mainly the older generation; and young radicals such as Jawaharlal Nehru and Subhas Chandra Bose who argued for complete independence. Bose was a militaristic young activist who liked to wear a uniform and thought of non-violence as an insufficient tool for gaining Indian independence. He was immune to Gandhi's charm, and critical of his limited strategic thinking; he felt independence would be won through at least some level of armed struggle.

In response to the perceived insult of the Simon Commission and the implicit suggestion that Indians could not produce their own working constitution, Motilal Nehru chaired a working committee of politicians who worked on what would be called the Nehru Report, which was ultimately to form much of the basis of the constitution of independent India. Its most important provision was universal suffrage, enfranchising men and women equally, a democratic advance that was enacted in Britain only in 1928, the year the Nehru report was produced.

At the Calcutta Congress at the end of 1928 Gandhi proposed a compromise between those who wanted a campaign for complete independence and those who argued for dominion status. He proposed they should set a deadline for the British: dominion status with a constitution along the lines of the Nehru Report before 31 December 1929, in the absence of which they would fight for complete independence. Gandhi backed Jawaharlal Nehru in his candidature for Congress president over Bose. For some time he had been favouring the younger Nehru for leadership, despite Jawaharlal's flirtation with socialism, a rival creed resisted by Gandhi as too materialistic. Nehru had the charm and ability to be a leader, but was short on ideas; those would be supplied by Gandhi. 'May God spare you for many a long year to come, and make you His chosen instrument for freeing India from the yoke,' he wrote.[28] The triumvirate of Motilal, Jawaharlal and Gandhi dominated the independence movement: wits said it was being run by the father, son and holy ghost.

The Viceroy Lord Irwin announced that the natural outcome of India's constitutional progress was the attainment of dominion status. But this was no more than had previously been stated – nationalists wanted a date. The British government, as well as parliament as a whole, were divided, however. Prime minister Baldwin said of dominion status that no one knows 'whether that date be near or distant'.[29] A round-table conference was to be held in London but Congress boycotted it. Congress moderates might well have wished to confer, but the radical wing, and those extremists outside Congress with their bombs and their incendiary language, forced the party to be radical or risk losing the initiative.

Britain refused to concede a timetable for dominion status; the two-volume report of the Simon Commission was still in preparation when the Congress deadline ran out. Jawaharlal Nehru raised the tricolour flag in Lahore at midnight on a very cold New Year's Eve in 1929, dancing rather stiffly round the flagpole. Gandhi called on all patriots to meet on 26 January 1930, to pledge independence and their willingness to break the law to obtain it. The pledge declared British rule a 'fourfold disaster': economic, political, cultural and spiritual.

Gandhi had been preoccupied with how to bring about the national mobilisation he had promised; he decided that first only his trained supporters would perform acts of civil disobedience, to be followed by untrained satyagrahis. If any violence could be justifiably attributed to his movement, he would call a halt to the campaign. But over what would they campaign?

In February 1930 Gandhi hit upon his spectacularly simple plan. He would declare to the world that he was going to break the law, then would walk two hundred miles to the coast in order to do it. The law he would break was that preventing the manufacture and sale of salt without paying a tax to the British. Such an absurd law demanded an absurd act of law-breaking: he would process salt and urge others to do so.

He had taken an interest in salt even while a student in London in 1891, remarking that 'there are thousands in India who have to live on one pice [one-hundred of a rupee] a day. These live on bread and salt, a heavily taxed article.'[30] The law forbade the production of salt except taxed salt; the possession and sale of contraband salt was an offence. Of the £800 million raised annually in revenue from India the tax represented £25 million, but the money came disproportionately from the poorest. Everyone had to have some salt, but those doing physical work needed it most, and the cost of it formed a higher part of their meagre incomes. The tax was also an abomination because there was salt in abundance in India: it could be had for the taking on parts of the coast, but it was a government monopoly. As a campaigning symbol salt had another attraction: it was needed equally by Hindus and Muslims, so was a unifying factor between them.

Personally, Gandhi had little use for salt – he had in fact tried excluding it from his diet. He wrote to a friend: 'By inducing an artificial appetite, it makes one eat more and arouses the senses gratuitously . . . I live on a saltless diet consisting mainly of fruit. It is not to mortify the body that I do this but so that the body, mind and *atman* [the soul] may be in fuller command of themselves and purer.'[31]

He wrote to the Viceroy ('Dear Friend') saying British rule was a curse that had impoverished the millions of India through an expensive military and civil administration, though he reassuringly asserted: 'I do not . . . consider Englishmen in general to be worse than any other people on earth.' He found the British administration of India the most expensive in the world, and cleverly invited Lord Irwin to compare his salary with that of the British prime minister: 'You are getting much over five thousand times India's average income. The British prime minister is getting only ninety times Britain's average income. On bended knees I ask you to ponder over this phenomenon.'[32] He declared: 'My ambition is no less than to convert the British people through non-violence, and thus make them see the wrong they have done to India.'[33] He would call a civil disobedience campaign unless the government conceded to a list of demands. He included in this the abolition of the salt tax, but did not emphasise it; others were alcohol prohibition, the reduction of official salaries and the right to bear arms.

Not for the first or last time, Jawaharlal Nehru was perplexed: 'What was the point of making a list of some political and social reforms – good in themselves, no doubt – when we were talking in terms of independence? Did Gandhiji mean the same thing when he used the term as we did, or did we speak a different language?'[34]

Gandhi announced his intention to agitate over salt on 5 March 1930 at a meeting at the ashram. Such politicians as Vallabhbhai Patel, Motilal and Jawaharlal Nehru were unimpressed. The salt tax was a minor imposition, no one was currently up in arms about it, the educated classes thought nothing of it. It did not appear to provide the empire-crushing stratagem that had been promised. The British dismissed the campaign as childish posturing, and it so escaped their sternest attentions – which of course was the point. They decided not to take any action but to let the protest fizzle out.

On 12 March the sixty-year-old agitator along with seventy-eight satyagrahis set off at 6 a.m. from the Sabarmati Ashram (sometimes called the Satyagraha Ashram), heading for Dandi where the Arabian Sea's tides had produced salt flats where the mineral could easily be garnered. Garlanded and accompanied by music, the marchers made their way through Ahmedabad saluted by tens of thousands who recalled great epic battles and many of whom wept, thinking, strangely, that the marchers were going to their deaths.

Gandhi wore a dhoti with a large watch pinned to it, and a shawl. He carried, as all the marchers did, a shoulder bag with a bedroll, a change of clothes, a hand-spindle for spinning, a diary and a mug. The plan was to march for twenty-five days along a carefully plotted path through the villages of the west coast. In order to maintain communication with the world, Gandhi was writing tens of letters a day and would sometimes be up at 3 a.m. to write his article for *Young India* before the day's march started. They passed through villages that had been primed in advance to supply the simplest food, a place for sleeping and a site for them to dig latrines. Townspeople came out in their thousands to cheer the march, villages were festooned and roads sprinkled with water to damp down the dust.

Gandhi made the march the occasion for promoting the messages in favour of spinning and against untouchability. At the village of Dabhan he walked past the temple to the untouchables' quarter, where he drew water from the 'untouchable' well and bathed. He then persuaded the high-caste Hindus of the welcoming committee to allow the untouchables to join the gathering. Most villages gave a warm welcome; others provided no reception committee and the marchers had to drum up interest on their arrival. A police officer reporting on the march informed his superiors: 'Gandhi is becoming weaker and weaker every day. This is seen from his care-worn face. He now takes more time to accomplish his afternoon marches than he used to take at the commencement. He also now hurries through his speeches. At times, he himself says "I am tired."'[35]

They covered 241 miles in the twenty-five days and reached Dandi on 5 April. Sarojini Naidu and other activists were there to receive them. For the last miles of the trek, the ashramites had been joined by thousands of supporters. The long build-up had allowed journalists from around the world to gather, to whom Gandhi issued the message: 'I want world sympathy in this battle of Right against Might.'[36] On 6 April he bathed in the ocean, breaking the salt laws by picking up a pinch of salt (in fact salty mud), the signal for people all over India to do the same. Along the coast, villagers waded into the sea or gathered salt from the saline earth; in the cities Congress volunteers sold illegally produced salt (of somewhat dubious quality) in the streets. Gandhi produced some salt, which was sold to the highest bidder and raised 1,600 rupees for the cause.

Thousands were arrested for producing and selling salt, or beaten for such offences as refusing to let go of salt they were holding in their hands. From the southern coast to Bengal and the North-West Frontier Province demonstrations took place that were mostly peaceful, but in Peshawar Indian soldiers refused to fire on unarmed demonstrators – for the British, a serious turn of events. In Bengal, long a hotbed of violent dissent, nationalists attacked an army depot in Chittagong and seized arms. The British banned nationalist newspapers including *Young India* and *Navajivan* and ruled by decree, bypassing the democratic legislatures.

Gandhi was planning to raise the stakes and lead a march on a government salt depot, but he was arrested after midnight in his hut on 5 May under an early-nineteenth-century law that allowed detention without trial. He collected his belongings, brushed his few teeth and obtained permission to have his leading cantor sing a prayer – the camp was already roused and waiting silently for his departure. He was taken by train and car back to Yeravda jail in Poona where he had previously been incarcerated. When he was examined he was found to weigh 100lbs and to be five feet five inches tall. He referred to the prison as Yeravda Pleasure House in the letters he wrote from there, as if he were glad of the tranquillity that imprisonment gave him.[37]

The proposed march on the government salt depot at Dharasana took place, led by Sarojini Naidu, with thousands of satyagrahis approaching the heavily fortified building and showing no resistance when they were beaten back with heavy sticks (lathis). The spectacular event was reported around the world; in the striking words of Webb Miller, the United Press correspondent: 'From where I stood I heard the sickening whack of the sticks on unprotected skulls . . . Those struck down fell sprawling, unconscious, or writhing with fractured skulls or broken shoulders.'[38] As the Viceroy Lord Irwin wrote to the king, 'the whole business was propaganda and, as such, served its purpose admirably well'.[39] The American media in particular found the image of Gandhi defying the British Empire to be irresistible, evoking the tea tax of 1776, with its iconic place in the history of the American Revolution.

Arrests continued at a fast pace, and as soon as leaders were led away more took their place. When Jawaharlal was arrested, Motilal Nehru became president of Congress in his place, followed by Vallabhbhai Patel, then Rajendra Prasad – a sequence of arrest and replacement that was duplicated at every level of Congress organisation. Some fifty thousand were jailed in all, but defying the government's expectations, repression had the opposite effect: civil disobedience became more aggressive and violence escalated.

The round-table conference (later known as the *first* round-table conference) on India's constitution called by Labour prime minister Ramsay MacDonald in London was opened on 12 November 1930 by George V. Despite such high-level support, it did not enjoy success as it was so clearly unrepresentative of the Hindu nationalist majority. Jinnah and the Aga Khan represented the Muslims and for the first time the princes were strongly represented at a political conference. Those who attended agreed on the principle of an Indian federation and on the desirability of immediate dominion status, the latter being close to what the Congress supporters had been demanding. It was the minimum the British could give, and much misery would have been avoided had they moved faster to make the concession. If the British were attempting to gather their forces in opposition to Congress, the ploy had failed. The Simon Report, when it was finally issued, proposed an All India Federation, which was to be an elusive goal for British constitution makers for the next seventeen years.

With such a level of agreement, the government of India was prepared to make a gesture towards a settlement with Congress, and on 26 January 1931 all leading protesters were released in order to make discussions possible. Gandhi gave a rather stiff statement to Associated Press on his release: 'I have come out of jail with an absolutely open mind, unfettered by enmity, unbiased in argument and prepared to study the whole situation from every point of view.'[40]

Motilal Nehru died that February; when Gandhi visited him the sick man had asked for a drink. Gandhi said he should be reciting the *Bhagavad Gita* and thinking of spiritual things. 'I leave unworldly things to you and my wife. While I'm still on earth, I will be earthy,' the old lawyer said.[41] With the wise cynic Motilal gone, the last restraining influence on Gandhi from the older generation was removed, for good or ill. Everything that followed from the Congress side, for perhaps the next ten years, was at his direction – its success or failure was in his hands.

Congress authorised Gandhi to negotiate a settlement of the civil disobedience campaign with the Viceroy, so he wrote to Lord Irwin and they met in February and March 1931. Winston Churchill was outraged, famously referring to Gandhi as a 'malignant subversive fanatic': it was 'alarming and also nauseating to see Mr Gandhi, a seditious Middle Temple lawyer [in fact, Inner Temple], now posing as a fakir of a type well-known in the East, striding half-naked up the steps of the vice-regal palace, while he is still organising and conducting a defiant campaign of civil disobedience, to parley on equal terms with the representative of the King–Emperor'.[42] Churchill had served in India and was well aware that the land swarmed with self-styled holy men in various states of undress, begging from already impoverished people and offering bogus panaceas. Gandhi was not such – he was entirely genuine; but it was not unreasonable for Churchill to confuse him with charlatans.

Churchill felt that for Britain to grant dominion status would be a 'crime' if it were attained 'while India is a prey to fierce racial and religious dissensions and when the withdrawal of British protection would mean the immediate resumption of mediaeval wars'. His view was that the political class represented a tiny self-interested fraction of the 350 million Indians and that no community could have the dignity of dominion status that 'brands and treats sixty millions of its members, fellow human beings, toiling at their side, as "Untouchables", whose approach is an affront and whose very presence is pollution'.[43] Thus he agreed with Gandhi on the horror of widespread Hindu–Muslim conflict and on the offence of untouchability; but whereas Gandhi was taking practical steps against them, Churchill presented these negative aspects of Indian society as reasons to delay moves towards independence, perhaps indefinitely. Churchill resigned from the Conservative shadow cabinet over his party leader Baldwin's support for Indian constitutional change – not the future war leader's most far-sighted move. Churchill was correct, however, in pointing out that the real importance of the meeting of the two sides was the perceived equality it gave to Indian leaders and the British administration: Gandhi approached Irwin not as a supplicant, but as an equal.

Irwin, later Lord Halifax, was to become infamous as the Foreign Secretary of appeasement in the run-up to the Second World War. Of aristocratic bearing (at six feet five inches), he towered over the diminutive sage of India. On Gandhi's 'indeed unfavourable' physical endowment he remarked in a letter: 'Small, wizened, rather emaciated, no front teeth, it is a personality very poorly adorned with the world's trimmings. And yet you cannot help feeling the force of character behind the sharp little eyes and immensely active and acutely working mind.'[44] He was unabashed by Gandhi's appearance in his loincloth and shawl, or the presence of Mirabehn (the former Madeleine Slade was a lady, after all) dancing attendance on Gandhi, bringing his dates and goat's milk to the viceregal palace when the discussions ran on past his dinner time. A diplomat who was present remarked, 'I remember Gandhi squatting on the floor and after a while a girl coming in with some filthy yellow stuff which he started eating without so much as a by your leave.'[45]

Irwin early assessed Gandhi's character and decided to appeal to his 'vanity of power and personality'.[46] Irwin was to be given the nickname Holy Fox (a pun on his title) because he was both religious and devious, and should therefore have been a fair sparring partner for Gandhi. But progress was slow. Irwin wrote to his father:

I kept asking myself all the time 'Was the man completely sincere?' I think that as our conversation went on I came to feel about this in rather double fashion. I came to have no doubt whatever that, if Mr Gandhi gave me his word on any point, that word was absolutely secure, and that I could trust it implicitly. On the other hand, I found what had always been my impression being confirmed, namely, that though intentionally he was completely sincere, yet in some matters he was the victim of unconscious self-delusion.[47]

They met eight times, and reached agreement on 4 March 1931 with what became known as the Delhi Pact, or the Gandhi–Irwin Pact. Gandhi called off the civil disobedience campaign and agreed to join in the second round-table conference. The British wanted Indians to stop the boycott of Lancashire cotton goods, as it was causing hardship among workers in the cotton towns. This was accepted, though encouragement of Indian textiles was also part of the deal. The non-violent picketing of liquor shops would be permitted. The Viceroy did not agree to abolish the salt tax but to permit people in certain villages to produce salt for their own use and sell it individually. He refused to launch an inquiry into police excesses during the campaign. He released all non-violent prisoners but would not reprieve from hanging the men who had been involved in bomb attacks. This led for the first time to Gandhi's having to face demonstrations against himself. Supporters of Bhagat Singh, who had thrown two bombs into the legislative assembly crowded with British and Indian members, and who later killed a young British policeman, greeted Gandhi when he arrived at the Karachi Congress in March 1931 with black flags and shouts of 'Gandhi go back!'

Congress members again felt sold out by Gandhi. For the second time he had called off a campaign, and with no particular gains. It could be said, however, that he had cannily brought a halt to both civil disobedience movements when they were losing momentum, thereby retaining strength. Jawaharlal Nehru wept bitterly, and told Gandhi such a settlement would never have been reached had his father been alive: 'Was it for this that our people behaved so gallantly for a year? Were all our brave words and deeds to end in this?'[48] Seats at a round-table conference with no preconditions as to dominion status had been on offer, after all, since before the start of the 'salt satyagraha'.

Thus ended the second campaign for Indian independence. Its only achievement, in the end, was the considerable one of the perception' that Gandhi was now in a position to negotiate. He then tremendously enhanced his prestige by leaning on his Congress colleagues to allow him to be the sole representative, even though the government had allocated sixteen places. Gandhi knew that the divisions within Congress would not be apparent if he were at the table alone; and he knew all eyes would be on him. His appearances in 1930–1 set the seal on Gandhi as a world icon.

9

World Icon

Gandhi travelled to London on the SS *Rajputana* on 29 August 1931, taking with him Mirabehn, Mahadev Desai, Pyarelal and his son Devdas. He was the sole Congress representative as well as having plenipotentiary powers to make decisions over last-minute proposals. Sarojini Naidu travelled with them as a delegate representing Indian women; G.D. Birla went representing the business community. Gandhi travelled second-class but spent most of his time on deck, dictating letters and holding court to those who were interested in seeing him.

He had been uncertain whether to go at all, in the absence of a settlement of Hindu–Muslim differences and because of non-observance of the Gandhi–Irwin Pact, but he eventually succumbed to divine guidance. 'My faith is in God,' he said, via Associated Press. 'He seems to have made my way clear for me to go to London. Therefore I expect He will use me as His instrument for the service of humanity.'[1] Asked by the press if he were going to take advisers he replied: 'My adviser is God. If I had any idea to take advisers I would have taken them as delegates.'[2]

An American preacher, John Haynes Holmes, described Gandhi at this time:

He has a shaven head, protruding ears, thick lips, and a mouth that is minus many of its teeth. But his dark complexion is richly beautiful against the white background of his shawl, his eyes shine like candles in the night, and all over is the radiance of a smile like sunshine on a morning landscape. What impresses you is not the physical appearance

but the spiritual presence of this man. You think at once of his simplicity, his sincerity, his innocence. He approaches you with all the nat-
uralness and spontaneity of a little child.[3]

There had been much discussion in India as to what Gandhi would
wear in the notoriously bad English climate; for him it was a test of
what he had become, and he was unhesitating. He went as a representative of 'the semi-starved, almost naked villager' and as such would
wear only his loincloth: 'My loin cloth is an organic evolution in my
life. It came naturally, without effort, without premeditation'; he determined 'to add nothing more to the loin cloth than the climate peremp-
torily demands'.[4]

It was raining when he disembarked at Folkestone; he was first taken
to the Quaker headquarters, the Friends' Meeting House, where he was
welcomed by a crowd led by the socialist writer Laurence Housman.
The composition of this welcoming committee showed where support
for Gandhi lay in England: in the churches, in the women's organisations and with the political left as represented by trade unions and the
Labour Party whose stalwart Fenner Brockway was present that day.

Gandhi went on to Kingsley Hall, a mission to the poor in the East
End of London, where he was a guest of Muriel Lester, a pacifist and
prohibitionist who had visited him at the Sabarmati Ashram. He had
been invited to stay in grand places in the fashionable West End but
made a point of saying he wanted to live among his own people, the
poor. 'There is no surplus furniture to be found in all the settlement,'
he reported excitedly, 'the inmates occupy tiny rooms called cells.'[5]

Gandhi had a cell leading from an open terrace. It was five feet wide
and seven or eight feet long with bare walls, furnished only with a table,
a chair and a thin pallet on the floor. He established a regime: at three
he was woken for prayer, then took a rapid walk through the streets,
followed by breakfast, a meeting with his secretaries and interviews. At
ten o clock he would take a car to the conference, 'followed by panting
detectives, and some of his staff clutching the famous spinning wheel
and the green rush basket containing his food', as an observer put it.[6]
At seven o'clock he conducted his evening prayers, then interviews and
conferences lasted into the night. His stamina was remarkable but his

busy schedule may have prevented him from getting the best out of the conference; he was often seen to be listening quietly to debates with his eyes closed, perhaps asleep.

The mission was besieged by well-wishers, the curious and journalists. American interest in Gandhi was shown by a half-hour broadcast on CBS in which he promoted his ideal of a bloodless revolution for Indian liberty. He already had a fascinated following in the US; *Time* magazine had made 'Saint Gandhi' 1930's 'man of the year'. He met one of the other instantly recognisable world icons, Charlie Chaplin. Gandhi had been unwilling to see Chaplin, as he said he did not have any interest in actors and had never seen a film, but on being told of Chaplin's childhood poverty he did meet him. He also met Lloyd George and gave a talk to his old friends of the Vegetarian Society.

His great pleasure in London was visiting the homes of the poor. Muriel Lester described how, followed by a large crowd as he usually was, he decided to visit families in a neighbouring street:

> In and out of the houses he went on both sides of the street. The women were inordinately proud. They had had no idea he was coming; some were at their ironing, some cleaning, but all were ready to display every corner of their little domain for him to inspect, and ask about and to admire. He wanted to know what work the men round about did, the rent of the houses, the work of the sanitary authorities so far as drains and cleanliness were concerned, what provision was made for the care of the family during unemployment . . . They showed him their pets, their rabbits and their chickens; occasionally there was a piano to be proud of, and always it was obvious how the best was being made of everything and how anything that possessed any sort of beauty was cherished.[7]

Sometimes irreverent East End children would shout after him: 'Gandhi, where's your trousers?'

His wit endeared him to a public used to strait-laced politicians and gave the world the typical Gandhi anecdotes that have been endlessly repeated. Asked what he thought of Western civilisation, he replied that he thought it would be a good thing. When asked, after meeting the king, whether he thought himself underdressed, he explained that 'the king had enough on for both of us'.

At the request of Charles Andrews he visited Lancashire mill towns, where he met workers who had been hit hard, at a time of economic depression and high unemployment, by the swadeshi policy of resisting foreign cloth. He described the living standard of the poor in India – far worse than that of the poor in England, he asserted – and explained how he was attempting to revivify the cottage industries in his own country. At one moment, captured on film, he was surrounded by the mainly women mill-hands who put their arms around him and cheered him. He also spoke to people in the great institutions of empire: boys at Eton and scholars at Oxford and Cambridge. One of the dons at Oxford, the missionary and historian Edward Thompson, remarked: 'Not since Socrates has the world seen his equal for absolute self-control and composure', but he was quite able to understand, he added, why the Athenians had made Socrates drink hemlock.[8]

Life at Kingsley Hall may have been more congenial to Gandhi but it was inconvenient for a conference that was being held eight miles away. So Andrews and Harry Polak, who were managing his affairs in London, rented 88 Knightsbridge, where Gandhi's staff stayed and which he used as an office.

As they prepared for the voyage to London, the political scene in Britain had been changing. On 24 August the Labour government had been replaced by a Conservative-dominated coalition, though with Ramsay MacDonald still prime minister. It was generally the case that nation-alists in India had best look to the Liberals or Labour for boons, but party policies were converging in the 1930s on the need for constitu-tional reform, and the process that resulted in the Government of India Act of 1935 was conducted in a parliament with a large Conservative majority. British parliamentarians had their own timetable; the reform of Indian political institutions continued almost despite the nationalists who, after all, were not asking for better government under the British.

When Gandhi arrived at the conference it was obvious why he had been in two minds as to whether to go: sitting with sixty-eight other representatives from British India, twenty-three from the princely states and twenty from the UK, he was just one voice among many. His claim to represent the whole of India was regarded with disdain by those who felt he represented only his own idiosyncratic viewpoint. His decision to attend alone and not take up the other Congress places had been splendid from the point of view of what would later be called public relations: all media attention was focused on him. But in the conference hall it left him isolated and looking unrepresentative. Nor was his performance exemplary; though Gandhi was clearly the most senior Indian at the conference, observers were disappointed. An anonymous writer in *The Times* said:

> The expectation formed in many quarters here of seeing a man of commanding gifts was not fulfilled. He had no mastery of detail: constitutional problems did not interest him. He was no orator; his speeches were made seated and delivered slowly in low, level tones, which did not vary whatever his theme might be. His interventions in discussion were mainly propagandist and often had little real connection with the matter in hand. He made no real constructive contribution to the work of the conference.'[9]

He explained his difficulties in a conversation with George Bernard Shaw, to whom he confided that the conference 'requires more than the patience of a Job. The whole thing is a huge camouflage, and harangues that we are treated to are meant only to mark time. Why not, I ask them, announce your policy and let us make our choice? But it does not seem to be in the English political nature to do so.'[10] In fact, it was not in Gandhi's political nature to appreciate that the procedure of holding discussions with interested parties until a solution was reached really *was* the policy. For Gandhi, public life was a search for truth which, when he satisfied himself he had found it, he then had to present to the rest of the world, using all means to have them accept it. British politicians would be happy with a compromise in which no one died.

In particular, before independence could be considered, the British were committed to a solution to the existing communal differences. They insisted that minorities had to be protected: Muslims, untouchables, Sikhs, Christians, Parsis and Europeans. In addition, no move the

British made towards independence or democracy could be binding on the whole of India, but only on the three-fifths of the nation controlled by Britain; the princes must decide their future in their part of the country. The Muslim League claimed to represent all India's Muslims, Gandhi's Congress claimed to represent all Indians; their differences were irreconcilable. Moreover, Gandhi had particular problems in his claims to represent the untouchables, who asked for separate electorates, as did all other minorities with the exception of the Sikhs. But the others were non-Hindus while untouchables were part of Hinduism, perversely, by virtue of being ritually excluded from it.

The untouchables' representative was Dr B.R. Ambedkar, who felt he had a better claim to represent the outcastes than did Gandhi. The son of an untouchable who served in the British army, he had attended primary school and, though segregated and treated with brutality, he had excelled. He was the first untouchable student at the Government High School in Bombay, despite cruel discrimination, and then the first untouchable to receive higher education. He won a scholarship to study at Columbia University in the US, where he took a PhD in economics; he continued his studies in London at the London School of Economics where he took another PhD and was called to the Gray's Inn Bar. Back in India in the 1920s he led civil rights movements campaigning to allow untouchables access to drinking-water and to temples.

Gandhi could lecture his high-caste friends like the Nehrus about suffering and the poor, but there was nothing he could tell Ambedkar. The untouchables' leader saw the elevation of his fellows as best taking place through education and improving living conditions. He felt untouchability was a product of a system that was itself pernicious; he argued that the caste system should be abolished – in counterpoint to Gandhi, who defended it but wanted it to embrace untouchables.

The two were bitterly divided on the issue of electorates: Ambedkar supported a separate electorate and reserved seats for untouchables; Gandhi opposed statutory protection except for the minority Muslim religious communities and the Sikhs. He felt Hinduism should reform so as to outlaw untouchability. He felt separate electorates would divide Indian society: 'I claim myself in my own person to represent the vast mass of the untouchables,' he said. A separate electorate for untouchables would enshrine the principle of their degradation in law: 'Will untouchables remain untouchables in perpetuity? I would far rather Hinduism died than that untouchability lived.'[11] Separate electorates would divide villages, subverting Gandhi's vision of a reformed Hinduism where caste Hindus would realise their responsibilities towards untouchables.

When Ramsay MacDonald, chairing the minorities committee, seemed to endorse the demand for separate electorates, Gandhi wanted to withdraw from it. The conference ended without agreement on the basis of a constitution; but three committees were to continue to work on aspects of the problem until the next conference took place. Gandhi argued at the plenary session of the conference that civil disobedience, not argument, was the answer to India's problems, with the suggestion that civil disobedience was the only alternative to terrorism.

Gandhi's return journey took him via Paris, where vast crowds greeted him at the Gare du Nord, then to Switzerland where he was a guest of Romain Rolland. Inquisitive Europeans troubled the great man: an Italian lady wrote to ask Gandhi the ten winning numbers in the next Lotto; Swiss-German nudists wanted to enlist him in their cause; the press set up camp around Rolland's villa and the hotels were full of people who had come to look at Gandhi in the celebrity-seeking Western model of darshan.

Rolland and Gandhi spent time together pondering the eternal principle of God, though Rolland found Gandhi so determined in his own views that little discussion was possible. In one revealing remark, speaking in English (translated into French by Rolland's sister), Gandhi said he had learned little from history: 'My method is empiric, all my conclusions are based on personal experience.'[12] He went on to Italy where he had an audience with Mussolini: independent India wanted a democratic constitution, he assured him – not, as Mussolini suggested, a dictatorship.

If, for the British, the round-table conference was a failure, in not having provided a constitutional solution, it was a huge success for Gandhi who had made of it a world showcase for himself. The Gandhi brand of ascetic living and devout, defiant speech, laced with a hint of mischief, was now compounded with the image of Gandhi the loinclothed spinner. For every newspaper reader, political cartoons made him an instantly recognisable figure.

For Congress the conference was a marked disaster. The party was now so closely connected with Gandhi that independent action was not possible; it would be sixteen years before Congress leaders were able to exercise action independently of him. Congress should have been at the conference pulling together all the different factions in India, doing deals and setting up a federation. The failure to do so was the first major mistake that set India on the road to partition. Gandhi was a great leader but a poor politician: he should have left the politics to men like Nehru and Rajagopalachari.

When Gandhi disembarked from the SS *Pilsna* at Bombay on 28 December 1931, it was to a tumultuous welcome; for the masses the Mahatma could do no wrong. There had, however, not only been no progress – in a number of ways the situation was worse than when he left the country: there was more violence and politics was more fragmented. The government was now using emergency powers to deal with the terrorist incidents and civil disobedience in Bengal and the North-West Frontier Province. With Gandhi's permission (from England) a no-rent campaign had been started by Congress in the United Provinces, aimed against the high taxes that were collected with the rents. The response from the new Viceroy Lord Willingdon, formerly known to Gandhi when he was Governor of Bombay, was to imprison the leaders. Gandhi suggested civil disobedience would have to be reintroduced, and he was duly arrested on 3 January 1932. Willingdon remarked that 'to have to deal with a man who is a mixture of a saint and a "bania" is very trying indeed'.[13] For the British the message was that negotiating with Gandhi had brought neither positive results constitutionally nor civil peace in India.

Gandhi was taken to his old 'home', Yeravda jail. Vallabhbhai Patel was at this time a fellow prisoner, and Gandhi's secretary Mahadev Desai later joined them. Gandhi was allowed to write and receive unlimited amounts of letters on non-political subjects.

New emergency ordinances were issued, providing the authorities with sweeping powers to suppress unrest. Thousands defied the ordinances and were imprisoned or beaten by police with lathis. If this was, literally, the stick of the policy, there was also the carrot of constitutional change wending its slow way through the corridors of power. 'The dogs bark but the caravan passes on,' said Secretary of State for India Sir Samuel Hoare in response to the disturbances in India. A history of the subcontinent told from the viewpoint only of Congress makes these civil disturbances seem a driving force of change, while in fact change was proceeding at its own pace. There were also many in the Indian political world prepared to trust the British to progress towards independence; while the key events of the 1930s saw Congress losing the initiative, the British succeeded in creating a more advanced democracy than existed anywhere else in the East. Gandhi realised the way forward and was now discussing whether Congress would stand for office under the new constitution. He even asked Patel which portfolio he would want in a home rule cabinet: 'I will take the beggar's bowl,' said Patel, telling Gandhi what he wanted to hear. He fully expected to be prime minister and, indeed, he came close to it.[14]

Gandhi's tacit acceptance of the ongoing constitutional developments was diverted when the government's provisional scheme for minority representation was announced in August 1932. The proposals were for separate electorates for Hindus and Muslims, as there had been previously, but also for untouchables or the 'depressed classes' as the British expression had it. Gandhi wrote to Ramsay MacDonald on 18 August 1932 declaring: 'I have to resist your decision with my life. The only way I can do so is by declaring a perpetual fast unto death from food of any kind save water with or without salt and soda.'[15] Characteristically, though this letter was written on 17 August, Gandhi declared the fast would begin on 20 September, thereby allowing maximum lead-in time to attract publicity so as to put pressure on the government.

MacDonald in a long and considered letter expressed surprise that 'you propose to adopt the extreme course of starving yourself to death . . . solely to prevent the Depressed Classes, who admittedly suffer from terrible disabilities today, from being able to secure a limited number of representatives of their own choosing to speak on their behalf in the legislatures.'[16] 'What a capacity he had to give shocks to people!' wrote Nehru, who was 'angry with [Gandhi] at his religious and sentimental approach to a political question' and because he had chosen 'a side-issue for his final sacrifice.[17] Congress leaders may have been disdainful of the fast, but they could not lose Gandhi; as well as being the subject of their genuine affection, he was the totem without which Congress could not claim to represent the masses.

As far as Ambedkar was concerned, 'the Mahatma's ways of thinking are strange and are certainly beyond my comprehension'; far from wishing to augment the minimal political power now within the untouchables' grasp, 'on the contrary he has staked his very life in order to deprive them' of the little they were being offered.[18]

On the day he began the fast Gandhi wrote to Mirabehn: 'As I wrote that first letter conveying my vow, I thought of you and Ba . . . How would you two bear the thing?'[19] For much of the fasting period he stayed in the prison yard nursed by Sarojini Naidu who had been transferred from the women's area of the prison. Kasturba was later moved from another prison to be with him. 'Again, the same old story,' the long-suffering wife commented.[20]

Pressure was now being applied to Ambedkar, who was aware that Gandhi's death would result in a massacre of untouchables throughout India. The leaders of Congress and wealthy supporters met with Ambedkar in Birla House, Bombay, on the day the fast started. They worked out together a complex scheme of nomination and reserved seats for untouchables and put it to Gandhi. Deputations were allowed to see him in jail – the authorities knew they would not be urging him to continue with the fast. His blood pressure had become dangerously high, putting him in real danger.

Ambedkar saw him on 22 September, when Gandhi was already weakened by two days of fasting; then returned on the second and third days and negotiated over issues such as the number of reserved seats untouchables would have and the proposed primaries for untouchable candidates. The final solution – not for separate electorates but for a larger number of reserved seats – was, as Ambedkar said, available at the round-table conference, but it was rejected by Gandhi. Ambedkar remarked: 'I responded to the call of humanity and saved the life of Mr Gandhi by agreeing to alter the Communal Award [the distribution of seats among the religious communities] in a manner satisfactory to Mr Gandhi.'[21]

The agreement known as the Yeravda Pact was drafted and signed by the chief negotiators, then cabled to London where Andrews and Polak submitted it to the government. It was a Sunday and not an easy day to assemble politicians, but realising the danger of delay Ramsay MacDonald and Sir Samuel Hoare met at 10 Downing Street until midnight and the government in India and in London announced approval of the pact on 26 September. Gandhi broke his fast with a glass of orange juice that same day.

Ambedkar thought of the fast as a political stunt but it was undeniable that Gandhi had moved caste Hindus to address the question of untouchability in a way that they had not done before. They opened temple doors to untouchables, allowed them to use wells and even fraternised with them. This was a short-lived reform, the temples were soon closed again, but the principle had been stated. It was said that the fast marked the turning point for untouchability: previously it had been socially improper to consort with untouchables; afterwards, to practise untouchability was the mark of a reactionary bigot. Gandhi's supporters presented the event as 'the epic fast', which was used as a title of a book by Pyarelal. In it Rajagopalachari compared Gandhi's fast to Socrates' suicide and Jesus' death on the cross. This was excessive; excruciating though it was, it was not even the most extreme fast that Gandhi had put himself through.

Gandhi had to some extent regained the initiative as national leader with his action over the untouchables. He consolidated his position by launching, in 1933, an eight-page English-language weekly, *Harijan*, replacing his paper *Young India* which had been suppressed by the government. At almost the same time, now adept at the newspaper business he launched the Hindu *Harijan Sevak* (Servant of Harijans) and the Gujarati *Harijanbandhu* (Brother of Harijans). 'Harijan', meaning 'children of God', was Gandhi's term for untouchables, which he started using in September 1932. Ambedkar considered it patronising and it is, at best, a euphemism for outcastes, its use a demonstration that Gandhi did not truly believe the untouchables would be assimilated into the caste system. Ambedkar represented the opinion of untouchables towards Gandhi: 'How can they believe him to be their friend when he wishes to retain caste and abolish untouchability, it being quite clear that untouchability is only an extended form of caste and that therefore without the abolition of caste there is no hope of abolition of untouchability?'[22]

Gandhi was interested in removing untouchability, but was constrained by wanting also to preserve Hinduism intact. He said: 'We must endeavour to bring orthodoxy to our point of view, if it is at all possible. In any case we may do nothing to hurt anybody's susceptibilities.'[23] He proposed a scheme whereby temples would be open some times in the day for untouchables and for those who supported their admission, but at other times closed to untouchables and open to others for whom untouchability was 'a deep religious conviction'.[24] A few years later, in 1935, he moved towards the abolition of caste, but again made it a matter of conscience – if collective conscience – rather than of policy, saying 'the sooner public opinion abolishes it the better'.[25]

Soon after his 'epic fast' Gandhi felt there was not enough response to his work on untouchability. He considered himself responsible, and also blamed members of the ashram who had failed to be sufficiently pure; an inmate of the ashram had been carrying on a clandestine affair and when letters were found, they were of course given to Gandhi – ashramites delighted in denouncing each other. Gandhi therefore declared he would fast again, for twenty-one days from 8 May 1933, against untouchability and for the spiritual strength of its opponents. Considering that a six-day fast had nearly killed him, this was a dangerous exercise. The government decided they had had enough, and not wanting to be considered in any way responsible for his death they set him free on the day he started the fast. He survived, finishing it on 29 May in a mansion in Poona. He was uncertain about the future of civil disobedience: he argued with Congress for it to continue, then announced it was at an end, then said individual acts of civil disobedience were to continue. His was a rudderless ship.

Gandhi proposed meeting the Viceroy to bring some solution to the conflict, but he was in no position to bargain. The Viceroy refused to see him. Gandhi held less fascination for Willingdon than he had for his predecessor: 'Gandhi is a sort of Jekyll and Hyde,' he said, 'and while he may have his saint-like side, on the other he is the most Machiavellian, bargaining little political humbug I have ever come across.'[26] The

Gandhi magic was no longer working, either on the British or on Congress, which was now splintering, radicals such as Subhas Chandra Bose leading one faction, the left wing leading another, and orthodox Hindus, another.

Gandhi had declared on the Dandi march that he would not return to the Sabarmati Ashram until victory had been achieved and the salt tax abolished. He did not return to make it his permanent home. The ashram had not been paying land tax and therefore its goods had been seized and sold by government collectors. The community had been restive without him, and he was doubtless sick of their squabbling. Eventually, in 1933, he closed the ashram; the site became a trust for the assistance of untouchables and was renamed the Harijan Ashram.

The same year he intended to undertake a march from the ashram to Ras in Kheda, in solidarity with peasants there who had lost their lands, but he and his thirty-two companions were arrested before they could do so. He was released and arrested again, for refusing to comply with orders restricting his movements. He sent ashram members to conduct individual acts of civil disobedience, but there were now too few to make a difference. Gandhi was again arrested, went on another fast and was released. Nothing was working for him – not the untouchability campaign, nor the ashram nor civil disobedience. He was soon telling ashramites to find jobs to keep themselves rather than courting jail again. He would finally call off civil disobedience in all its forms in April 1934.

Late in September 1933 he moved to Wardha in the Central Provinces, close to India's geographical centre, where he was the guest of a leading financier and cotton merchant, Jamnalal Bajaj. He gave Gandhi the land to set up a new ashram beside the nearby village of Segaon. Another reason for Gandhi's going there was that one of his followers, the scholarly and ascetic Vinoba Bhave, had been working near Wardha. The location for the new ashram, which he called Sevagram (Village of Service), was terrible even for that region: the climate was harsh and the land was flat, baked dry in the long summers and whipped by dusty whirlwinds. Before the ashramites came, the place was home only to scorpions and poisonous snakes – and these remained, to be non-violently removed with tongs away from the living areas. Relief came with the monsoon, but then the waterlogged land was a breeding ground for mosquitoes. A dirt road connected the ashram to Wardha, the nearest town. The village of Segaon was populated mainly by untouchables stricken by disease and malnutrition. There were no shops or facilities, except for a well. A follower described Gandhi in the village: 'One of my earliest memories of Bapu is seeing him trudge along the tracks sweeping up the excrement that the villagers had left around like dogs, even by the well. This was his way of setting an example, of teaching the villagers the most elementary lesson of all the lessons he wanted to teach – that human and animal filth was the main cause of disease throughout the land.'[27]

The ashram was a collection of mud and bamboo huts around a gravel courtyard; the inhabitants set up communal latrines and used the effluent as fertiliser for growing their staple crops of sugar cane and vegetables. A typical day was described by a former ashramite. A clock in the dining hall was synchronised to Gandhi's ever-present watch (he liked to make use of all the time allotted to him). At 4 a.m. when the gong sounded, Abha, a girl who tended to Gandhi's needs (and later married his grand-nephew Kanu), came with a lamp and his toilet articles. These consisted of an iron bowl, a tumbler of water, a powder made from charcoal and the shells of almonds and walnuts, and a twig from a neem tree. Gandhi would set about brushing his remaining teeth (before they were removed in December 1936) or his gums and cleaning his tongue, while Abha took away the brass spittoon that he kept by his bed. He would put on a clean dhoti and his spectacles and walk to a tree at the end of the courtyard where he sat cross-legged on a cushion. The ashramites, including Kasturba, gathered for prayers at 4.20 precisely. The ashram had its own prayer book, the *Ashram Bhajanavali*, which incorporated prayers and hymns from various traditions, added to by ashram visitors. A typical prayer meeting would involve a Buddhist chant, a Hindu prayer, a reading from the Koran, a Zoroastrian (Parsi) prayer and a Christian hymn – Gandhi's favourite was 'Lead, Kindly Light'. The ashramites would chant invocations to God under various names of the Hindu tradition – 'Hare Krishna', 'Hare Ram' and so on. Gandhi enjoyed the chant more and more as it grew faster and louder: 'Nothing thrilled Bapu more. He was in ecstasy as the names of God rolled over us.'[28]

Gandhi would return to his hut for his morning drink of bicarbonate of soda, honey and lemon juice in hot water, then settle in for one and a half hours of work. He worked on an upside-down soap box with a khadi cloth covering it. On this makeshift desk were a few sparse and often handmade items, old pens, loose nibs and ink. He was attended by Mahadev Desai and Pyarelal who was now joined by his younger sister Sushila Nayar, a Western-trained doctor who used to monitor Gandhi's blood pressure and would also take Hindi dictation. When Mirabehn was staying with him she would work with the English-language material, but he kept her at a distance after 1935. Gandhi was also constantly in contact with his workers in the field, people who were promoting his ideas for national improvement and who reported back to him.

At 6.30 a.m. he would take his morning walk, accompanied by ashram children and revered by pilgrims and local peasants along the way, some of whom would prostrate themselves as he passed. In 1932 he had stopped the practice of putting his hands on the shoulders of accompanying women to support himself. He explained: 'I was unconscious of doing any wrong, so far as I can recollect, till some years ago at Sabarmati an intimate of the ashram told me that my practice, when extended to grown-up girls and women, offended the accepted notion of decency.'[29] Still unconvinced that there was anything wrong in it – and it does not look out of place in the many photographs of Gandhi taken during the last ten years of his life – in 1936 he resumed walking with physical support from ashram girls, usually Abha and Sushila. He called them his 'walking sticks'. His first question to them would be 'Did you have a good bowel movement this morning, sisters?'[30] His preoccupation with bowels was unabated – he taught these ashramites how to administer enemas to each other, as he had at other ashrams.

Sushila Nayar had been visiting Gandhi since her mother had taken her, aged six, to see him in 1920. As she sat on his lap he told her mother to gift the girl to him. She later visited the ashram as a teenager and, after taking a medical degree, became his personal physician. Like other ashram members, she thought little of his physical requests – perhaps they seemed less bizarre because so much in the ashram was outside the realms of ordinary behaviour. Sushila often slept with Gandhi. She said: 'There was nothing special about sleeping next to Bapu . . . I used to sleep with him, just as I would with my mother. He might say, "My back aches, put some pressure on it." So I might put some pressure on it or lie down on his back and he might just go to sleep. In the early days, there was no question of calling this a brahmacharya experiment. It was just part of the nature cure.'[31] In these 'early days' of Sushila's life with Gandhi he still had a wife, Kasturba, with whom he might have slept chastely. There was no conflict between these women, however. Kasturba had a close relationship with Sushila. If Sushila had a rival for Gandhi's affections, it was the now exiled Mirabehn.

His relationship with Abha was particularly warm; she described their banter: 'Once, I was bathing him and he asked me to hurry up. He had an appointment. He told me to hurry up three times and I said, "You are a renowned Mahatma and yet you are so impatient, like any other common mortal. What does it matter if you're a little late?"' Gandhi liked her spirit – he laughed: 'Only a mother would dare talk to her child the way you talk to me.'[32]

After his walk he would return to his quarters and 'spend at least twenty minutes squatting on the commode' in his bathroom. According to a woman ashramite who spoke with the writer Ved Mehta in the early 1970s, Gandhi 'was completely unselfconscious about urinating and defecating, rather like a child. He believed that these bodily functions were as natural and as sacred as eating, and used to say "The bathroom is a temple, it should be so clean and inviting that anyone would enjoy eating there." If any of us wanted to talk to him, we could go in and out as we pleased.'[33] Gandhi frequently drew comparisons between eating and defecating: 'The process of eating is as unclean as evacuation, the only difference being that, while evacuation ends in a sense of relief, eating, if one's tongue is not held in control, brings discomfort.'[34] After performing this function, Gandhi would be helped on to a high bamboo table and Sushila and Abha massaged his body with mustard oil and lime juice. He would return to the bathroom for a bath, sitting in the tub while Pyarelal shaved him. He then settled down for another hour's paperwork before visiting the sick of the ashram, giving massages or administering enemas as his notions of nursing might lead him.

The ashramites all ate together at 11 a.m.; more than 100 people would be in the hall, many of them vying for Gandhi's attention. They had learned they could most easily attract his attention by being ill, so the ashram often gave the impression of being a home for the sick. In order to eat, Gandhi had to be brought his dentures in a bowl of water, which he would fish out and insert. He chewed the food thoroughly, taking about an hour over a meal and finishing with goat's milk. As a relish with the steamed vegetables he ate ground neem leaves and crushed garlic, both of which he believed were good for health. After lunch he went to sleep in his hut with a mud poultice on his head and stomach that had been prepared by Abha. He would write or give interviews in this state. Mahadev Desai recorded: 'In the hot season a mud bandage on the head is an additional item', and Gandhi delighted in describing to visitors 'the wonderful properties of mother earth'.[35]

Gandhi continued to try to educate Kasturba, and after his sleep would have her reading from a Gujarati primer and copying out letters; although she could read by now, she was said to forget the following day what she had been taught. Her strength was in practical work, in organising the ashram as a giant household. She controlled the kitchen and subverted the austere regime as much as she could. She kept sweets for the ashram children and secretly served guests tea and coffee.

Gandhi would spend another twenty minutes on the commode, then proceed to an hour or two of spinning cotton. He would sometimes receive visitors while spinning, workers from the constructive programme of village service, Congress members and various officials seeking his advice. Secretaries were constantly in attendance taking notes, which Gandhi reviewed, and if he thought they were of sufficient interest he would have them published in one of his weekly newspapers. His day continued with another sleep, then more reading and writing until the evening meal at five, another long walk and an evening prayer meeting illuminated by kerosene lamps. This meeting would incorporate a sermon by Gandhi on sanitation, celibacy or some other favourite topic. There would be a roll call of the ashramites to check how much yarn each had spun during the day, and they were free to talk or sleep while Gandhi returned to his hut to read and have an enema before retiring. By 9.30 the lanterns were out and the ashram asleep.

Birth-control pioneer Margaret Sanger visited Gandhi in 1935 and inspected the cotton-growing, paper-making, oil-pressing and turn-wheel irrigation that he promoted. She wrote: 'I was not enthusiastic. It seemed so pitiable an effort, like going backward instead of forward.' The principle of trying to extend this to all of India amounted to 'trying to keep millions labouring on petty hand processes merely in order to give them work to do by which they might exist'.[36]

As his grandchildren grew up, Gandhi engaged them in his version of public service. His son Ramdas's eldest daughter Sumitra was an intelligent, self-willed child who resisted Gandhi's attempt to deny her education as he had her father. He wanted all his grandchildren to go to his Basic Education Centre at Sevagram Ashram but Sumitra refused to have anything to do with it. 'It led to a lot of dissension between grandfather and me,' she later recalled. 'He was very angry.' When she was ten, however, and was obviously not bending to his will, he let her go to a high school that was a little like an English boarding school. After she had graduated from there, Gandhi again tried to steer her away from education: 'What is the need for further formal education?' he said. 'Come and be my secretary – I will train you.'

Sumitra replied: 'I don't want to be one of your inferior secretaries who wash your clothes and utensils, organise your meals, make appointments, usher people in and out, and are filled with self-importance.' She had noted, she later said, that 'the really superior people, like Nehru, were never Grandfather's secretaries. They had been educated in England and were so independent they didn't feel the need to live with him at all'.[37] Whatever his faults, Gandhi always admired honesty and courage, and he allowed her to go to university in India. Later Sumitra studied in the US and returned home to become a member of parliament.

Despite Nehru's respect for Gandhi's power over the masses, he was extremely critical of his attitude to sex which he described in 1936 as 'unnatural and shocking . . . I think Gandhiji is absolutely wrong in this matter. His advice may fit in with some cases, but as a general policy it can only lead to frustration, inhibition, neurosis and all manner of physical and nervous ills.'[38] Nehru felt he had a personal life in which sex played a part but did not obsess him or divert him from other activities.

Early in December 1935 Margaret Sanger attempted the thankless task of trying to persuade Gandhi to support birth control. She suggested easily available contraceptives as a means of promoting planned parenthood. He argued that sex was sinful except explicitly for the production of children. He referred to his own life: 'I know from my own experience that as long as I looked upon my wife carnally, we had no real understanding . . . The moment I bade goodbye to a life of carnal pleasure, our whole relationship became spiritual. Lust died and love reigned instead.' If Kasturba's opinion on these matters were ever canvassed, it has not been recorded, though he did reveal that 'very often she would show restraint, but she rarely resisted me although she showed disinclination very often.'[39]

Sanger gives an illuminating picture of Gandhi in his sixties, not appearing to entertain new ideas, but just stating his own well-rehearsed opinions, 'I felt his registering of impressions was blunted,' she said. 'While you were answering a question of his, he held to an idea or train of thought of his own, and as soon as you stopped, continued as though he had never heard you . . . In fact, despite his claim to open-mindedness, he was proud of not altering his opinions.'[40] Desai remarks, however, that Gandhi was moved to approve of the rhythm method of birth control, which he felt at least provided for some self-restraint over the 'unsafe' periods. He was plagued with erotic thoughts during an illness a few days after seeing Sanger: 'I was disgusted with myself,' he said in the pages of *Harijan*. 'The moment the feeling came I acquainted my attendants and the medical friends with my condition. They could give me no help . . . The confession of the wretched experience brought much relief to me.'[41]

Primabehn Kantak, one of his principal women supporters, felt this article was a little opaque and asked in a letter for more information. 'I had a discharge,' he replied, but added reassuringly: 'but I was awake and the mind was under control.'[42] Presumably she enquired further because he later went on to explain with candour:

I have always had involuntary discharges. In South Africa they occurred at intervals of several years. Here in India they have been of months . . . If my brahmacharya had been completely free from discharges, I would have been able to place before the world very much more than

I have succeeded in doing. But it seems practically impossible that a person who has indulged in sex gratification from the age of fifteen to thirty, maybe with his own wife only, can, on taking a vow of brahmacharya, control the discharge of his vital fluid completely.[43]

In the mid-1930s he was still writing to Harilal, who was attempting a reconciliation. 'Have you touched liquor any time after you wrote your first letter to me from there? Have you indulged in sexual pleasure through mind, speech or body? Do you smoke?' he demanded, with the usual threat – to a man who was now forty-six – 'If at any time you break your word to me or if it is proved that you have deceived me, I should fast for at least seven days.'[44] Later he wrote that Harilal had visited him and seemed to have stayed off alcohol and had no 'carnal passion' except a desire to marry, but was still addicted to smoking; Gandhi allowed him 'three cigarettes a day with my permission.'[45]

Harilal relapsed. His whole life seemed an angry tirade against his treatment by his father: he would get drunk in public, consort with prostitutes, and he engaged in dubious business dealings, using the Gandhi name. On 14 May 1936 he made a public conversion to Islam in Bombay. Gandhi responded in a press statement: 'Harilal's apostasy is no loss to Hinduism and his admission to Islam is a source of weakness to it if, as I apprehend, he remains the same wreck that he was before . . . excessive indulgence has softened his brain and undermined his sense of right and wrong, truth and falsehood.'[46] He was offended by the public rejoicing among Muslims over the incident, for which he could see no religious motivation.

In 1933 Gandhi toured the country, covering 13,000 miles by third-class train, by car and on foot, preaching against untouchability, holding as many as five meetings a day. He raised money for the drilling of wells for untouchables and the funding of schools. While clean water and education were good in themselves, a separate provision for those denied the use of community facilities confirmed the separateness of untouchables.

His visits were the occasion for informal dinners and concerts to bring the communities together, and sometimes there would be a ceremonial opening of temples to untouchables. The change may have been short-lived in many places, and the temples closed again when he left, but the statement had been made. More seriously, from the point of view of a sincere reformer, Gandhi was suffering the curse of fame: people came to *see* him, for the darshan of this celebrated figure – they were not particularly interested in what he had to say. He pleaded: 'I have no new religion to give, no new truth to expound. My humble role is that of a scavenger both literally and spiritually. I know the outward art of cleaning the streets, commodes and latrines, and I am endeavouring to the extent of my ability to clean my inside also, so that I may become a faithful interpreter of the truth as I may see it.'[47] Gandhi could be frank about the ignorance of the crowds; to a questioner who asked why untouchables should not choose to convert to Islam or Christianity to escape Hindu oppression he replied: 'Some of the untouchables are worse than cows in understanding. I mean they can no more distinguish between the relative merits of Islam and Hinduism and Christianity than a cow.'[48] He was still anxious to keep untouchables in the Hindu fold, though, particularly after 1935 when, disgusted with Hinduism's inability to provide for basic human rights, the untouchables' representative Ambedkar declared his intention to convert to a new religion.

Gandhi's stand against untouchability prompted violent orthodox Hindus to hold alternative meetings at venues where he was due to appear, burn pictures of him and wave black flags when he arrived. At one time, in Poona, a bomb was thrown at a car in which he was believed to be travelling and seven people were injured.

A large part of Bihar province suffered a severe earthquake on 15 January 1934. Thousands died and tens of thousands were left homeless. Gandhi took a detour to embrace the stricken area, walking between villages and bringing comfort but also, surprisingly, chastisement. The earthquake, he said, was a punishment for sin, particularly the sin of untouchability.

The first time he addressed this line of thought, at a public meeting in Tinnevelly, he said: 'A man like me cannot but believe that this earthquake is a divine punishment sent by God for our sins.'[49] Then later: 'Believe with me that for this absolutely unthinkable affliction in Bihar your sins and my sins are responsible . . . I tell you the conviction is growing on me that this affliction has come to us because of this atrocious sin of untouchability.'⁵⁰ Addressing the questions Why punish now for an age-old sin? Why punish Bihar and not the south of the country, for example? he said: 'I am not God. Therefore I have but a limited knowledge of His purpose.'⁵¹ His practical explanation of the mechanism in play here, if one can call it that, was an association of ethical principles with cosmic phenomena: 'Physical things originate from the same source of energy as spiritual, and so there is no impassable gulf between physical and spiritual things.'⁵² Gandhi was widely criticised by his more sophisticated supporters, notably by Rabindranath Tagore, who pointed out that he had opened the way for the orthodox to claim the earthquake was a result of divine anger at Gandhi's work against untouchability.

He resigned from Congress in October 1934, unable to unite its feuding factions. The future, at least the immediate future, was going to be constructed by the constitution builders, precisely the area of leadership for which Gandhi had no time. He correctly judged he had little to offer the political process at this stage. 'Hand-spinning by the Congress intelligentsia has all but disappeared,' he lamented, 'the general body of them have no faith in it.' He was being blamed for the hypocrisy and evasiveness of Congress personnel, paying lip-service to his principles but following their own political ends.⁵³ He explained: 'I am leaving Congress to lift the weight which has been suppressing it, in order that it may grow, and I may grow myself.' In reply to questions he was even more explicit: 'I feel today that I have lost the power to persuade you to my view. I have become helpless. It is no use keeping a man like me at the helm of affairs, who has lost his strength.'⁵⁴

The prize for nationalists was now real power in the legislatures – a course gingerly approached by Congress, then embraced with enthusiasm. In what was a triumph for patient constitution-building by the British, all sections of Indian society joined in the elections held in 1935 under the old electoral regulations (the Government of India Act of 1935 was not yet in force). The result was a picture of a divided India: the government and their supporters gained two-fifths of the seats, Congress and the orthodox Hindu 'Congress nationalists' two-fifths, and the independents (mainly Muslims) a fifth. Jinnah emerged as the leader of the Muslim independents; his skill in wielding the votes of his balancing group showed him as the political master of this cohort of Indian democrats.

The Secretary of State for India Sir Samuel Hoare had worked diligently to produce a workable constitution. A select committee was set up to consider the results of the round-table conferences. After almost two years, 1933–4, against fierce criticism from the Conservative right wing led by Winston Churchill, the result was the new Government of India Act. Its provisions for federation, including the princely states, were never put into effect – discussions were still proceeding when the Second World War broke out – but provincial autonomy under eleven directly elected governors and legislatures was highly successful.

The election of 1937 showed Congress leaders demonstrating their ability to make contact with the people – Nehru covered 50,000 miles using every conveyance from elephant to aeroplane; a total of ten million people saw him. Gandhi made no political speeches but walked from village to village promoting his new All-India Village Industries Association for the improvement of the poor, in what was now a nationwide application of the ideas he had taken from John Ruskin and Leo Tolstoy and burnished himself.

The Congress secured absolute majorities in five of the eleven major provinces and was the largest single party in three others. After the usual dithering over whether to assume any power that was short of absolute, Congress took office in March 1937, forming ministries in six provinces. The Muslim League made a poor showing, with less than 5 per cent of the total Muslim vote. Congress members showed their political inexperience with a triumphalism that implied the current balance of power would last for ever; they felt no need to ally with the Muslim League, even though the League's social and economic programmes were similar to their own. They treated the League more as a political opposition than fellow Indians striving for a common goal.

Muslim League candidates were refused cabinet positions unless they joined Congress. Mohammad Ali Jinnah contacted Gandhi over the situation in Bombay where the League had done particularly well amongst the Muslim electorate, but the sage replied with a mystic pronouncement: 'My faith in unity is as bright as ever; only I see no daylight out of the impenetrable darkness, and in such distress, I cry out to God for light.'[55] Jinnah wanted to meet Gandhi but he said he was guided by Abul Kalam Azad, a Muslim member of Congress, and Jinnah should speak to him. Thus easily and with no apparent appreciation of the dangers, Gandhi cast aside the chance of Hindu–Muslim unity at the highest political level. The haughty Jinnah did not take rejection lightly: he would soon be speaking of Congress as a Hindu party that was conspiring to deny Muslims a say in government. The end result of this thinking would be separatism, a notion that was fast gaining acceptance in Muslim circles.

In a move that had attracted little attention at the time a scholar called Choudhary Rahmat Ali, inspired by discussions at the unglamorous third round-table conference that finished in 1933, had suggested a name for a Muslim nation that could be carved out of India. Taking letters from the names Punjab, Afghan Province (the North-West Frontier) Kashmir, Sind and Baluchistan he made the semi-acrostic 'PAKISTAN', which was close to the Urdu word 'Pakistan': land of the pure. Now the Muslims had something to aim for.

10

Quit India

As one of the world's supreme moralists, Gandhi might have been expected to have something to say about the state-inspired violence of the 1930s. The imperialists who were recolouring the map of Asia that decade were closer to home than the Europeans who had previously made their mark there: the Japanese, who felt the Europeans had dominated for long enough, had their sights on French, Dutch and British possessions in the Far East and on conquering China.

The Japanese annexation of Manchuria in 1931 was followed by a full-scale invasion in 1937, accompanied by rape and massacre on a previously unprecedented scale. Gandhi suggested non-violent resistance: 'It is unbecoming for a nation of 400 millions, a nation as cultured as China, to repel Japanese aggression by resorting to Japan's own methods. If the Chinese had non-violence of my conception, there would be no use for the latest machinery for destruction which Japan possesses.'[1]

The assaults in Germany on the Jewish population resembled more closely Gandhi's own remit in South Africa and India, featuring as they did the imposition of unjust laws against one section of the population. 'My sympathies are all with the Jews ...' he said. 'They have been the untouchables of Christianity ... If there ever could be a justifiable war in the name of and for humanity, a war against Germany, to prevent the wanton persecution of a whole race, would be completely justified. But I do not believe in any war.'[2] His advice was: 'If I were a Jew and were born in Germany and earned my livelihood there, I would claim Germany as my home even as the tallest gentile German may, and challenge him to shoot me or cast me in the dungeon.'³ This weak response, which was much criticised at the time, is all the more remarkable because when Gandhi's close friend Kallenbach visited him in the 1930s they discussed Jewish persecution at length; and one of Gandhi's permanent disciples, Margarete Spiegel, known as Amala, was a Jewish schoolteacher who had fled Nazi persecution.

Adolf Hitler was an unmarried, non-smoking, non-drinking, vegetarian nationalist with a strong sense of personal mission. He was just the sort of person Gandhi admired – a remark that can be made without sneering, since Gandhi genuinely perceived such choices as what a person ate and whether or not they smoked as moral indicators. He said: 'I do not want to see the Allies defeated. But I do not consider Hitler to be as bad as he is depicted. He is showing an ability that is amazing and he seems to be gaining his victories without much bloodshed.'⁴ Instead of addressing the quality of the evil that was being unleashed on the world in the 1930s, Gandhi sought a moral equivalence. He considered that the British were just as bad as the Nazis: 'We resist British Imperialism no less than Nazism. If there is a difference it is in degree.'⁵ 'I see no difference between the Fascist or Nazi powers and the Allies. All are exploiters, all resort to ruthlessness.'⁶

Announcing 'I own no foes', he wrote a letter to Hitler, addressing him as 'Dear Friend', in December 1940, at a time when Britain was being bombarded nightly: 'We have no doubt about your bravery or devotion to your fatherland, nor do we believe that you are the monster described by your opponents [though] many of your actions are monstrous and unbecoming of human dignity, especially in the estimation of men like me who believe in universal friendliness.'⁷ For his part, Hitler's notion of how to deal with Gandhi had been expressed to the former Viceroy Lord Irwin in his later incarnation as Foreign Secretary Lord Halifax. 'All you have to do,' the dictator remarked briskly, 'is to shoot Gandhi. If necessary shoot more leaders of Congress. You will be surprised how quickly the trouble will die down.'⁸

Gandhi at least had the moral courage to admit his impotence. As early as 1938 he remarked that when he contemplated what he would do in a country invaded by aggressors, 'my head starts reeling. You may well argue how much the non-violence that has made only this much progress even after fifty years' experience can help us in our struggle. If you think like this, you may give it up. For me there is no question of giving it up. My faith in it is unwavering. I shall however ever regret that the Lord has not favoured me with such clarity of expression that I could explain my ideas to others.'[9] His failure to comprehend the orchestrated evil of state-inspired violence had already been apparent in his inability to acknowledge the genocide (committed by the Turkish army) against the Armenians when he was proclaiming the moral validity of the Khilafat. In itself, this was no great failing – why should he comment on every world event? one might ask. However, it does reveal a persistent, underlying failure to understand radical evil. His vision of the calamities of the twentieth century would culminate, horrifyingly, in a metaphysical conceit that welcomed a chaos out of which supposedly would come order as India moved towards the disaster of partition.

Congress politicians were learning about the difficulties of government. They had formed ministries in seven provinces in July 1937, and an eighth followed a year later. Their campaigns for mass literacy and agrarian and social reform were constrained by cost and lack of administrative experience, but their enthusiasm for reform made up for much. Gandhi contributed little save for promoting such long-term aims of his as the prohibition of alcohol, which he described as 'perhaps the greatest moral movement of the century'.[10]

Though the provinces were now under Indian political control, the peasant marches, strikes and picketing did not stop. Corrupt time servers were joining the Congress Party, lured by the promise of power and vitiating the moral message of the leadership. Power was being used as an instrument of domination. The crude nationalism of many Congress leaders made Muslims feel they were being Hinduised. Attention often focused on education: children would be made to perform idolatrous acts such as singing 'Vande Mataram' with its invocation of Mother India as Durga (an incarnation of the goddess Parvati). Children were also said to be obliged to pay homage and sing hymns of praise to Gandhi's portrait – certainly not something Gandhi himself would have encouraged. Provincial Congress governments attempted to prevent the slaughter of cows and the eating of beef while making no commensurate efforts to safeguard Muslim culture.

Jinnah complained: 'The present leadership of the Congress, especially during the last ten years, has been responsible for alienating the Mussalmans of India more and more by pursuing a policy which is exclusively Hindu, and since they have formed the governments in six provinces where they are in the majority they have by their words, deeds and programmes shown more that the Mussalmans [Muslims] cannot expect any justice or fair play at their hands.'[11] Communal violence continued, now with Congress ministers calling out the military to quell rioters, as in March 1938 in Allahabad, to Gandhi's distress. For all his fine words about Hindu–Muslim unity, the common people refused to acquiesce, instead acting out their ancestral hatreds.

Belatedly acknowledging Jinnah as the main player on the Muslim side, Gandhi was prepared to meet him in April 1938 in an attempt to recover some remnants of Hindu–Muslim unity. The meeting was cursed, however, by a uniquely Gandhian event. As he lay with his aides in the ashram on 7 April, he had suffered an involuntary ejaculation. This was important both because he felt he had by now completely controlled his sexual nature, and because of his almost magical belief in the power of seminal fluid. 'One who conserves his vital fluid acquires unfailing power,' he wrote. 'Why should I lose my vitality for the sake of a momentary pleasure?'[12] Exactly a week later the same thing happened again. He described it to Mirabehn: 'That degrading, dirty, torturing experience of 14 April shook me to bits and made me feel as if I was hurled by God from an imaginary paradise where I had no right to be in my uncleanliness.'[13]

He explained to the rest of the women of his entourage what had happened, an exercise which must have taxed even Gandhi's considerable powers of description. His next response was to distance himself from them, but he felt he had to give way to the entreaties of these women who so needed to be close to him: 'Once I intended to give up all personal services from Sushila [Nayar] but within twelve hours my soft-heartedness had put an end to the intention. I could not bear the tears of Sushila and the fainting away of Prabhavati.'[14] He was plunged into a 'slough of despond'. 'For the first time in my public and private life I seem to have lost self-confidence,' he wrote in a press release. 'I do not consider myself fit for negotiations or any such thing for the moment . . . I ask the public not to attach any exaggerated importance to the interview.'[15] With such forebodings he approached the three hours of talks with Jinnah.

The meetings in spring 1938 came to nothing. Jinnah wanted Gandhi to acknowledge him as the leader of the Muslims while Gandhi was that of the Hindus; but Gandhi claimed to represent all India. By the end of the year Jinnah was answering Gandhi's charge that he, Jinnah, had abandoned nationalism for sectarian politics: 'I have no hesitation in saying that it is Mr Gandhi who is destroying the ideal with which the Congress was started. He is the one responsible for turning the Congress into an instrument for the revival of Hinduism. His ideal is to revive the Hindu religion and establish Hindu Raj in this country.'[16]

Gandhi was at this time assailed by fits of trembling at night – perhaps from the cold, or perhaps it was psychosomatic. He was comforted by having young women lie with him. As noted earlier, he habitually had women around him while he performed personal functions, once explaining when challenged: 'Sushila has been present in the bathroom while I have bathed in the nude and in her absence Ba [Kasturba] or Prabhavati or Lilavati have attended on me.'[17] The provision of personal services to Gandhi was a much sought-after sign of his favour and aroused jealousy among the ashram inmates. Mirabehn advised him to keep his distance from female ashramites. She had never been a participant in his 'experiments' with brahmacharya, perhaps because he feared she would show insufficient restraint – or that he would. She might well have felt jealous at the physical closeness (and therefore trust) that was permitted these other women.

He asked Mirabehn: 'Should I deny myself the service rendered by Sushila? Should I refuse to have malish [massage] by Lilavati or Amtul Salaam for instance? Or do you want to say that I should never lean on girls' shoulders?'[18] He followed Mirabehn's advice in denying himself those personal services requiring women's physical contact with him, and issued an apology to ashram inmates, who may have been showing signs of revolt. He apologised for denying them 'the freedom I have given myself . . . my action was impelled by vanity and jealousy . . . My experiment was a violation of the established norms of brahmacharya.' These sexual 'experiments' were indeed a violation of the accepted norms. Physical contact with women and sleeping with them were Gandhi's own contribution to the practice of celibacy. They were not sanctified by any tradition and were, in fact, forbidden in texts on the subject.

He took responsibility for not only his own, 'moral lapses' but also for those of others in the ashram.[19] 'Even a woman's proximity, speech, look, letter etc., may work the evil as her touch might,' he pondered. In an Oedipal remark he declared, 'I must put out my eyes, rather than have the animal in me be aroused.'[20] He discussed sex in some detail with Sushila, who in 1938 was twenty-four. Addressing a letter to her with an affectionate insult – 'Stupid girl' – he wrote: 'If you too have experienced desire, it is as well. For then we are both in the same plight and we both ought to be on our guard . . . After my 69 years the vikara [lust] in you cannot affect me. I burn with my own vikara. Because of my vikara I regard myself as unfit to take service from any woman.'[21] Within three months he had abandoned the whole of this 'experiment' in restraint: he resumed resting his hands on women and the personal services to his body were reinstated. He explained to those closest to him in 'A Circular Letter' in September 1938 how innocent were the baths he and Sushila took together: 'The bathing arrangement is this: she bathes in the space behind the bathtub and while she is bathing I keep my eyes tightly shut. I do not know the manner of her bathing – whether she bathes naked or with her underwear on. I can tell from the sound that she uses soap. I have seen no part of her body that everyone here will not have seen.' She then massaged him while he lay naked.[22] He blamed the morally derelict condition of Congress on deficiencies in his brahmacharya.[23]

He would continue to be sufficiently troubled about the services he received from women to maintain a commentary on the subject, reporting to Vallabhbhai Patel in February 1939: 'As from yesterday I have stopped sleeping close to them. That is, the girls sleep far enough to be out of reach of my arms.'[24] Questioned in the 1970s, Sushila revealingly placed physical contact with women as part of a lifestyle; the elevation of it to a brahmacharya experiment was a response to criticism of this behaviour. She said: 'Later on, when people started asking questions about his physical contact with women – with Manu [his grandniece], with Abha [another grandniece], with me – the idea of brahmacharya experiments was developed.'²⁵

When war was declared on Germany in September 1939, India was automatically involved and was also at war. The dominions made their own decisions, committing themselves to stand alongside Britain (as India almost certainly would have done if given the choice). It was a serious mistake on the part of the British to fail to give the semblance of a democratic consultation before committing the subcontinent to the war. Memories of the Rowlatt Acts were still strong in India – it was reasonable to fear that emergency powers adopted as a wartime measure would be extended.

Congress declared they wanted to be involved in a war to defend democracy, but they also wanted full democracy to be established in India, with Indian politicians having the right to determine their own constitution. Invited to see the Viceroy to talk about the war, Gandhi said he felt tears welling up at the thought of Westminster Abbey and the Houses of Parliament being bombed. But he was unable to communicate this affection to members of the Congress: at the working committee he said he was 'sorry to find myself alone in thinking that whatever support was to be given to the British should be given unconditionally'.²⁶ Instead, on 14 September 1939 Congress put out a wordy statement drafted by Nehru that said, crucially: 'If Great Britain fights for the maintenance and extension of democracy, then she must necessarily end imperialism in her own possessions, establish full democracy in India, and the Indian people must have the right of self-determination by framing their own constitution.'²⁷

Gandhi then loyally went along with the Congress line: his policy of supporting the British in the forthcoming war, as in the Zulu rising, the Boer War and the First World War, was ended. There was not even a proposed programme of action. Nehru wrote: 'Our position is one of non-cooperation but we have not as yet thought of anything more.'²⁸ Jinnah, on the other hand, was prepared to give the support of the Muslim League, but on condition that they were accepted as the sole voice of Muslim India and no constitutional changes were made without the League's consent. The British were unwilling to concede this but though the League were not therefore wholeheartedly supportive of the British war effort, they would do nothing to impede it.

The then Viceroy Lord Linlithgow invited leaders including Gandhi, Nehru and Jinnah for an interview with him, issuing a statement on 17 October that dominion status was the goal of British policy in India and that the Government of India Act would be open to modification at the end of the war. Linlithgow's lack of either imagination or administrative flair contributed to the already serious problems of his long period in office (1936–43), which encompassed some of the most dramatic events in Indian politics and which also saw the entirely avoidable Bengal famine.

As usual with British policy statements, Linlithgow's remarks were too little too late; but if the British approach was wrong, that of Congress was disastrous. Congress thinkers had boxed amongst themselves into a corner with their own internal disputes over the issue of dominion status versus complete independence. After more argument amongst themselves, Congress was reduced to expressing a petulant refusal to cooperate with the British, thus throwing away their electoral advantage and giving up what was for many their only experience of government. They also sacrificed what influence they had with the British, who were still and would remain the umpires in the game of constitution-making for whatever kind of an India was going to emerge.

The Congress working committee met in Wardha on 22 and 23 October 1939, condemned the Viceroy's statement and ordered all Congress governments to resign by the end of the month. If there was one action that could be credited with handing India over to the separatist Muslims, this was it – as a political failure it was exemplary: Congress emasculated itself politically, with gains to no one but the Muslim League.

Jinnah declared a 'Day of Deliverance and thanksgiving as a mark of relief that the Congress regime has at last ceased to function . . . [they have] proved the falsehood of the Congress claim that it represents all interests justly and fully, by its decidedly anti-Muslim policy.'[29] Other minority groups, notably Ambedkar and his untouchables, supported Jinnah. Jinnah had already decided in favour of a separate Muslim nation, but was a sufficiently calculating politician to keep this quiet. It was the following year, in March 1940, that the Muslim League would declare for a separate Pakistan.

Jinnah was a sick man. He had advanced tuberculosis and had collapsed on his way to the central legislative assembly in Delhi just days before the mass meeting in Lahore where he had announced what would be termed the 'Pakistan resolution' (though he never used the word himself). Weak though he was, for two hours he addressed a crowd of a hundred thousand, only a small fraction of whom could understand him, as he spoke in English. 'The Mussalmans are not a minority. The Mussalmans are a nation by any definition,' he said. If the British were seriously interested in peace and happiness 'the only course open to us all is to allow the major nations separate homelands, by dividing India into "autonomous national States".'[30] He rejected Gandhi's claim that Hindus, Muslims, Parsis and untouchables were all alike: 'Why not come as a Hindu leader proudly representing your people?' Jinnah asked him, 'and let me meet you, proudly representing the Mussalmans?'[31] The League later passed a resolution explicitly stating that the north-western and eastern zones of India should be independent states.

Gandhi was appalled: 'I believe with my whole soul that the God of the Koran is also the God of the *Gita* and that we are all, no matter by what name designated, children of the same God. I must rebel that millions of Indians who were Hindus the other day changed their nationality with their religion.'[32] He was arguing, therefore, that even if they were not Hindus, Muslims were still Indians. Gandhi was not even, however, speaking for all Hindus. Members of the extreme orthodox Rashtriya Swayamsevak Sangh echoed Jinnah's views, arguing that non-Hindus had no place in India.

To the disappointment of Congress, their great sacrifice of power for principle was not reflected in equal enthusiasm from the people of India: young men flocked to the recruiting stations, more volunteering for war service than the government could use.

In May 1940 Churchill assumed the premiership. He was always an implacable opponent of Indian nationalists though he was a complex figure, having declared five years earlier that Gandhi had risen in his estimation since he had started standing up for the untouchables. In July 1940, at the time of the Battle of Britain, Gandhi wrote:

I appeal to every Briton, wherever he may be now, to accept the method of non-violence instead of that of war for the adjustment of relations between nations . . . Your soldiers are doing the same work of destruction as the Germans. The only difference is that perhaps yours is not as thorough as the Germans . . . I want you to fight Nazism without arms or, if I am to retain the non-violent terminology, with non-violent arms . . . You will invite Herr Hitler and Signor Mussolini to take what they want of the countries you call your possessions. Let them take possession of your beautiful island, with your many beautiful buildings. You will give all these, but neither your souls nor your minds. If these gentlemen choose to occupy your homes, you will vacate them. If they do not give you free passage out, you will allow yourself, man, woman and child, to be slaughtered but you will refuse to owe allegiance to them.[33]

HM Government replied: '[We] do not feel that the policy which you advocate is one which it is possible for us to consider.'[34]

An alternative to Congress's non-cooperation with the British was to join with Britain's enemies. Subhas Chandra Bose, against Gandhi's judgement, had been president of Congress in 1939, from which position he proposed the British should be given an ultimatum: to leave in six months or face total civil disobedience. Gandhi and other Congress leaders thought India was not ready for such a battle, which would not only fail but would 'bring discredit on the Congress [and] spell disaster for the Congress struggle for independence'. Bose was defeated on the policy,[35] took his defeat with bad grace and left Congress to form his own party, Forward Bloc, which imitated the violent nationalism of the German, Italian and Japanese regimes.

With the Muslim League now making the running in national politics, Congress was sidelined and its working committee divided. Nonetheless they decided, in September 1940, to invite Gandhi to come back to lead them in a new campaign of civil disobedience. Gandhi was not willing to lead such a campaign, for which he felt the country was unprepared, but he declared that individual acts of satyagraha should take place, specifically Congress figures speaking out against the war. Nehru, Rajagopalachari and others informed the authorities of what they were going to do and courted arrest with speeches – Nehru was arrested even before he could make his speech and sentenced to four years in prison. After the leading members had been arrested, ordinary members joined in and eventually, by summer 1941 there had been twenty thousand convictions – not many considering the size of the membership of Congress and the population of India. The fact was that the public had failed to comprehend what the protest was about, and the British administrators were equally baffled. The war was good for the Indian economy; it was helping India in stimulating her industries, bringing employment and money. In order to deal with the pressure of war work the Viceroy had expanded his executive council to twelve, eight of whom were now Indian, indicating a continued intention to transfer power to Indians. Furthermore, the new executive council successfully urged the Viceroy to release those civil disobedience figures, including Nehru, who were still detained, as a conciliatory gesture.

They were released shortly before the Japanese launched their attack on Pearl Harbor and began their advance through South-East Asia, ultimately taking Hong Kong, Malaya, Singapore and Burma. The Chinese leader Chiang Kai-shek visited India in February 1942, meeting Gandhi, Nehru and other leaders to impress on them the importance of India's playing a role in the war against Japanese aggression. When he met Gandhi, Chiang painted a vivid picture of the atrocities committed by the Japanese in China. Gandhi kept on spinning throughout the meeting and at the end presented a doubtless bemused Chiang with the yarn he had spun.

Subhas Chandra Bose attempted a deal with the new imperialist power, and set up his Indian National Army, mainly comprising Indian prisoners of war, under the auspices of Japan. Few Indians at home were foolish enough to believe that life under a Japanese empire would be benign, and Bose's ideas had little success within India. An exception was Bengal, where terrorist incidents directed against the British took place throughout the rest of the war. In early 1944, Bose and his INA were to cross the Indian border but the tide of war was against Japan and her allies by this time, and the INA surrendered.

By 1942, with the Japanese advances, the war in which India was expected to participate was no longer far away in Europe but in the neighbouring country, Burma. When India's very borders were threatened, a new consensus might have arisen. Against Gandhi's advice – as usual he wanted to put non-violence first – Congress offered full cooperation against the Japanese in return for a national government immediately and a promise of independence after the war. But Churchill was not interested – Congress had not been reliable in the past, and India was supporting the war well enough without it.

The deputy prime minister, Labour leader Clement Attlee, had a genuine understanding of India. He had been on the Simon Commission and now chaired the India Committee, set up in 1942, which drew up the terms of reference of a delegation to be sent to India to negotiate a political settlement. This became the Cripps Mission, led by Sir Stafford Cripps, a member of Churchill's coalition government and a good choice for dealing with Gandhi. An austere socialist, teetotal and vegetarian, a pacifist in the First World War, Cripps was a man of firm principles that had had him expelled from the Labour Party at one time. Cripps had previously met Gandhi, had visited Wardha in 1939 and had distinguished himself by taking off his shoes when he entered Gandhi's hut – a courtesy mastered by few English visitors.

Cripps was a close enough friend of Nehru's to be present during the preparations for his daughter Indira's wedding to Feroze Gandhi. Feroze, a Parsi, was not a relation of Mohandas Gandhi, but it did no harm to Indira's impressive political career that many people thought he was. 'Mahatma' Gandhi had no more than his usual success in urging celibacy on the bride and bridegroom; they were to have two children, the first of whom, Rajiv, became prime minister as had his mother and grandfather; Rajiv's wife Sonia was to lead Congress.

Cripps was sent with an offer but had no negotiating room; Churchill had tied his hands. The deal was that India would have dominion status and a constituent assembly would frame a constitution, with the right of provinces to opt out of whatever constitutional arrangement was reached. This meant the princely states or the Muslim states could choose to stay with Britain. India's defence policy would also stay under British control. Churchill, always a fervent imperialist, did not want Cripps to succeed but he wanted to placate British, Indian and (increasingly importantly) American public opinion. The Americans were proud of having broken away from the British Empire – they did not want to be seen fighting to keep others in subjection. Cripps, who had discussed constitutional solutions with Nehru and Attlee in Britain in 1938 (when Nehru was a houseguest of Cripps), was entirely genuine in his approach.

Gandhi went to Delhi to meet him. He rejected the offer comprehensively, especially because of the proposed inclusion of the princely states in a future India, whatever form it might take. Even if they were represented in the constituent assembly, their delegates would be nominated by their rulers, enshrining an undemocratic procedure. He also rejected the possibility of Muslim-majority and other states opting out; and, rather unspecifically, opposed the defence proposal.

Gandhi was widely credited with the aphorism that the Cripps offer was 'a postdated cheque', though the phrase does not occur in his writings or in Cripps's account.[36] He did not add 'on a failing bank', which was a journalist's invention – Gandhi took no pleasure in Britain's difficulties. His implacable attitude has been blamed for the failure of the Cripps mission, though the refusal of the proposal to recognise Muslim 'nationhood' was enough for Jinnah to reject it also. There was certainly widespread disappointment over the rejection. Attlee later wrote: 'It was a great pity that eventually the Indians turned this down, as full self-government might have been ante-dated by some years.'[37]

While these discussions had been taking place, Japanese naval forces had moved into the Indian Ocean, sinking six British ships in the port of Colombo in Ceylon. Two British cruisers followed, then twenty ships were sunk in the Bay of Bengal in one day. Further attacks continued on Indian ports and defending aircraft bases. Gandhi sent a resolution to Congress calling for resistance, namely non-violent non-cooperation, against the Japanese if an invasion were launched. This clearly ruled out any active participation in the war effort designed to stop an invasion in the first place. Some Congress leaders were opposed to his proposal: Nehru wanted to organise guerrilla warfare against the Japanese if they invaded; Rajagopalachari wanted to form a united front with the Muslims and others.

Gandhi's thinking now took a curious turn: 'I feel convinced that the British presence is the incentive for the Japanese attack', he said. 'If the British wisely decided to withdraw and leave India to manage her own affairs in the best way she could, the Japanese would be bound to reconsider their plans.'[38] He thought it 'likely the Japanese will not want to invade India, their prey having gone.'[39] This is exactly what Japanese propaganda broadcasts said – that one of Japan's war aims was to free India from British rule. This was doubtless true, because the ultimate objective was for India to serve the Japanese empire. The attraction of India for Japan was the same as it had been for the British and the Moguls: India's huge wealth and manpower. Had Japan been allowed to invade, and had the Japanese been given an opportunity of committing in Calcutta the sort of atrocities they carried out in Nanking, the difference between the British and Japanese empires would have been readily apparent.

Gandhi hoped that with the withdrawal of British power 'wise leaders will realise their responsibility, forget their differences for the moment and set up a provisional government'. He did concede, however, that 'after the formation of the national government my voice may be a voice in the wilderness and nationalist India may go war-mad'.[40] But did that matter? he mused. If 'a non-violent struggle has been started at my behest and later there is an outbreak of violence, I will put up with that too, because eventually it is God who is inspiring me and things will shape as He wills. If He wants to destroy the world through violence using me as His instrument, how can I prevent it?'[41]

Cripps had felt that Gandhi 'may be actually desirous to bring about a state of chaos.'[42] This may be a fleeting comment made in frustration at the failure of his constitutional mission, but some of Gandhi's statements at this time seem perilously close to proposing a metaphysical experiment in which a churning of national passions would ultimately produce sanity and order. 'Let them entrust India to God or in modern parlance to anarchy. Then all the parties will fight one another like dogs, or will, when real responsibility faces them, come to a reasonable agreement.'[43] He seemed to be welcoming a period of chaos after the British withdrawal, for 'that anarchy may lead to internecine warfare for a time or to unrestrained dacoities [banditry]. From these a true India will rise in the place of the false one we see.'[44] He saw in the destruction that air raids wrought in Europe the end of technologically advanced civilisation, a vindication of his faith in the spinning-wheel: 'The age of cities is coming to an end. The slogan of "Back to the villages" was never so true as today.'[45]

Gandhi tried to impress upon sceptical colleagues the merit of making the subcontinent a testing ground for non-violence, a cauldron of chaos with non-violence supposedly the solution for everything. Gandhi's resolution to the Congress working committee would have bound it to say it was 'of the opinion that the British should withdraw from India ... The committee hopes that Japan will not have any designs on India.' In the event of an attack 'the Committee would expect all those who look to Congress for guidance to offer complete non-violent non-cooperation to the Japanese forces and not render any assistance to them.'[46]

Gandhi's resolution was significantly altered by Nehru and other colleagues at a working committee meeting so as to remove apparent sympathy for the Axis Powers and replace it with intimations of sympathy for the Allies. This became what was known as the 'Quit India resolution' (the phrase was not Gandhi's), which was finally passed on 14 July 1942 by the working committee and placed before the full Congress in Bombay on 7–8 August. By now it included, in deference to the wishes of those who wanted to continue the war against Japan, a reassurance that Allied armed forces could stay in India in order to resist Japanese aggression and to help China. It was doubtless also a consideration that Congress did not wish to offend America when the US was sympathetic to Indian independence. Nehru was reluctant to cause problems for the British, preoccupied as they were in fighting fascism, but went along with Gandhi.

Gandhi gave the committee a mantra: 'Do or Die. We shall either free India or die in the attempt; we shall not live to see the perpetuation of our slavery.'[47] The resolution certainly achieved unanimity among non-Congress Indians: all condemned it, from the Muslims and Liberals to the untouchables and the princes. Jinnah considered the objective of British withdrawal with no constitutional settlement in place would mean the creation of a Hindu raj in which minority interests would be violently crushed. Congress had lost its sense of the future, they were fighting the battles of the past: if even Churchill, the arch-opponent of India's independence, had accepted that dominion status would follow the war, then the struggle was no longer with the British for independence. Congress needed to focus on the disparate groups within India after the war, particularly the Muslims and the princely states.

Gandhi's scruples about attacking an enemy when that enemy was suffering misfortunes unconnected with the matter in hand seem to have fallen by the wayside. Three years earlier he had warned Subhas Chandra Bose that India was not ready to call on the British to leave, and nothing had since occurred to make the nation any readier. He also declared his intention not to call off the campaign if violence broke out – which he did not intend as an incitement to violence but which certainly did not discourage it.

Churchill's war cabinet, having had their best offer rebuffed, were prepared for the chaotic alternative and authorised the Viceroy to take severe measures against Congress. The mistake, as they saw it, of 1930 had been not to arrest Gandhi soon enough, to allow the salt protest to gain momentum. They would not make the same mistake again. The 'Quit India resolution' was passed on the night of 8 August; in the early hours of the next morning all members of the Congress working committee were arrested. Those who remained free went underground and instructed Congress supporters to paralyse the government in any way possible. Rioting crowds now attacked British property and symbols of British rule such as railway stations and post offices, of which hundreds were destroyed or damaged. In more organised protests, attempts were made to sabotage the war effort: telephone and telegraph wires were cut and bridges blown up. Troops remained loyal, however: the authorities were able to hit back hard, hundreds were killed and the uprising died down within weeks. If proof were ever needed that non-violence was the right strategy for Indian nationalism, it was surely this failure of violence to achieve any political objectives.

Gandhi was interned with Sarojini Naidu, Mirabehn and Mahadev Desai in the Aga Khan Palace near Poona, which had been requisitioned by the British for war service. Desai was not with him long; less than a week after his arrest Gandhi's faithful secretary suffered a massive heart attack. Gandhi called out his name, saying 'If only he would open his eyes and look at me he would not die', but Desai, who was just fifty, was already dead.[48] Gandhi was upset that national reaction to Desai's death was so muted and restrained; there was no great outpouring of grief. Gandhi had failed to recognise the difference between a man who was important to him and one who was important to the nation, perhaps considering that the two were the same.

Pyarelal was allowed to join Gandhi as his secretary in Desai's place. As usual Gandhi showed his best qualities as a leader when most challenged, rallying his colleagues to deal with the death by filling every day with a busy timetable: study, prayer and other activities. 'We should keep ourselves so busy that there is no time for idle thought, depressing or otherwise,' he said.[49] One diversion he was persuaded to adopt was telling his own life story to his companions, so his principal biographers Pyarelal and Sushila Nayar heard many details that do not appear in his autobiographies.

Kasturba, though not arrested in the original sweep, had been taken in within a day because she threatened to make a speech at a protest meeting in place of Gandhi. Sushila Nayar, who had accompanied her, was also picked up. Kasturba was able to berate her husband: 'Did I not tell you not to pick a quarrel with this mighty government? You did not listen to me and now we have all to pay the penalty.'[50]

The Viceroy blamed Gandhi for the violence taking place across India, an accusation which so upset him that from 9 February 1943 he went on a twenty-one-day fast. The authorities fully expected him to die and had arranged such contingencies as a short news blackout, so that in the event of his death local government would have time to prepare for such unrest as it might produce. In fact this fast, during which his drinking water was supplemented with lime juice, salt and other minerals, passed without incident. Lord Linlithgow cabled Churchill that Gandhi was 'the world's most successful humbug' – both suspected a level of fraud in the fast, but none was proved. 'It now seems almost certain that the old rascal will emerge all the better from his so-called fast,' replied Churchill.[51] It may be that someone else, perhaps Sushila, was adding glucose or other nutrients to his water without his knowledge, though she explicitly denied this.

Reports of Gandhi's life in prison include his continuing the instruction of his wife that he had started when they were first married: he was now teaching her the history and geography of India. She is said to have inquired innocently: 'Why do you ask the British to quit India? Our country is vast, we can all live there. Let them stay if they like, but tell them to stay as our brothers.'[52]

Kasturba was suffering from an uneven heart rhythm, breathlessness and chest pains; she had a first heart attack late in 1943, and two more early the next year. She would sit up on the veranda with Gandhi beside her holding her hand. Medicines, whether Western or ayurvedic, ceased to have any beneficial effect, and Gandhi halted them. Her children and other family members came to see her, excepting Harilal, for whom she asked. Gandhi asked the police to look for him and it was found that he had attempted to visit his mother but had turned up at the gates of the Aga Khan Palace so drunk that he had been rejected. Later he was able to see her, and as Ramdas and Devdas were visiting too she was able to see three of her four sons (Manilal was in South Africa). When next Harilal visited he was drunk again, which so upset his mother that she began to beat her forehead with her fist; he was hustled out and not allowed to return.

Kasturba died on 22 February 1944, with Gandhi holding her, after more than sixty years of married life. He joined the women in bathing her body, and wrapped it in a sari made of yarn spun by him, as she had wished. The government did not want a big public funeral which would have taken on the nature of a demonstration, so she was cremated in the palace grounds on wood brought to the palace for Gandhi's own funeral, had he died on his last fast. Friends and relatives were allowed into the compound. She was cremated in a corner of the grounds where the cremation of Desai's body had taken place previously. Gandhi waited beside the pyre until it had burned down to ashes. Several times it was suggested he should go and rest but he refused, saying: 'How can I leave her like this after sixty-two years of companionship? I am sure she won't forgive me for that.'[53] Kasturba's bangles were found intact in the ashes – a good sign for those who believe in signs and tokens.

'It was as if a part of Bapu departed,' Mirabehn said of Kasturba's death.[54] He learned to be reflective about it, and a year after her death was able to write: 'Perhaps you do not know how many of my plans came to nothing because of Ba's imperfections. I exercised as much strictness as I could. But the limitation would always show itself.'[55] In later years he was pleased to say how much he had learned from Kasturba's resistance to his will. She so often went against his rules that, according to one resident, 'Bapu, in the end, had to accept defeat and declare that Ba was exempted from the regulations of the ashram.'⁵⁶ Their grandson Arun Gandhi remembered his first visit to the ashram when he was four years old. He had a fever when he arrived and Gandhi prescribed a week-long fast for him. After the third day the fever had abated and his mother appealed to Gandhi to ask if he might now eat. When Gandhi said no, the child began to wail. Kasturba, without arguing the matter, gave him a glass of orange juice saying: 'I am not going to let this child starve.' Gandhi desisted, and Arun remembered his 'quizzical smile and small sign of resignation'.⁵⁷

Gandhi had admonished her, however, when she transgressed rules relating to national campaigns. All of his followers were supposed to boycott Hindu temples that refused entry to untouchables. On a visit to Orissa, Kasturba and Mahadev Desai's wife visited the Jagannath Puri temple, one of the most important in India but that persisted in excluding untouchables. Gandhi denounced her behaviour at a public prayer meeting that evening, but chiefly blamed himself and Mahadev for not better educating their wives; both undertook a fast. Kasturba was never a convert to 'Gandhism'; she was ever the orthodox Hindu but, being that, she had to side with her husband. As one of her friends said to her: 'We must stick to our orthodox views and not allow untouchables in our houses and not drink water touched by a Muslim, but these things are not for you. For you the higher ideal is to follow your husband.'⁵⁸

Whether she was really, as Gandhi gallantly put it, 'my teacher in the art and practice of non-violent non-cooperation', she certainly shared his miseries.⁵⁹ Gandhi had truly lived the lesson of his boyhood hero King Harishchandra whose family suffered for his noble principles: Harilal was to die, of tuberculosis exacerbated by alcoholism, in 1948 at the age of fifty.

As well as the deaths of his wife and his secretary, Gandhi was also stricken by the deaths of two close friends, Charles Andrews in 1940 and the cotton merchant Jamnalal Bajaj in 1942. About this time he suffered a severe attack of malaria; his blood pressure was as high as it had been for years. Sushila, monitoring his health, noted that he was suffering from anaemia, hookworm, dysentery, a high fever and depression. The new Viceroy Lord Wavell felt that a third death in custody would re-invigorate the Quit India movement, which was currently moribund. The military situation was also less threatening: the Indian army was at its most numerous, in good shape, and the Japanese were in slow retreat. On 6 May 1944 Gandhi was released from jail for the last time. Of his seventy-four years he had been in prison, in South Africa and India, for more than six.

1 1

Partition and Death

Lord Wavell, a career soldier, was more interested in efficiency than in quibbling. He welcomed Congress and others addressing the problems of India in a practical manner; he had no respect for 'Quit India' or any other sloganising. He quickly organised relief for famine-stricken Bengal, a task that had been neglected by his aristocratic predecessor. A cultured and versatile man who wrote verse, Wavell was appalled at the poor quality of the administrators who had been left behind to run India while better men were doing war work. He freed Gandhi despite his own musings on the subject: 'Personally I could not see that we gained much credit by releasing him at the point of death; and if he was not at the point of death there was no need of such hurry.'[1]

Churchill had agreed to free Gandhi partly because it was felt unlikely that he would ever be well enough to return to active politics. But with his usual knack of surprising his enemies, Gandhi's spirits rose with his recuperation in the houses of his wealthy supporters and he was soon his old self again. He asked to see the (still imprisoned) Congress working committee members and the Viceroy. The United Provinces Governor Sir Maurice Hallett considered Gandhi 'cunning as a cartload of monkeys' and advised Wavell not to see him.[2] Churchill, wondering why Gandhi was not dead yet, was opposed to the Viceroy's giving imperial attention to a prisoner recently released on the grounds of ill-health. Wavell merely suggested that if Gandhi had 'a definite and constructive policy to propose for the furtherance of India's welfare' he would be glad to consider it. 'Quit India' had cost the nationalists dear in terms of the latitude the British were prepared to extend. Wavell's wish to be at least courteous in his correspondence was frustrated by the fact that he was expected to get London's approval for everything he wrote to Gandhi, so that his drafts were sharpened up and made more arrogant by the intervention of Whitehall.

Gandhi often declared: 'I consider the vivisection of India to be a sin', but there had in fact been a major shift in attitudes.[3] The senior Congressman Rajagopalachari had not taken part in the Quit India movement and had therefore remained at liberty. Both as a respected politician and as a family member (his daughter was married to Gandhi's son Devdas) he had access to Gandhi, and he visited the Aga Khan Palace in February 1943. There he floated a scheme, which Gandhi accepted, for a Congress–Muslim League national government and a plebiscite to determine whether the Muslim-majority provinces wanted to secede. In the event of separation, mutual agreements would cover such matters as defence, commerce and communications. This would be a federation with a promise of local Muslim rule in the Muslim-majority provinces. The far-sighted Rajagopalachari, who was to become the first Indian Governor General, had two objectives. One was to maintain India's integrity during the war and address the challenge of Japan, which he saw as his country's major foe. Second, he wanted to keep India entire, as a joint Hindu and Muslim state, after the granting of independence when the fears of invasion and resentment of the British would be things of the past; and a popular government would have to work out the nation's future.

By July 1944 Rajagopalachari was ready to present his formula to the public. He told Jinnah that Gandhi was not inflexible, but Jinnah needed to hear it from Gandhi himself, and talks between the two on the constitutional future of the country were announced. Gandhi's meetings with Jinnah had the long-term effect of stimulating the supporters of Vinayak Savarkar, the Hindu extremist with whose views Gandhi had clashed in London thirty-five years previously, and in response to whose arguments he had written *Hind Swaraj*. When it was announced that Gandhi would meet Jinnah, two of Savarkar's followers, Nathuram Godse and L.G. Thatte, led some supporters to Gandhi's ashram at Sevagram, intending to form a picket to stop him from leaving. The police arrested the leaders and found a dagger on Thatte, who said that a martyr would kill Gandhi. As president of the All-India Hindu Mahasabha Savarkar warned the Secretary of State for India Leo Amery: 'Hindusabhites can never tolerate breaking up of union of India their fatherland and holy-land.'⁴

Gandhi talked with Jinnah fourteen times, each time walking from where he was staying with the Birlas on Mount Pleasant Road to Jinnah's house in the same exclusive Malabar Hill area of Bombay. Gandhi found the meetings with Jinnah exhausting; Jinnah had first asked what the point was in talking to him if he represented only himself. 'It was a test of patience,' Gandhi explained to Rajagopalachari. 'I was amazed at my own patience.' Pressed on Pakistan, Gandhi conceded to Jinnah: 'I endorse Rajaji's [Rajagopalachari's] formula and you can call it Pakistan if you like.'⁵

Gandhi was therefore prepared to ask Congress for a post-independence secession by plebiscite, as in Rajagopalachari's formula. It still did not go far enough for Jinnah, who wanted his Pakistan to be larger and with more sovereign powers than those which Gandhi was prepared to endorse, and he wanted it *before* independence. The principle was conceded, nevertheless, but Gandhi later backed off. He began again to criticise the entire principle of the Muslims in India constituting a separate nation, particularly given that if there were a plebiscite, Jinnah did not want non-Muslims to have a right to vote on the issue in Muslim-majority provinces – hardly a democratic procedure.

While Wavell thought both leaders were 'obstinate, intransigent, crafty old men', he at least felt they could achieve something. But his conclusion was: 'The two great mountains have met and not even a mouse has emerged.'⁶ Wavell analysed the differences between them: Jinnah wanted Pakistan first and independence afterwards, 'while Gandhi wants independence first with some kind of self-determination for Muslims to be granted by a provisional government which would be predominantly Hindu.'⁷ Jinnah simply did not believe that a Hindu-majority government would grant any significant level of Muslim self-determination. He was betting on getting Pakistan from the British before they left.

They were unable to continue their meetings, which had anyway become less than cordial, in January 1945 because both were ill, Jinnah with pleurisy. If Gandhi was often distinguished by putting this whole body into the national struggle, Jinnah was no less so: he maintained a glassy outward persona while his body was racked with disease; every public appearance took an effort of will.

Jinnah unwound enough to mention to Gandhi that he was troubled by a nervous rash on one foot. Gandhi knelt on the floor and insisted he remove Jinnah's shoes and socks, then held the affected part, saying: 'I know what will heal you. I will send it tomorrow morning.' He sent a box of healing earth, which Jinnah accepted with his usual good manners, declaring he had already seen improvement, but in fact he made no more use of that than of anything else Gandhi had to offer.[8] As to his own health, Gandhi was suffering from exhaustion, amoebic dysentery and a bronchial cough. His cure for these ills was, of course, to propose a fast. With exquisite diplomacy, Rajagopalachari suggested a 'work-fast' for a month. Gandhi succumbed to his love of novelty, and had what anyone else would call a rest.

Wavell lobbied British politicians for the release of the other Congress leaders – Churchill had kept them locked up long after detention served any useful purpose. Finally the Viceroy was able to announce in a radio broadcast the release of the Congress working committee in June 1945. Indian leaders were now invited to talk with the Viceroy at Simla about the composition of a new interim government council. Gandhi was invited, and went to the town to be consulted but did not attend the meetings. In his progress by train he was greeted by crowds 'delirious and deaf with love or joy.'[9] Jinnah thought the choice not to attend the conference was 'another trick of Gandhi's, he pretended not to belong to Congress when it suited his book, but when necessary appeared as the Dictator of Congress which everyone knew he was.'[10]

The proceedings at Wavell's conference were blocked by Jinnah's insistence that the League alone should represent Muslims. In part this was attributable to Jinnah's nature, but it was also a result of government policy. Neither Wavell nor Churchill was prepared to see a Congress-dominated constitutional conference, so they elevated the League to parity with Congress, a danger Congress should have foreseen in 1939 when they withdrew from the provincial ministries and left a political vacuum for the Muslim League to fill. Jinnah's intransigence was the correct stance for him politically: he gained ground against non-Muslim

League co-religionists who now felt progress could not be made outside the League.

Events in India were accelerated by the British elections in 1945 with Labour coming to power in July; a Labour or Liberal victory had always been good for progressive Indian politics. The government was now led by Clement Attlee, who had sent Cripps to offer dominion status in 1942. Having been a member of the Simon Commission, he knew both the constitutional problems and the strength of Indian nationalist feeling.

Elections were to be held in India in 1945–6 for the central assembly and the provincial legislatures. The elections were held – and independence was voted for – under the prevailing legislation, the Government of India Act of 1935. Congress campaigned on the principle of independence, the Muslim League on the creation of Pakistan. In what was virtually a straightforward battle between them, the Muslim League won all the assembly seats reserved for Muslims and more than 80 per cent of the Muslim seats in the provincial legislatures; Congress became the largest single party in the assembly, and won 90 per cent of the provincial seats, forming ministries in eight provinces with a share in a coalition in another.

Gandhi took no interest in these matters. 'For years I have not been taking any part in elections,' he explained.[11] He argued with Jawaharlal Nehru about his vision of India as expressed in *Hind Swaraj* and frequently expressed thereafter, of a village nation sustained by farming and home spinning, enjoying the purifying influence of physical labour. Nehru argued for progress through science and industrialisation.

Gandhi had promoted Nehru as the next president of Congress, meaning that he would, in the course of things, become prime minister. He had not been the only candidate, but Gandhi pressed the other two, Vallabhbhai Patel and J. R. Kripalani, to withdraw. Nehru was therefore selected as head of the interim government that would bridge the gap between British rule and independence. Nehru was the natural leader, anointed by Gandhi as his heir despite their differences. Subhas Chandra Bose would not be coming back from the Far East: he had died in a plane crash. Patel, the other realistic option, was dominated by Gandhi and would do as he was told.

From August to October 1945 Gandhi reverted to his passion for healing the sick, working in a clinic near Poona. He used to prescribe the repetition of the name of God (Ramanama), sunbathing, hip baths and simple eliminative diets of milk, fruit and fruit juices with plenty of clean fresh water. He explained: 'All mental and physical ailments are due to one common cause. It is, therefore, but natural that there should be a common remedy for them, too . . . I therefore prescribed Ramanama and almost the same treatment to all the patients who came to me this morning.'[12] He also used to visit the homes of patients and comment on their cleanliness and sanitary arrangements.

He did not comment on the atomic bomb after its use on Japan in August 1945, answering a journalist quixotically: 'The more I think the more I feel I must not speak on the atomic bomb. I must act if I can.'[13] He used it as a metaphor, however, for a cycle of violence: 'The world has reached the stage of atomic warfare in returning violence for violence. Let us pray to God that he will save us from this atom bomb mentality. I have been persuading everyone to observe silence in reply to abuse or violence.'[14]

He had returned to the ashram, ever irritated by the quarrels, the differences of opinion and the temperaments of the ashramites; sometimes he wondered whether to close it down and take up a peripatetic life. In early 1946, sidelined by the political process – for he was neither standing for election nor negotiating with the government – Gandhi travelled to Bengal, Assam, Orissa and south India where people would walk for miles just for a glimpse of this exalted person.

In this restless spirit he moved on to ever more testing experiments in brahmacharya. 'I deliberately want to become a eunuch mentally,' he explained. 'If I succeed in this then I become one physically also.'[15] He detailed the precise difficulty, that of controlling ejaculation in sexually challenging circumstances: 'I did have experiments with Ba, but that was not enough. If emission took place then, it would have been less regrettable morally than any emission occurring now. Emission was a possibility then. I feel it is not a possibility now.'[16] It is unclear precisely what was taking place, but it is quite possible that the 'experiments' did not merely entail his being in the presence of naked women but that some further stimulation was involved during which he must withhold ejaculation for the experiment to be considered a success.

He had blessed the celibate marriage of his submissive ashram manager Munnalal Shah to the rather more wilful Kanchan, and was not short of instructions as to how they should behave. To Munnalal: 'You should not meet alone, nor touch each other . . . You should not talk with each other, nor work together, or take service from each other. I would advise you to go away for some time.'[17] In a later letter Gandhi was to describe to Munnalal how he had obliged Kanchan to sleep with him: 'Abha slept with me for hardly three nights. Kanchan slept one night only. Vina's sleeping with me might be called an accident. All that can be said is that she slept close to me.' This is an interesting remark, implying that really getting into the spirit of the experiment was something more than just sleeping close to Gandhi. He continued: 'Kanchan's case was rather tragic. I didn't understand her at all. What Abha or Kanchan told me was this: that she [Kanchan] had no intention whatever of observing brahmacharya but wished to enjoy the pleasure of sex. She, therefore, stayed only reluctantly, and undressed only for fear of hurting me. If I remember rightly, she was not with me even for an hour.'[18] How that information left the state of Munnalal Shah's marriage can only be imagined.

Despite criticism of his behaviour, he continued having physical contact with women, justifying himself via the circular argument that ceasing now would be to concede that he was wrong to have started. 'If I stop sleeping together for all time it will mean that I have been mistaken. Otherwise why should I stop it? There is a limit to abstaining from it for the sake of my friends.' It was not a path for others to follow, however: 'The experiment is not to be imitated. But if I can become a perfect brahmachari thereby, would I not be able to contribute more to the welfare of the world?'[19] He was, therefore, connecting the degree of sexual restraint he could achieve with the contribution he could make to humanity. The more he could resist increasing sexual challenges, the better he would be.

Following Kasturba's death Gandhi showed signs of valuing his family more. His grandson Arun, Manilal's son, visited his father in 1945 and 1946. He was 'amazed at his capacity to be loving and grandfatherly one moment, and a serious politician the next. He spent an hour with me every day, and he told me stories and examined my lessons.'[20] Manilal, who had been editing *Indian Opinion* in South Africa, noticed how much Gandhi's attitude had changed since his own childhood:

> It seemed to me that he spoilt those near him by his extreme love and affection. They had become his spoilt children, as it were, and much more so after my mother had been called away from this life . . . One of the things that struck me was the extreme softness in father's attitude compared with what it was when we four brothers were under him . . . When I saw this, many a time I chafed him and said to father, 'Bapu, you have vastly changed from the time we were under you. You never pampered us; I remember how you made us do laundry work and chop wood; how you made us to take the pick and shovel in the bitterly cold mornings and dig in the garden, to cook and to walk miles. And I am surprised to see how you now pamper these people around you.

Gandhi would listen, then burst into hearty laughter. 'Well children,' he would say, 'are you listening to what Manilal is saying?' And he would love and caress them as his own children had so wanted to be loved.[21]

The principle of Indian independence was conceded without fanfare on 15 March 1946 by prime minister Attlee in the House of Commons. A British journalist, H.N. Brailsford, found Gandhi 'happy when I met him, for Mr Attlee's speech in the Indian debate had just opened the road to Indian independence. He looked well and very much less than his age . . . His manner was never solemn and often he relaxed in a humorous chuckle.'[22]

The Labour Secretary of State for India was an old friend, Frederick Pethick-Lawrence, once a leading backer of the suffragette movement; Gandhi had seen his wife Emmeline speak in London before the First World War. As a pacifist, a socialist and someone who himself had been imprisoned for his actions in support of women's suffrage and had been on hunger strike, he was more Gandhian than most British politicians. Pethick-Lawrence and Stafford Cripps were sent as part of a cabinet mission in March 1946 with the objectives of forging an interim national government and resolving the problem of Pakistan with a constitutional settlement. Pethick-Lawrence visited Gandhi in the colony of untouchables where he was living on the Reading Road in Delhi, and attended some of his prayer meetings.

It would take more than goodwill to square the circle of communal aspirations in India, however. Wavell and the cabinet mission met Gandhi on 3 April – 'naked except for a dhoti and looking remarkably healthy,' noted Wavell despondently. He remarked how Pethick-Lawrence 'began with his usual sloppy benevolence to this malevolent old politician, who for all his sanctimonious talk has, I am sure, very little softness in his composition.'[23] Gandhi began talking about the salt tax; Wavell noted in his journal that he had never heard anyone but Gandhi suggest it was oppressive, but Gandhi wanted it removed as a sop to his vanity as he had gone to prison over it. Wavell felt the cabinet mission showed 'absurd deference' to Gandhi, who had 'brought to a fine art the technique of vagueness and of never making a statement which is not somehow so qualified or worded, that he cannot be pinned down to anything definite.'[24] Gandhi stayed out of the detailed negotiations, though he put forward his ideas of government to the mission: independence first, before any moves toward the creation of Pakistan, with Jinnah leading the government if that was what it would take to keep him in the process.

The cabinet mission negotiated the perilous waters of Indian politics with not only the Muslims and Hindus but the Sikhs and untouchables also wanting a say in the future constitution. Another Simla conference was convened in May 1946; again Gandhi did not attend but stayed nearby, and leaders went to see him every morning in his bungalow. Wavell noted that Gandhi 'seemed quite unmoved by the prospect of civil war. I think he has adopted Patel's thesis that if we are firm the Muslims will not fight.'[25] The Muslims knew this line of reasoning, and had every intention of fighting; if anything, Jinnah had trouble holding back his co-religionists.

On 16 May 1946 the cabinet mission declared a plan for a federated India with strong provincial governments and a central government retaining responsibility for defence, foreign affairs and communications. They rejected a separate Pakistan but the provinces would form three groups for intermediate administration: the Punjab, the Afghan Province (North-West Frontier), plus Sind and Baluchistan together – as one big provincial grouping. The second group would contain Bengal, which was heavily Muslim, and the next-door province Assam; and the third would contain all the rest of India. The mission wanted this to be the constitutional basis on which an assembly would meet – a compromise on the framework on which everyone was agreed.

There seemed to be slow progress towards agreement. Cripps and Pethick-Lawrence retained their faith in Gandhi until 20 May when he called for the British to leave, whatever the constitutional position, saying there should be an Indian national government before a constitutional assembly was called. This would mean the British would leave without a settlement of the claims of the Muslim League. It was effectively what he had been asking for in 1942 – for the British to leave the Indians to their disputes, which, given the Hindu majority, meant their domination over the Muslims – exactly what Jinnah was attempting to prevent. Wavell enjoyed the scene: 'I have never seen three men taken more aback by this revelation of Gandhi in his true colours . . . Cripps and the Secretary of State were shaken to the core.'[26] They were learning the facts of Gandhian logic: he did not lie, but he had his own interpretation of the truth. Pethick-Lawrence declared that only cabinet mission members should see Gandhi in future, and notes should be taken of all meetings.

After many weeks of wrangling, Congress accepted the mission's long-term constitutional assembly plans – the 'grouping' of provinces into a proto-Pakistan – which, as he had opposed them, was an indication of Gandhi's declining influence in Congress. Pyarelal recorded the moment when he admitted defeat and the Congress working party, chaired by Abul Kalam Azad, who was a Muslim but opposed to the Muslim League, let him go: 'A hush fell on the gathering. Nobody spoke for some time. [Abul Kalam Azad] with his unfailing alertness at once took in the situation. "What do you desire? Is there any need to detain Bapu any further?" he asked. Everybody was silent. Everybody understood. In that hour of decision they had no use for Bapu. They decided to drop the pilot. Bapu returned to his residence.'[27]

Jinnah and the Muslim League had accepted the plan on the grounds that if they accepted it and Congress rejected it, Wavell would ask Jinnah to form the interim government. The cabinet mission returned to Britain at the end of June, believing they had achieved their objective.

Presumably under Gandhi's influence, Nehru scuppered the agreement at the beginning of July, after a Congress meeting called to ratify it. He said that 'grouping' would not work – they had agreed only that they should operate as an assembly and that that assembly would be free to do what it chose, thus snatching away assurances that had been built in to satisfy Jinnah. The Muslim League felt betrayed – they had accepted an Indian union only under the proposals ratified by the cabinet mission. If all these agreements were off, they would not enter into an Indian union. They reverted to their objective of a fully independent Pakistan, 'to vindicate their honour and to get rid of the present British slavery and the contemplated future Caste-Hindu domination'.[28]

Nehru had been too candid – a better politician such as Patel or Azad would not have betrayed the underlying intention before the deal was in the bag. Even Gandhi told him his commentary on the agreement 'does not sound good. If it is correctly reported, some explanation is needed.'[29] Gandhi was much better at weaving a web of words to confound the listener. The end result was that the cabinet mission's plan was wrecked – Gandhi's position (independence first, without strings, then a constitutional settlement) was left as the policy of the Congress president. Wavell believed Gandhi had undermined both his Simla conference and the cabinet mission plan. Despite this, Gandhi was declining in influence with the politicians, who were now looking towards their own positions and power in the future.

With no agreement between the parties, Wavell asked Nehru as head of Congress, the largest party, to form an interim government. The Muslim League could come in as they chose. Jinnah and the League raised the political temperature with a trick they had learned from Gandhi: they announced their own Muslim hartal – strike – for 16 August.

The date became known as the start of the 'Great Calcutta Killing'. It was described at the time as the worst communal riot in India's history, though it is now seen as a foretaste of worse things to come. Muslim youths armed with sticks and daggers roamed the city shouting pro-Pakistan slogans and looking for weak and unprotected Hindus to kill; homes and shops were sacked and burned. On the second day Hindus responded with equal vehemence, and Sikhs joined in on the attacks on

Muslims. For four days there were riots, and a final toll of more than five thousand dead and twenty thousand injured. One feature of the destruction was the immunity of the Europeans: they were already being sidelined – the battles to come would be between Indians.

In the aftermath of the Great Calcutta Killing Wavell called Gandhi and Nehru to the Viceregal residence to make one last attempt to bring them to accept the cabinet mission's statement, which Congress had previously endorsed and whose interpretation Nehru had subsequently questioned. Wavell wanted a clear and unequivocal statement that they accepted the 'grouping' of provinces before a constitutional assembly would take place.

Gandhi started picking over legalistic points and Wavell snapped that he himself was 'a plain man and not a lawyer'. As the discussion became heated Gandhi, according to Wavell, said: 'If India wants her blood-bath, she shall have it.'[30] Wavell said he was shocked to hear such words from him. We have only Wavell's record of this remark, but it is startlingly close to others made by Gandhi about India resolving her conflicts after the British had left. 'There might be a blood-bath,' he told Woodrow Wyatt who had accompanied the cabinet mission. 'It will be settled in two days by non-violence if I can persuade India to go my way, or the ordeal may last longer.'[31] Even Gandhi's friend and admirer Lord Pethick-Lawrence 'was coming to believe Gandhi did not care whether two or three million people died and would rather that they should than that he should compromise.'[32]

There was some consistency in this view of Gandhi's. In 1941 in response to British concerns about the gulf between the Muslim League and Congress he had said that if the British withdrew,

I promise that Congress and the League and all other parties will find it in their interest to come together and devise a home-made solution for the Government of India. It may not be scientific; it may not be after any western pattern; but it will be durable. It may be that before we come to that happy state of affairs, we may have to fight amongst ourselves. But if we agree not to invite the assistance of any outside power, the trouble will last perhaps a fortnight. And it will not mean even one day's destruction of human heads such as goes on in Europe today, for the simple reason that thanks to the British rule we are unarmed.[33]

He minimised the dangers: 'It is the politically conscious Muslims and Hindus who will fight. They will fight with sticks, staves and soda-water bottles, but they will soon tire, and there will be wise men enough among us to bring about an honourable peace.'[34] Gandhi was fully aware of the inflammatory nature of communal passions in India. He correctly judged that the communal riots in four regions in spring 1941 were 'a rehearsal for a civil war' or, as he said later, 'like a miniature civil war.'[35] He was not prepared to do anything to avoid violence if 'anything' meant conceding a move towards the break-up of India. His intransigence spoiled the best chance of a settlement that would have secured peace, at least in the short term.

Nehru took office as prime minister on 2 September 1946. Early that morning, he and his ministers went to the untouchables' quarter where Gandhi was living. It was Monday, a day on which Gandhi still maintained silence (a discipline he had first imposed on himself back in 1921), so his advice to the prime minister of India was in written form: 'You have been in my thoughts since the [morning] prayer. Abolish the salt tax, remember the Dandi March. Unite Hindus and Muslims. Remove Untouchability. Take to Khadi.'[36] Gandhi gave each of the ministers his blessing and thus armed they went off to confront India's problems; the old magician could offer them nothing new.

Jinnah commemorated the day as one of mourning – millions of Muslims appeared on the streets in black-flag demonstrations. The Muslim League joined the government the following month, but merely obstructed its functioning so as to demonstrate that a Congress–League coalition was not practical: they had no interest in making a united India work.

Gandhi contemplated returning to his ashram at Sevagram but was diverted by the news of massacres in Noakhali in East Bengal, where a small Hindu minority had been attacked by a large Muslim majority. Refugees told of mass killings in which well organised gangs went from village to village carrying out murder, forced conversions, rape, forced marriages, the destruction of homes, forcible feeding with beef and the defiling of temples. Gandhi felt he could most usefully go to the villages of Noakhali to try to bring peace. Whatever his faults, he had a supreme sense of duty towards his fellows that drove him to put himself in the place of maximum hardship and danger, if he could help. The seventy-seven-year-old therefore boarded the train for Calcutta on 28 October 1946, his progress disturbed, as ever, by people who clambered on to the train and crowded the windows, calling for him and demanding darshan. He sat with his fingers in his ears to keep out the shouting.

By the time he reached Calcutta on his way to Noakhali there had already been retaliations against Muslims by Hindus in Bihar. Other leading Congress members were also active in an attempt to contain what was potentially the start of an Indian civil war. Nehru threatened to use aerial bombing to quell the disturbances (which, in practical terms, suggests a lack of understanding of the capabilities of air power). Gandhi responded: 'But that was the British way. By suppressing the riots with the aid of the military they would be suppressing India's freedom.'[37] He went on a minimal diet and threatened to fast in the near future. Gandhi now wrote in leaflets that were widely distributed to the Hindus of Bihar, where perhaps seven thousand Muslims had been killed: 'You should not rest till every Muslim refugee has come back to his home which you should rebuild and ask your ministers to help you to do so . . . What you have done is to degrade yourselves and drag down India.'[38]

On 6 November he travelled with his entourage and a number of provincial government officials to Noakhali in a train arranged by the Bengal government. At Chandpur they boarded a steamship to take them upriver to the remote lush region where the wealthy landowning Hindu minority had been under attack from their more numerous, poorer Muslim neighbours. He set up in Srirampur where a cottage was found for him, and he held prayer meetings and acted as a focus for polit-icians: the provincial commerce minister worked with Gandhi and the local police to draw up a plan for restoring harmony in a place where some three hundred homes had been plundered and burnt down. His mind was filled with the example of Jesus, 'a man who was completely innocent [,who] offered himself as a sacrifice for the good of others, including his enemies'. Answering a rhetorical question as to the truth of Jesus's story he said: 'To me it is truer than history because I hold it to be possible and it enshrines an eternal law – the law of vicarious and innocent suffering taken in its true sense.'[39]

He trudged from village to village, saw the destruction of homes, people's skulls and charred remains, the ashes of public buildings. He went barefoot, considering it part of his penance despite the broken glass, brambles and filth sometimes deliberately strewn in his path. His tramping through the villages produced one of the iconic images of the bare-legged Gandhi with his shaven head, dhoti, large pocket-watch and sometimes a shawl, and carrying a long bamboo staff.

But the image of the lone sage striding out against the world's evils was a journalistic invention. He was accompanied – as well as by the press themselves – by his usual entourage, by the police and by local volunteers including Nirmal Kumar Bose, a professor who acted as an interpreter, and a local 'fixer', Charu Chowdhury. Chowdhury remarked: 'Since all the paraphernalia he needed – the buckets, the bathtubs, the commode, the syringes, and whatnot – had to come with us, it was no easy task getting from village to village.'[40] This is something of an exaggeration – there was just one commode and one hand basin. The inclusion of syringes indicates Gandhi was maintaining his regime of enemas. He also had a travelling library of twenty books including the *Sayings of Muhammad*, *A Book of Jewish Thought* and Bengali language primers. He was taking regular lessons in Bengali to help him communicate with the locals; this urge for self-improvement never left him – he was studying a Bengali primer on the day he died.

One morning when he had been there less than two weeks he gathered his followers together then sent Pyarelal, Sushila, Abha and others off to live in seven riot-torn villages, to act as focuses for peace. They protested – as one recalled, they 'said we would all be killed if we didn't stay together. But Bapu insisted that only by being on his own could he find his bearings and test his faith in truth and non-violence but also in God.'[41] The absence of most of his entourage meant Gandhi had less support when facing the Muslim peasantry, but at the same time he was unencumbered by direct challenges over the brahmacharya 'experiment' that he was now conceiving as a yajna or sacrifice.

In what was probably not a coincidence, on 17 December 1946 he was heard arguing with Sushila when she came to visit him. They were alone and shouting excitedly at each other at about 3.20 a.m., some forty minutes before normal waking time. When Bose went to see what was going on he found them both crying, Gandhi motioning Sushila to go away. It would be many months before they would be close again. It may not be unconnected with this outburst that within days Gandhi was to start his sexual experiments with a woman almost half Sushila's age.

He wrote to the father of nineteen-year-old Manu Gandhi, saying he needed her support. Manu was his grandniece, whom he often called his granddaughter. She had lost her mother at twelve and been cared for by Kasturba, and in her turn, when she was sixteen, had nursed Kasturba in her final illness in the Aga Khan Palace. After Kasturba's death Gandhi became a 'mother' to the girl, telling her how to do her hair, how to wear her clothes and taking an interest in her physical development, though there were quite enough women surrounding Gandhi who were in a position to advise a girl on intimate matters – his involvement was not a matter of necessity. He found her sexuality – or lack of it – fascinating. Pyarelal records that 'she claimed to be a complete stranger to sexual awakening generally associated with a girl of her age', and Gandhi felt magnetically attracted to such natural chastity.[42]

When he contacted her father he had already written to Manu from Noakhali, telling her: 'I shall be happy if you come over and have a talk with me. I do not wish to put any pressure on you. It is my earnest desire that you should remain a pure virgin till the end of your life and spend your life in service.'[43] She arrived at his temporary headquarters in Srirampur on 19 December. Early on the morning of the 20th Bose entered Gandhi's room and found them in bed together. Gandhi later explained to Bose that they had been discussing 'a bold and original experiment' whose 'heat will be great'. Only those who realised this and were prepared to remain at their posts should be with him.[44]

Gandhi explained to Sushila, as she later recounted, that 'even on the first night Manu was snoring within minutes of getting into his bed'. When, some time later, he said to Manu: 'We both may be killed by the Muslims at any time. We must both put our purity to the ultimate test, so that we know that we are offering the purest of sacrifices, and we should now both start sleeping naked', she acceded.[45] He was able to report to Pyarelal at the end of December: 'She sleeps naked but she sleeps soundly.'[46]

Gandhi described his concept of a brahmachari thus:

One who never has any lustful intention, who, by constant attendance upon God, has become proof against conscious or unconscious emissions, who is capable of lying naked with naked women, however beautiful they may be, without being in any manner whatsoever sexually excited ... who is making daily and steady progress towards God and whose every act is done in pursuance of that end and no other.[47]

Thus far, his reasoning was spiritual, but in the maelstrom that was India approaching independence he began to see his sex experiments as having national importance: 'I hold that true service of the country demands this observance,' he stated.[48] Pyarelal examined his thought processes in relation to Manu:

Gandhiji had claimed that he was mother to her and she had endorsed the claim. If the truth of it could be tested, it would provide a clue to the problem that baffled him. Incidentally it would enable him also to know how far he had advanced on the road to perfect Brahmacharya – complete sexlessness ... He did for her everything that a mother usually does for her daughter. He supervised her education, her food, dress, rest, and sleep. For closer supervision and guidance he made her sleep in the same bed with him. Now a girl, if her mind is innocent, never feels embarrassment in sleeping with her mother.'[49]

Manu apparently accepted the word – one of the books she wrote about her time with Gandhi is titled *Bapu – My Mother*.

Pyarelal explained how this related to the challenge India faced: 'If his sincerity could impress itself upon her and evoke in her all the excellences that he aimed at, it would show that his quest of truth had been successful. His sincerity should then impress itself upon the Muslims, his opponents in the Muslim League, and even Jinnah, who doubted his sincerity, to their own and India's harm.'[50] Gandhi thus connected his own physical state with the very survival of a united India. He is reported to have said of his sex trials: 'If I can master this, I can still beat Jinnah.'[51]

Gandhi's behaviour was widely discussed and criticised. He wrote to his son Manilal: 'Do not let the fact of Manu sleeping with me perturb you. I believe that it is God who has prompted me to take that step.'[52] In response to criticism at a prayer meeting reported in his newspaper *Harijan* in February 1947, he maintained that his 'experiments' were an integral part of the yajna he was performing. He conceded that many friends had become upset because of his behaviour, but found a way of regarding the objections as a further reason why he should continue: 'If I do not appear to people exactly as I am within, wouldn't that be a blot on my non-violence? . . . If I don't let Manu sleep with me, though I regard it as essential that she should, wouldn't that be a sign of weakness in me, and in that case would not my death, since I would have failed to realise perfect ahimsa, be the best thing for me?'[53]

He used frequently to wake Manu up at night to talk to her and to scribble in his diary. On 2 January 1947 he wrote: 'Have been awake since 2 a.m. God's grace alone is sustaining me. I can see there is some grave defect in me somewhere which is the cause of all this. All round me is utter darkness. When will God take me out of this darkness into His light?'[54] There was no doubt that Manu was going into real danger when she willingly went to him in Noakhali. Violence was ever present, and Gandhi's mission was resented. At one time the superintendent of police showed him printed placards put up by hostile Muslims demanding his expulsion. They tramped every day, Gandhi haranguing the villagers they passed and engaging in dialogues. She tended his cut feet in the evenings when they stayed in bare huts blasted by cold winds.

He lost two people who had been with him in Noakhali: R.P. Parasuram, who had acted as his secretary, and Nirmal Kumar Bose; both of them wrote criticising Gandhi's behaviour with Manu. Two supporters who were editing *Harijan* in his absence also resigned after refusing to print parts of Gandhi's sermons dealing with his sleeping arrangements. His son Devdas wrote to tell him that he was taking the wrong path. Congress leaders Patel and Kripalani (Congress president since November 1946) expressed their disapproval, despite the latter's engagement with brahmacharya – he had a celibate marriage with a woman called Sucheta who was also sometimes part of Gandhi's entourage.

His habit of sleeping with Manu was discontinued in March that year to please Amritlal V. Thakkar, one of Gandhi's leading disciples and a kingpin of his organisations helping untouchables and developing villages. Thakkar had spent a week with Gandhi at the end of February and impressed upon him that gossip about the practice was adversely affecting their work. He wisely also asked Manu to ask Gandhi to stop. Her intervention on the matter seems to have been the deciding factor: Gandhi stopped sleeping with her, but with no admission that he had done anything wrong. Manu was well aware of the controversy; at one point she is recorded as translating for Bose a letter in Gujarati from a critic to the effect that 'Gandhiji was obviously suffering from a sense of self-delusion in regard to his relations with the opposite sex.'[55]

Manu's devotion to Gandhi was genuine. She wrote (or was involved in the writing of) five books and booklets about her time with him, and made no complaint in them about her sleeping arrangements, though she did complain about being sent on petty errands by Gandhi. She describes the fierce rains, strong winds, the slippery roads and pathways and the soft marshy puddles that they had to cross with the help of improvised bamboo bridges. Her recollections of Gandhi, despite their occasional quarrels, are profoundly loving and sympathetic. She wrote in her diary of 'my good fortune in having the chance to travel with the saint who pilgrimages barefoot in this stinging and oppressive cold weather'. Once on a river crossing, Gandhi put his head in Manu's lap and went to sleep. She wrote: 'I was alone in the boat, except for one boatman who was no company, with one of the world's most exalted souls, with him lying cosily on my lap and with my palm on his forehead. It was just a fleeting five minutes, but a five minutes that were full of bliss for me.'[56] Given the attractions of fame, all accounts suggest there was no shortage of young women eager to serve Gandhi in any way he wished.

Even the ever-loyal Pyarelal, despite Gandhi's urging him to report the brahmacharya experiments in full, is surprisingly coy. He reports Gandhi's activities with Manu, but not with his own sister Sushila.

There was a further dimension in the endless psychodrama of Gandhi and his disciples in that forty-seven-year-old Pyarelal was obsessed with Manu and wanted to marry her. Gandhi disapproved of his pursuit of her, but Sushila pressed her to accept Pyarelal, presumably because that would wrest her from Gandhi and leave a vacancy that she herself could again fill. Gandhi tried to be understanding of Pyarelal: 'I get the impression that you have been terribly disappointed,' he wrote. 'You do not know how much I have talked to her and tried to persuade her.' But he finally remarked to his assistant: 'I can see that you will not be able to have Manu as wife.'[57]

There were genuine achievements at Noakhali – some looted property was returned and some abducted women restored; Hindus who had fled returned. The attention that Gandhi and his followers attracted discouraged bad behaviour. Journalists, too, played a part in assuring wrongdoers that their deeds were observed by the world. Gandhi always enjoyed a good press. Many showed no pretence to objectivity: two of the journalists who travelled with him, from UPI and *The Hindu*, took over typing Gandhi's letters for him as a labour of love.

Muslims had taunted Gandhi that here he was, caring for the suffering Hindus, but what about the Muslims who had been attacked in Bihar? There, Hindu mobs had killed at least seven hundred Muslims. He had received no call from within, he said, but when the government of Bihar sent him a message inviting him, he left, in March 1947. This pleased the Governor of Bengal, Sir Frederick Burrows, who told Wavell that he 'was very relieved that Gandhi had left Bengal, as it had taken twenty of his best police to protect him; and he was sarcastic over an American correspondent's article headed "Gandhi walks alone".'[58]

The violence in Bihar was felt the more deeply by Gandhi because in some places the Hindu crowds had committed barbarities against Muslims while shouting 'Mahatma Gandhi ki jai.' Again he begged the Hindus to make what amends they could: 'Rebuild their houses with your own hands, clean their wells, sink new wells to replace the ones filled with the corpses of massacred Muslims.'[59] He told Congress workers, some of whom he believed had taken part in the disturbances: 'I have vowed to do or die. I will not rest or let others rest. I would wander all over on foot and ask the skeletons lying about how that had happened. There is such a fire raging in me that I would know no peace till I have found a solution for all this.'[60]

While Gandhi was witnessing the horrors of communalism being visited on his beloved village life, India was inching towards the end of British rule and its unified state. Attlee announced that the transfer to Indian control would take place no later than June 1948, even if that meant transferring power to provincial governments. He also announced the departure of Wavell; the Viceroy gave Gandhi a copy of his anthology of verse, *Other Men's Flowers*, as a parting gift. His replacement was the Supreme Allied Commander of liberated South-East Asia, Lord Mountbatten, cousin of the king and naval officer. When Mountbatten arrived in March 1947 it was with the objective of setting up a unitary government in accordance with the cabinet mission's plan. If he had failed in this by 1 October, he was to report back with realistic alternative proposals of how to hand over power.

The Muslim League had succeeded in making India ungovernable at cabinet level and were now refusing to take part in the constituent assembly. The realists in Congress were coming to terms with the fact that they had a choice between partition and civil war – any civil war probably ending in partition, anyway. Unrest in the Punjab was such that by March that year they were already resigned to the partition of at least that province into Muslim and non-Muslim areas. Congress had therefore sent a proposal secretly, but with Wavell's consent, to London, suggesting the transfer of power to two governments, both of which would have dominion status under the Crown. So dominion status, long the shibboleth of Congress hardliners, was now to be accepted, five painful years after it had been proffered as part of the Cripps mission.

In his first days in office Mountbatten met all the major figures in Indian politics including Gandhi, who impressed the Viceroy with his strength of personality, as he always did at first meetings. He suggested calling on Jinnah to appoint his own administration, in an attempt to maintain the unity of India, a notion that initially rather engaged Mountbatten; but Congress rejected the idea and the Viceroy's advisers identified it as an old and impractical proposal. Gandhi's experiences in Bengal and Bihar had not led him to alter his opinion on the causes of the problem; Mountbatten's press secretary recorded Gandhi's position thus: 'The British system of "divide and rule" had created a situation in which the only alternatives were a continuation of British rule to keep law and order, or an Indian blood-bath. The blood-bath must be faced and accepted.'[61]

At Mountbatten's instigation Jinnah agreed to sign an appeal to end the violence and incitement to violence, but the Muslim leader insisted that only two people should sign it, he himself representing the Muslims and Gandhi representing the Hindus, thus making a humanitarian appeal into a political statement. Gandhi returned to Bihar and the powers in Delhi moved towards a resolution without his input. Nehru told Mountbatten that partition was accepted but that it was the provinces themselves that must be partitioned – they could not break off in their entirety. Jinnah was outraged, but Mountbatten explained that any argument for the partition of the nation of India into Muslim and non-Muslim applied equally well to the partition of its provinces.

Jinnah's urgency to see his new nation materialise was hastened not merely by the departure of the British: he knew his days were numbered; he was hollow-eyed and skeletal, conserving his energy at every turn. If he wanted a Pakistan, he would have to move fast. Eventually he was to come round to accepting a 'moth-eaten' Pakistan, as he put it. The Mountbatten plan for partition was formally announced on 3 June 1947, with Muslim-majority provinces in the west of India breaking away and the non-Muslim parts of East Punjab and West Bengal going with India. Gandhi was appalled: 'It is not for the British Government to change the map of India,' he said. 'All it has to do is to withdraw from India, if possible in an orderly manner, maybe even in chaos, but withdraw in any case.' He now saw the merits of the cabinet mission's position, which he had previously dismissed, saying he would 'urge every patriot and certainly the British power, irrespective of the worst kind of violence, to leave India under the Cabinet Mission's document'.[62]

Mountbatten already had the agreement of Hindu, Sikh and Muslim leaders to partition, so it was with some trepidation that he moved to clear the agreement with Gandhi, as he was fearful the old sage would wreck the plan. To Mountbatten's delight, when Gandhi arrived at the viceregal palace on 2 June 1947 he entered the room with his finger on his lips: it was his day of silence. Mountbatten explained the plan and Gandhi responded by scribbling notes on the backs of old envelopes. There was a provision allowing him to break his vow of silence on Mondays in order to talk to someone as senior as the Viceroy on urgent matters, but clearly he had decided there was nothing in it for him.

Mountbatten, still worried that Gandhi would sabotage the plan, later saw him again and urged him to consider the settlement not as a Mountbatten but as a Gandhi plan, for the Viceroy said he had striven to incorporate in it Gandhi's major concepts of non-coercion, self-determination and the earliest possible date for British withdrawal. It is a testament to Mountbatten's diplomacy that at his prayer meeting that night Gandhi said: 'The British Government is not responsible for partition. The Viceroy had no hand in it. In fact he is as opposed to division as Congress itself, but if both of us – Hindus and Muslims – cannot agree on anything else, then the Viceroy is left with no choice.'[63]

Some agreement on partition was long anticipated, but the timetable came as a surprise when Mountbatten announced it at a press conference on 4 June: the transfer of power would take place on 15 August – the British Raj was to be wound up in seventy-two days' time. 'My life's work seems to be over,' Gandhi remarked sadly. 'I hope God will spare me further humiliation.'[64] As an enduring symbol of the nation's rejection of what Gandhi had to offer, the flag of the new India was the Congress tricolour but without the spinning-wheel that he had placed at its centre. In its place was the wheel of Asoka, the third-century BC king of a unified India.

Gandhi was on the move to Bihar but as he passed through Calcutta he was urged by the city's Muslims to stay on at least until after independence. He agreed to do so if they would use their influence with the Muslim League to ensure Muslims did not attack Hindus at Noakhali. He took up residence in one of the houses abandoned by Muslims who had fled the looting and murder, and he was now berated by Hindus who accused him of siding with the Muslims. He exerted a calming influence on his surroundings; compared to the Punjab, Bengal was a haven of peace. Mountbatten gallantly paid tribute to him as a 'one-man boundary force.'[65]

He had stopped sleeping with Manu at the end of February 1947, but in May he resumed the challenges of chastity in the belief that if he had perfect equilibrium it would dispel the violence around him – and the continued violence meant that he must demonstrate ever more spiritual purity. 'This is the culmination of my striving for the last sixty years,' he told Manu. 'You have become an instrument in this. In this yajna I got a glimpse of the ideal of truth and purity for which I had been aspiring.'[66]

Eighteen-year-old Abha, the wife of Gandhi's grandnephew Kanu Gandhi, rejoined his entourage in July, and by the end of August he was sleeping with both girls at the same time. Abha had been sleeping with him since she was sixteen, though less willingly than Manu. Abha later recalled: 'He did ask me to take my clothes off. But, as far as I remember, I usually kept my petticoat and choli [bodice] on.'[67] The men from Gandhi's entourage, including Kanu, asked him to stop, but he continued. It may have been that he felt he required added spiritual strength for the challenges of the times. Resistance to the charms of one naked teenage girl was not sufficient – perhaps two would provide the necessary power in these difficult days. It is hard to imagine what sexual experiment he might have thought of next.

The greatest opposition to Gandhi came not from Muslims but from violent Hindu nationalists who believed he had sided with the Muslims and sacrificed India. Pakistan was shaping up to be unworkable as a nation, with a large western wing and, more than a thousand miles across India, a populous eastern wing carved out of Bengal. The possessions of the old united India – government offices, railway lines, military hardware, finances – were now shared out between what remained of India and the new state.

Asked to give media statements on the final victory of the nationalists, Gandhi refused, sadly – it was no time for celebration. He spent 15 August, Independence Day, fasting and spinning. Manu wrote: 'His visage was grave. While the people in his room rejoiced, his mind kept thinking of the suffering people in riot-torn regions.'[68]

Worse was to come. The report of the boundary commission for the division of Bengal and the Punjab was delayed until after the independence celebrations. Within days of the announcement, Sikhs and

Hindus attacked the Muslims of eastern Punjab while Muslims attacked Sikhs in the west. The slaughter triggered a further exodus of refugees until there were millions of people crossing over the Indo-Pakistan border – perhaps as many as eleven million, probably the largest human migration in history in such a short period. No one had realised how bad the situation would be, though the shock was compounded for Congress leaders because they had previously clung to the comforting delusion that communal violence was a product of imperialism – as Nehru had said: 'When the British go, there will be no more communal trouble in India.'[69] Huge marching convoys with their carts and bundles were attacked; refugee trains would arrive at their destinations with no living passenger on board – all had been slaughtered. Gandhi's belief that any violence accompanying independence could not be extreme because Indians had been denied arms by the British was shown to be monstrously wrong: this violence between neighbours was all the more intimately horrendous *because* they had no arms – killing was done with farming and kitchen implements. Tens of thousands were butchered with the most primitive tools, sometimes suffering humiliation and torture beforehand. Though Gandhi did not know it (and he never did appreciate the full horror of what happened in the Punjab), some half a million people perished in a month-long orgy of killing, and countless numbers of women were raped or abducted. Gandhi commented: 'I am told that I should count the figures. What figures should I count? ... And what will I do, knowing the figures?'[70]

Two weeks after Independence Day an angry crowd of young men bent on violence forced their way into the house where Gandhi was staying in Calcutta, smashing doors, windows and ceiling fans. Gandhi was in bed between Abha and Manu. He got up and approached the invaders, touching his palms in a traditional salutation. A blow was aimed at him, and a brick meant for him struck a Muslim beside him. Manu and Abha stayed by his side. Even though it was his day of silence, he spoke to them, saying: 'What is it? Kill me, kill me ... Why don't you kill me? My God asks me, where are you? ... I am deeply pained.'[71] The police arrived, chased the marauders out of the house and dispersed the crowd outside with tear gas. Gandhi recorded that he had shouted at the crowd but was unable to command silence, and as they were Bengali and he was speaking in Hindustani it was a futile effort. 'I feel totally lost,' he wrote to Vallabhbhai Patel the next morning.[72] Some Congress leaders had taken Gandhi's Hindu message but ignored the non-violence part of it, which was felt to be merely an opportune tool against the British. They also rejected the universalism, feeling, along with Patel, that it was better to cut off the 'gangrenous arm' of Muslim power in India than to allow it continued influence.

Gandhi decided to fast after seeing the bodies of some Muslims killed when a hand-grenade was thrown into a truck being used to take them to safety. To those who would dissuade him from putting himself in mortal danger he said: 'If the riots continue what will I do by merely being alive? What is the use of my living? If I lack even the power to pacify the people, what else is left for me to do?'[73] As soon as it was announced on the evening of 1 September, the fast began to have an effect: murders and looting abated. Many police and other Calcuttans went on a symbolic one-day fast in sympathy, university students gathered weapons from streets and homes and delivered them to Gandhi. Hooligan bands went to his bedside to see him and pledged to desist from violence. Weapons were piled up at the gates of his house. On 4 September the police reported the city had been at peace for twenty-four hours.

He went on to Delhi, intending to continue to the Punjab where he hoped to promote peace, but found himself staying there with his entourage, including Manu and Abha; Pyarelal later joined them. They could not stay in the untouchables' quarter as usual as it was occupied by refugees, so instead went to Birla House as guests of Gandhi's rich industrialist friend. There was work enough for him in Delhi, where violence had broken out on 5 September. Hindu and Sikh refugees had run wild, attacking Muslim homes and businesses, thereby making many Muslims refugees in their own city. Refugees from West Punjab crowded into three camps. Gandhi prayed to God to let him die rather than see the suffering of India. He determined to stay in Delhi until it had recovered itself, proposing to go to the Punjab later. 'I have to do or die here,' he said, 'If heart unity is not restored in Delhi, I can see flames raging all over India.'[74]

The authorities were overrun. Nehru did what he could, sometimes placing himself between gangs of killers and their victims. He visited Gandhi every evening for spiritual comfort. The Viceroy's wife Edwina also frequently visited Gandhi, while undertaking a self-imposed mission to organise sanitation and health facilities in the refugee camps. Nehru's daughter Indira worked with the refugees camped around her father's house until Gandhi asked her to work in the Muslim camps. She was still weak, having just given birth, but was willing to go. She asked who would be with her and Gandhi replied: 'My dear girl,' if I had someone else to go, I wouldn't ask you.'[75] She reported back to him each day, or if there was no time he would send a flower or a message.

Sushila Nayar tells of how she was in a car in Delhi with Gandhi when they came to a point where an angry, menacing crowd of Muslim refugees had gathered on the road. The driver accelerated to escape quickly. Gandhi told him to stop, but he refused. Gandhi was furious and shouted at the driver to stop, which he finally did. The crowd, which had been left a little distance behind, quickly surrounded the car. Sushila wrote:

> Gandhiji stepped out – a sad, frail figure – and placing his hands on the shoulders of two angry young men on either side for support, asked them all to move on to the lawn. As they sat down, Gandhiji addressed them. They could see and feel the force of his love and his desire to help them. The eyes which were emitting sparks of hatred a moment earlier were filled with tears and they told him of their sufferings and their grievances of various kinds, including the lack of medical care.

Gandhi sent Nayar to look after them in her capacity as doctor.[76]

After partition the accession of the princely states, whether to India or to Pakistan, became the major constitutional problem for the subcontinent. Most of the princely states that had a Hindu population acceded to India, some under threat though none with bloodshed. Kashmir had a Muslim population with a Hindu ruler, though the Muslims of Kashmir had been traditionally closer to Congress than to the Muslim League. Pakistan claimed Kashmir (it was, after all, what the K in the name represented) but the Maharaja of Kashmir acceded to India. Kashmir had been invaded by tribesmen, encouraged by Pakistan's leaders, in order to force accession to Pakistan. India then sent troops in by air, the Pakistani army invaded, and the first war between India and Pakistan began.

The government of India attempted to pressure Pakistan by withholding the 550-million-rupee balance of the agreed portion of the assets of old India. Gandhi felt the government of India was behaving dishonourably. Gandhi was always scrupulous about money and about debts being paid. This was a fine attribute for the marketplace but, as Patel said, the Pakistanis would be using the money to buy arms with which to kill Indians. It would not have been too much of a stretch of principle to use money as a bargaining counter to save life in Kashmir. Nevertheless, Gandhi started a fast on 13 January 1948 for peace in Delhi, the money symbolising peace between Hindus and Muslims. This time he had less support than usual; opponents picketed outside Birla House with banners saying 'Let Gandhi Die.'

Valabhbhai Patel offered to resign if that would end the fast but Gandhi wanted him and Nehru to stay in the government together. Three days later, on 16 January, the government of India announced its decision to release the cash balances due to Pakistan. Patel was in tears at the cabinet meting where the decision was taken – as well he might be. The failure to settle the problem of Kashmir then was egregious; more than sixty years later the province was still seeing conflict resulting from it.

On the positive side, the gesture was appreciated in Pakistan: offers were made to help rescue abducted Hindu and Sikh women. A representative delegation of the religious communities called on Gandhi to pledge themselves to encourage Muslims in Delhi to feel able to return to their homes, and to return mosques that had been seized. Thus reassured, Gandhi ended his last fast with a glass of orange juice on 18 January.

On the evening of the 20th, as he was giving his post-prayer discourse there was a loud bang – an explosive charge had been set off by a wall near where Gandhi sat. Manu clung to his legs in fright. 'Suppose someone really came to shoot us down, then what would you do?' Gandhi asked her.[77] As the audience panicked Gandhi said, in a voice clearly recorded by All India Radio: 'Listen! Listen! Listen! Nothing has happened.' Order was restored and he resumed speaking – his physical courage was always beyond reproach. The bombers' courage failed, however. They had planned to attack Gandhi with revolvers and grenades after the explosion, but they panicked and made off in the confusion – except one, a refugee from Pakistan called Madanlal Pahwa, who was arrested.

Ten days later, just after 5 p.m. on 30 January, Gandhi walked out of Birla House with his hands on the shoulders of Manu and Abha. As he passed along the cordoned lane through the prayer congregation, he took his hands off the shoulders of the girls to acknowledge greetings, his palms pressed together. A stocky young man in a khaki bush-jacket elbowed his way towards them. Manu thought he was attempting to touch Gandhi's feet and remonstrated with him, saying they were already late for prayers. He pushed her away violently, causing the notebook, spittoon and rosary that she was carrying to fall. She stooped to pick them up and the man stood in front of Gandhi and fired three shots at point-blank range from a 9mm Beretta. Gandhi fell, with the words 'Hey, Rama' or 'Raa . . . m.'[78]

Abha caught his head as he fell and the crowd surged forward to catch him, too. But he was already dead, at 5.17 p.m., with blood soaking through his white clothes as he lay on the floor. His body was taken back into Birla House. Manu, temporarily deafened by her proximity to the gunshots, her clothes stained with Gandhi's blood, tried to help. Sushila's first-aid box 'had no effective remedies in it', she remarked pathetically.[79]

Gandhi had said he hoped to meet death 'calmly, with a smile, and all the while remembering my chosen God.'[80] He had told Manu: 'If it occurs to me to utter the name of Rama with my last breath, it should be taken as a proof of the success of my attempt [to attain perfect non-attachment].'[81] Manu also wrote of his thinking about finding a good death. Only she mentioned his last words; when the assassin was interviewed he remembered Gandhi saying nothing. It may be that she merely thought she remembered his last words being the name of God. Perhaps he did, quite reasonably in the circumstances, cry out 'Oh God!' when he was attacked. Or, given his constant repetition of the name of God, it would not be unlikely that this was his last word anyway.

A doctor arrived and made a detailed examination, pronouncing him dead from three bullets, one of which was still lodged in his right lung. Nehru, Patel and Mountbatten arrived on the scene. An angry crowd had gathered. Someone said a Muslim had murdered Gandhi. The quick-witted Mountbatten countered: 'You fool, everyone knows it was a Hindu!' He knew nothing of the kind, but he realised violence would follow if a Muslim were implicated.[82] Nehru was said to be beside himself, sobbing over Gandhi's body for a few moments; then he recovered himself and became the statesman again. Mountbatten pressed him into making a speech to the nation to defuse the tension. Rising to the occasion, Nehru made a great and memorable opening:

> Friends and comrades, the light has gone out of our lives and there is darkness everywhere. I do not know what to tell you or how to say it. Our beloved leader, Bapu as we called him, the Father of the Nation, is no more. Perhaps I am wrong to say that. Nevertheless, we will not see him again as we have seen him for these many years. We will not run to him for advice and seek solace from him, and that is a terrible blow not to me only but to millions and millions in this country... The light has gone out, I said, and yet I was wrong. For the light that shone in this country was no ordinary light... For that light represented something more than the immediate present, it represented the living, the eternal truths, reminding us of the right path, drawing us from error, taking this ancient country to freedom.[83]

Manu with Gandhi's son Devdas performed the last service for Gandhi, washing his body. They anointed it with sandalwood paste, and placed his rosary in his hands, along with a garland of hand-spun yarn. The body was arranged in a room filled with flowers; 'He Rama' was written in rose petals near his head. Gathering crowds were now calling to see the body, and it was taken to the balcony of the house and placed on a raked catafalque so that as many people as possible could view it.

The following day, 31 January, flags flew at half-mast as the hastily arranged state funeral took place. The body was carried on the five-and-a-half-mile route to the cremation ground on an army weapon-carrier covered in a white sheet. In deference to Gandhi's opposition to machines, the vehicle was pulled by two hundred uniformed servicemen. Crowds shouted: 'Mahatma Gandhi has become immortal!' and blew holy conch-shells as the cortège proceeded slowly by. People swarmed on rooftops, up telegraph poles and trees as far as the eye could see. Planes of the Indian Air Force circled showering flowers, bringing to mind the flying chariot described in the *Ramayana*. A raised platform twelve feet square had been constructed at Rajghat near the River Jamuna. Gandhi's son Ramdas performed the Vedic rites; sandalwood was piled on top of the body and the pyre was ignited, sending red flames high in the sky. Manu buried her face in Patel's lap and wept. The pyre burned for fourteen hours during which time priests recited the entire text of the *Bhagavad Gita*.

Manu, who preserved Gandhi's fingernail clippings as a last relic, was speedily removed from the scene. Despite Gandhi's having written to Ramdas: 'I have asked her to write about her sharing the bed with me', the protectors of his image were now eager to silence her.[84] Devdas, Sushila and others accompanied her to Delhi station. The train was late and Devdas took the opportunity of taking Manu aside and talking with her. She wrote: 'His particular topic of conversation was my diary... Kaka [Uncle] warned me not to disclose the contents of my diary to anyone and at the same time forbade me to divulge the contents of important letters... He said "You are very young but you possess a lot of valuable literature. And you are also unsophisticated."'[85] Though she wrote five books about Gandhi (or were they ghost-written from her recollections?), she was never to disclose her side of the brahmacharya experiments.

Gandhi's ashes were scattered in the Ganges, the Hoogli, the Sabarmati and other major rivers of India on 12 February, and at four points in the sea. The assassin, thirty-seven-year-old Nathuram Godse, editor of the Marathi journal *Hindu Rashtra* (Hindu Polity),was one of the conspirators who had exploded the bomb days previously. Among at least eight others involved in the conspiracy were thirty-four-year-old Narayan Apte, the journal's manager, a hotel keeper, and Nathuram Godse's brother Gopal.

The Hindu extremist leader Vinayak Savarkar with whom Gandhi had argued in London in 1909 before writing *Hind Swaraj*, was associated though not directly connected with the conspiracy. Godse and Apte were known to have been with him in August 1947 and may have been, twice, in January 1948. At the trial, at which Savarkar was acquitted, it was testified that they had visited his house and he had wished them luck days before the first assassination attempt.

Godse had been immediately arrested and had expressed no remorse. He was one of the men who had appeared at Gandhi's ashram in 1944 in a picket attempting to stop him from meeting with Jinnah, and he had been a member of various Hindu extremist groups. His motive was his resentment of Gandhi's sympathy for Muslims, and he also hated non-violence and all that the spinning-wheel stood for; in his view Gandhi was weakening Hindu society.

The assassination had political repercussions. A professor in Bombay who had been trying to help Madanlal Pahwa was shocked when he read that the young refugee from Pakistan had been arrested for the first attack. He remembered Pahwa's talking of a conspiracy to assassinate Gandhi and had informed the authorities, alerting leading members of the Bombay government to the plot. The information was passed on to Patel who spoke to Gandhi, but Gandhi refused to have a police presence at his prayer meetings or to allow attendees to be searched for weapons. Leads to other conspirators were not followed up, leaving them free to launch their second attack. Patel's poor handling of the case discredited him and weakened him in his battles with Nehru. He would never regain his earlier prestige.

As the messages of condolence from all parts of the world pouring into India demonstrated, whatever differences people may have had with Gandhi, he had been the best-known and most respected Hindu on earth. The nation had lost one of her greatest assets. Some weeks after his death, in his inimitable style, both intimate and grandiloquent, Nehru wrote an article for Gandhi's newspaper *Harijan*: 'Our memories of him will be of the Master, whose step was light to the end, whose smile was infectious and whose eyes were full of laughter. We shall associate no failing powers with him of body or mind. He lived as he died at the top of his strength and powers, leaving a picture in our minds and in the mind of the age that we live in that can never fade away.'[86]

Legacy

The most trenchant criticism of Gandhi and Gandhism came, perhaps unsurprisingly, from the man who murdered him, Nathuram Godse. He chose the role of assassin, fully expecting to be caught and making no plans to escape, precisely because the trial would give him a platform from which to condemn Gandhi. He spoke for five hours in English on 8 November 1948. Gandhi would have wryly acknowledged that his killer had used a very Gandhian trick: accepting a punishment for an action he considered righteous, in order to use the resulting trial as a vehicle for his ideas.

Born in 1910 to a Brahmin family in Maharashtra, Godse was an early follower of Gandhi. A committed nationalist, he was also a supporter of Hindu reform: 'I publicly joined anti-caste movements and maintained that all Hindus should be treated with equal status as to rights, social and religious, and should be high or low on merit alone'; he used to attend anti-caste dinners in which thousands of Hindus broke intercaste rules by dining together.[1] He subsequently joined pro-Hindu organisations and came under the influence of Savarkar, who gave him funding to start a newspaper to propagate their views.

He could not object to Gandhi's principles of truth and non-violence: 'No sensible or enlightened person could object to these slogans. In fact there is nothing new or original in them. They are implicit in every constitutional public movement.' But it was a mere dream, he went on, to consider that non-violence could apply to every situation, when honour, duty, love of family and of one's country might require force. Gandhi was, 'paradoxical as it may appear, a violent pacifist who brought untold calamities on the country in the name of truth and non-violence'.[2]

Godse praised Gandhi's work in South Africa, but said when he returned to India

> he developed a subjective mentality under which he alone was to be the final judge of what was right or wrong. If the country wanted his leadership, it had to accept his infallibility . . . either Congress had to surrender its will to his and had to be content with playing second fiddle to all his eccentricity, whimsicality, metaphysics and primitive vision, or it had to carry on without him. He alone was the judge of everything and everyone . . . 'A satyagrahi can never fail' was his formula for declaring his own infallibility and nobody except himself knew what a satyagrahi was. Thus the Mahatma became the judge and counsel in his own cause. These childish inanities and obstinacies, coupled with a most severe austerity of life, ceaseless work and lofty character made Gandhi formidable and irresistible.[3]

Far from being the father of the nation, according to Godse Gandhi had encouraged and appeased the Muslims, assisted them in dismembering the nation; he was not the father of India, but the father of Pakistan. He felt Gandhi's was a continuing malign influence on the government and the only way to stop him was to kill him. Despite requests for clemency by Manilal and Ramdas Gandhi, Godse and Apte were hanged on 15 November 1949.

Godse's reading of the situation could not have been more wrong. Gandhi had been a declining influence at least since the blunder of the Quit India campaign. The success of his fast for the immediate payment of the money owed to Pakistan was probably his last gasp. His next move was going to be to call for Congress to disband as a political party and for its supporters to dedicate themselves to good works around the country. His expectations of high-mindedness among politicians would surely have been disappointed: few people who had fought for so long for political independence would renounce the opportunity of power, not to mention personal position and wealth. The decline in his status was set to continue.

Politically, the most important thing Godse did in martyring Gandhi was to discredit the Hindu hardliners, who were not to revive their fortunes for another fifty years. It was not until 2002 that the Hindu Bharatiya Janata Party (BJP) felt able to acknowledge Gandhi's old adversary Vinayak Savarkar as its hero and cult figure. In terms of Gandhi's reputation, Godse's act completed the process of deifying his victim. Gandhi is an enduring symbol of India; along with Buddha he is one of two Indians of whom everyone has heard, whose image can be immediately brought to mind.

Gandhi was always proud of his achievements, many of which have stood the test of time. In the modernist first decade of the twentieth century his ideas looked out of date, particularly to such progressives as Nehru. But the twenty-first century brought a world in which many ideas of his that had been considered eccentric have become mainstream. Gandhi would find common cause in the developed world with his intolerance of smoking, which he considered worse than drinking alcohol; it is certainly less well tolerated in Europe today. His dietary experiments were in his own times the mark of an oddity. Today many millions of people pay minute attention to details of diet such as eating no more than a certain number of calories a day, eating only single kinds of food, eating no carbohydrates, eating five vegetables a day and other seemingly endless permutations. Gandhi could certainly be a modern dietitian, and such qualities of his as thrift and self-reliance have made a comeback as virtues, now being represented as saving the planet.

Gandhi is enduringly remembered for public fasting, a spiritual exercise that he adapted for political ends. He successfully fasted for peace in Calcutta but also fasted when members of his ashram were guilty of what he considered to be moral lapses by finding each other attractive. When he engaged on the 'epic fast' for a joint electorate for the caste Hindus and the untouchables he was successful not because of his spiritual purity but because there would have been a massacre of untouchables had he died in what he saw as their cause.

Controlled fasting is a standard practice in major religions. Those who attempt a fast unto death to attain political ends, however, have usually been linked to terrorist organisations such as the Irish Republican Army, the Tamil Tigers and animal-rights militants. The act of fasting is associated with the militancy of violence contained, a violence that can do no more damage but turn in on itself. The power of the faster is that of the anorexic or the voluntary mute, who has control over a tiny area, that of their own body functions, and determines to dominate it to an extreme degree. In the end fasting to death is an aggressive act, like the suicide who says: 'I will really hurt myself and then you will be sorry.' Gandhi has had few imitators in this field, and governments have generally been prepared to see fasters die rather than concede.

The week before Indian independence Gandhi wrote: 'So long as my faith burns bright, as I hope it will even if I stand alone, I shall be alive in the grave and what is more speaking from it.'[4] No friend to false modesty, he said: 'If I can say so without arrogance and with due humility, my message and method are indeed in their essentials for the whole world.'[5] In fact it took some time for him to apply his message of equal human rights more widely than just to Indians of his own class. His argument in South Africa was that the white political masters should treat Indians more like themselves in terms of political rights, and less like the native Africans; in this he showed a tacit acceptance of African inferiority. As time passed, however, Gandhi was to see other nationalist campaigns in the same light as his own. In 1944 he was arguing that 'freedom for India will bring hope to Asiatics and other exploited nations. Today there is no hope for the Negroes, but Indian freedom will fill them with hope.'[6]

The American civil rights movement came to cite Gandhi as a godfather. African-Americans had been reading about his message of righteous resistance in such periodicals as *The Crisis* since the 1920s. Martin Luther King, sometimes referred to as the 'black Gandhi', spent a month in India in 1959. 'To other countries I may go as a tourist. But to India I come as a pilgrim,' he said.[7] As a young man, having heard a lecture on Gandhi, he went out to buy half a dozen books on his life and works. These taught him, he said, that the Christian injunction to non-violence, which he had felt to be valid only in conflicts between individuals, could be applied to racial groups in conflict with nations. He interpreted Gandhi's message as 'non-violent resistance to evil'. When he went as a pastor to Montgomery, Alabama, and found himself spokesman of the civil rights movement, he said he was driven back to the Sermon on the Mount and the Gandhian method.[8]

Nelson Mandela cites Gandhi's influence in his battle against apartheid in South Africa. Gandhi was 'the archetypal anticolonial revolutionary. His strategy of noncooperation, his assertion that we can be dominated only if we cooperate with our dominators, and his nonviolent resistance inspired anticolonial and antiracist movements internationally in our century.'[9] Gandhi's ideals were the inspiring force for nationalist movements on the African continent up to the 1960s. He conceded, however, that the African National Congress had been able to take Gandhi's ideals only so far, maintaining a non-violent resistance as long as possible but then feeling constrained to launch a guerrilla war in 1961 with its founding of the Spear of the Nation wing. It was for his involvement with this organisation that Mandela suffered imprisonment for more than a quarter of a century before being freed to become the first president of a democratic South Africa.

Gandhi did not value sexual diversity any more than did the average conservative of his time, which makes it ironic that some of the most quintessentially Gandhian protests have been sexual. After the arrest of two men for kissing in public in central London, the homosexual activist group OutRage! staged a kiss-in at the statue of Eros in Piccadilly Circus in September 1990 in which, in an ultimate act of non-violent civil disobedience, demonstrators simply kissed, thereby challenging the police to do their worst, secure in the knowledge that any act of repression would reflect badly on the authorities. Similarly, the filmmaker Michael Moore, for a television programme he was making, drove a 'sodomobile' through US states where sodomy laws were still in place, proclaiming that forbidden acts were going on in the van. Clearly, any action to enforce such absurd laws would bring ridicule on the authorities while generating publicity for Moore. The spirit of Gandhi's salt protest shines through such prankish gestures of defiance.

The Campaign for Nuclear Disarmament too likes to consider Gandhi a spiritual godfather even though, he explained to a journalist, he very much doubted that the advent of the atomic era would basically affect human problems.[10] Pressed on the matter he later said: 'Ahimsa is a mightier weapon by far than the atom bomb. Even if the people of

Hiroshima could have died in their thousands with prayer and good-will in their hearts, the situation would have been transformed as if by a miracle.'[11] Gandhi cannot be challenged for not having all the answers to a nuclear arms race that had hardly begun when he died, but this points up a recurrent failing in his perception: his moral vision was profound, but it was about individual fulfilment. He could conceive of personal animosity, but genocidal destruction was beyond his understanding. Confronted with massive evil – the Armenian massacres, the Japanese massacres, the Nazi Holocaust – his philosophy faltered. It offered endless suffering but no salvation. Gandhi was a great nationalist, but his adversary Churchill was a better role model for the challenges the world's nations faced in the 1930s.

Gandhi's contribution was an approach that worked where there was a common principle and an expectation of civil obedience; where there was a legal framework in which courts showed at least a pretence to objectivity; where there was a standard of common decency to which he could appeal; where there was a free press to publicise injustice and a population concerned about it; where his opponents' ranks contained sympathisers with the nationalist cause who were free to express their views. In the case of India he was operating in a situation where the British had already conceded the principle of ultimate independence; the question was when it would take place. There was no comparison to life under a totalitarian state; Gandhi's suggestion of a moral equivalence between the democracies and the Axis Powers shows he did not know or was not interested in knowing what real dictatorship was.

In turning his back on the Western constitutional model of nationalist progress embraced by Jinnah and insisting on a village model, Gandhi promoted division among the nationalists. His ideas, his belief in the action of spiritual forces working on the elements here on earth, his apocalyptic notions of what independence would achieve, all played well in the countryside but they were not the stuff of statesmanship.

Aside from the democide of the partition process itself and of the Bangladesh conflict, partition was disastrous for the subcontinent for long-term reasons. Partition was also an administrative catastrophe: it destroyed the military, economic and administrative unity developed by the British over more than a century. One result of this has been the poor economic performance of Pakistan as compared to India; Pakistan has become the underdeveloped theocratic state that Gandhi hoped India would be. Partition did not even end the communal problems in India; communal violence has taken place every year since independence and there is evidence the situation is getting worse. India and Pakistan have fought a war almost every decade since independence, and both are now armed with nuclear weapons.

Was Gandhi in any way responsible for partition, the primary charge levelled by his assassin? Indian nationalists were equipped with two misconceptions, which Gandhi fostered: that communal tension was a result of the imperial system, and that the East was spiritually elevated as compared to the West. Gandhi explained: 'It is the British statesmen who are responsible for the divisions in India's ranks, and the divisions will continue so long as the British sword holds India under bondage.'[12] Indian nationalists witnessing communal cruelties consoled themselves with the fiction that Hindu–Muslim disunity was a function of a British divide-and-rule policy; without the British there would be no disunity. It did not take a very profound thinker to realise that the disunity had to be present in the first place, to be exploited by a ruler.

Gandhi, his followers and such spiritual adventurers as Annie Besant and Charles Andrews had promoted the notion of Indian moral superiority. This suffered a collapse in the very first days of the new nation, when atrocities took place worse than anything that had happened under the British Raj. Muslims, Sikhs and Hindus behaved as badly as each other; none were distinguished by the restraint of their creeds or the control of responsible leadership. Gandhi's contribution to peacekeeping was courageous and welcome, but in most places there was no Gandhi, or he arrived after the massacres. It is a grim truth, but it was not the spiritual superiority of the East and the ethical demise of the West that became apparent in the events of the 1940s, but a rather more sobering fact: the moral oneness of humanity – each is as bad as the other.

These misconceptions meant that the very basis on which nationalists operated – that everything would be for the best after independence – was grievously wrong. The cynical British and the determined Jinnah had a better grip on life's realities. For Gandhi, politics was the art of the impossible – the centuries-old conflicts between Hindus and

Muslims could be reconciled within a united India by imposing a morally improved model of village relationships. More experienced politicians begged him to accept a solution to India's constitutional problems. The creation of Pakistan had been rejected by the cabinet mission because it would not solve the communal problem – a grouping of provinces into Muslim-majority areas was preferred. Whether 'grouping' would have worked it is not possible to tell, but we do know that Jinnah would be dead within thirteen months of independence. Had the cabinet mission's scheme been in place, even with Jinnah *wishing* to secede his Muslim-majority provinces from the rest of India, without his skill and determination perhaps Pakistan would not have been created. Gandhi certainly bears some responsibility for refusing to back the cabinet mission's proposal until it was too late, by which time the creation of Pakistan was inevitable.

Gandhi has to take responsibility for the Muslims' *wanting* Pakistan so badly that they were willing to dismember India to get it. He could be said to be responsibile for the Hinduisation of politics, making Muslims feel increasingly isolated within a nation where the Hindu majority hoped for a return of the Rama Raj. Gandhi's political objectives were tied up with the reform of Hinduism. His achievement was in bringing the masses of the Hindu devout into politics; his failure was in linking independence so closely with goals of Hindu reform that there was no place, politically, for the huge minority of Muslims or for the untouchables, for whom Hinduism offered no boons, only curses. Worse was his suffusing Indian politics in a religious haze so that everything had to be interpreted in terms of spiritual attainment – an atmosphere that alienated Jinnah and other secular politicians but empowered hypocrites whose mouthing of religious sentiments proved sufficient for advancement.

Gandhi's work on behalf of untouchables, the other large minority in India, bore fruit, but not in the way he expected. In resisting a separate electorate for untouchables he wanted Hindus to realise their spiritual obligations to this despised class and embrace them. What has happened subsequently has been grounded rather more in self-interest. In Gandhi's time, the untouchables were a small percentage of the total population of united India. The 'depressed castes' constitute about 20 per cent of the population of modern India. Their needs cannot be ignored by politicians hoping to be elected; political parties need to have untouchables on their slate if they want to claim to be representative of local populations. A separate electorate, as requested by Gandhi's adversary B.R. Ambedkar, would have confirmed their assumed difference; the joint electorate undermines it.

Ambedkar drafted the constitution of India to outlaw the practice of untouchability, and great progress has been made in the cities. Ironically, it is in Gandhi's idealised villages that the 'sin of untouchability' is most apparent in today's India. His anti-industrial model of Indian life was not accepted by other nationalist leaders: Nehru, for instance, pushed on with nationwide industrialisation and with an ambitious nuclear programme. India's economic strength is now a matter for national pride. It has given great satisfaction to Indians that the richest man in Britain at the beginning of the twenty-first century was the Indian industrialist Lakshmi Mittal; and the Indian Tata Group took over the once mighty British steel industry in 2007. Tata family members had been contributing to Gandhi's work since his days in South Africa. A future of industrialisation and concomitant prosperity was not one that Gandhi predicted for India, or desired. It would appal him that between 15 and 25 per cent of Indians (depending on the criteria used) still live in abject poverty; but it can give quiet satisfaction to his successors that, whatever measurement is used, this figure has been falling rapidly since the mid-1970s, in keeping with industrial growth.

To the public, Gandhi is better known from Richard Attenborough's adulatory *Gandhi* rather than from Feroz Abbas Khan's film *Gandhi My Father*, which described his troubled relationship with his family. If Gandhi is any kind of role model, it is not as a husband and father. He behaved worst towards Kasturba, badly towards his sons and not always well towards his friends and supporters, but wonderfully towards people he did not know, and with an outflowing of spontaneous benevolence towards those toiling masses that he would never know in person.

His poor treatment of his own children stemmed from a disgust at the carnality of their creation, as if he saw in his own sons nothing but the embodiment of the copulatory urge that had to be tamed. As noted earlier, Gandhi's resentment against his own childhood marriage was that it obliged him to explore his sexuality before he had the opportunity to renounce it and address his spiritual nature. A soul contaminated with sex, even in youth, needed higher levels of discipline to purify it than could be achieved by simple abstinence as an adult. Gandhi's sexual preoccupations were well known and were already damaging his reputation when he was alive. The Congress Party hierarchy warned him of this as did members of his entourage and others who worked for him, including those left to edit his newspaper while he was in Noakhali, who resigned rather than print Gandhi's own reports of his sexual behaviour. Some of his supporters, including Nehru, could overlook his sexual peccadilloes or treat them with exasperated tolerance, but his opponents would not. Sir C.P. Ramaswami Iyer, prime minister of Travancore, told Mountbatten that Gandhi was 'a most dangerous, semi-repressed sex maniac'.[13] This was no passing insult: the premier was negotiating to prevent the riches of his state, including thorium deposits, falling into the hands of a Congress Party that had put itself in thrall to a man such as Gandhi.

Gandhi's musing on sex was not occasional or cursory: his accounts were frequent and detailed. His amanuensis Pyarelal, knowing he would himself be criticised, defended his dwelling on brahmacharya in writing about Gandhi on the grounds that it was 'fundamental and integral to Gandhiji's philosophy of life, and on account of the great importance he himself attached to it and his own injunction to me in that behalf'.[14] Gandhi was very clear as to the relative importance he placed on his political as compared to his spiritual life: 'My mahatmaship is worthless. It is due to my outward activities, due to my politics, which is the least part of me and is therefore evanescent. What is of abiding worth is my insistence on truth, non-violence and brahmacharya.'[15]

Gandhi's thoughts and writings were suffused with sex. In dealing with it so publicly he was very much in tune with the last part of the twentieth century and the beginning of the twenty-first, which have seen the increasing sexualisation of society. The difference is that, though Gandhi's discourse was apparently aiming to discourage sex, he referred to it constantly, so sex was ever present.

If 'having sex' means genital penetration, then for the last forty years of his life Gandhi was, as he would have put it, pure. But if we think of the sex urge as becoming more generalised with age, he was not. Had Gandhi spent more time understanding sex rather than suppressing it, he might have noticed that for men in their later years, with declining testosterone production, sex tends to become more diffused. Where for a young man penetration and ejaculation are imperative, a less specific eroticism seems sufficient for elderly men – the sound of women's voices, a female touch, the sight of nakedness. One could, of course, argue that it is because old men have less opportunity for active sex that they have to be satisfied with less. However it is viewed, Gandhi certainly maximised his sexual opportunities; in his terms, he did so in order that his renunciation might be all the more pronounced – to the disdain of Congress colleagues who were more men of the world than he. Gandhi in his sixties and seventies, with his daily naked massages, joint bathing and young women bedfellows, was getting a good deal more intimate female contact than any but sex industry moguls and rich sybarites do. The honest Sushila, whose concept of truth corresponded more closely to an accepted norm than did Gandhi's, made the point that his sleeping with women came first, while the notion that it was some kind of a spiritual experiment emerged after his behaviour had been challenged. Sushila died only in 2001, unmarried; in her sixties she transferred her spiritual affections to another guru, Sathya Sai Baba. Abha died at sixty-eight in 1995; she and her husband Kanu Gandhi had devoted their lives to running the Kasturba Ashram, one of the few memorials to Kasturba. Manu Gandhi married one Surandra Mashruwala, and died in 1969 at the age of forty.

While there are celibates in the Hindu as in the Christian religion, Gandhi was remarkable for the importance he attributed to celibacy. The impact of his sexual experiments and of his views on chastity on the world, however, has been nil or has worked to the detriment of his teachings. His admirers normally revere his non-violence, but not the chastity that he considered a supremely important aspect of his life. Gandhi was explicit about what people must do who would follow his path, and why they should do it. He recognised that truth can be a subjective matter, so anyone seeking after truth – which he identified with God – must standardise his or her conditions, just as conditions in a scientific experiment have to be standardised in order that that experiment can take place. He declared: 'Those who would make diligent search after Truth – God – must go through these vows: the vow of truth – speaking and thinking of truth – the vow of brahmacharya, of non-violence, poverty and non-possession. If you do not take these five vows you may not embark on the experiment.'[16]

His wish to divest himself of the things of this world led him to an ostentatious poverty, a kind of show pauperism that had to be underwritten by his wealthy backers, as it had to be kept on the road during Gandhi's travels around India in specially hired trains with only third-class carriages. 'If only Bapu knew the cost of setting him up in poverty' was Sarojini Naidu's oft-repeated remark.[17] The ultimate criticism that might be made of Gandhi is that of pettiness: there is always the suspicion that his preoccupation with clothes, food and sexual abstinence was a waste of his great gifts. To such a challenge he would have replied that his body was the instrument of his teachings and that he had to refine that instrument.

Gandhi is widely seen as having secured Indian independence, and he was certainly the best-known of India's leaders at the time of independence. His principles of non-violence are more often cited as moral exemplars than put into practice, but they nonetheless have been an inspiration to others. His renunciation of sex, alcohol and even interesting food did not spawn a world of imitators. His resistance to racism and an appreciation of the value of all religions, however, strikes a thoroughly modern note. As a man, he is most remarkable for making every day, perhaps every minute, a matter of reaching forward, for never settling in any one place in his long, intricate spiritual journey.

He never gave up. In his seventies he was still striving, feeling that his vision of truth and non-violence 'is becoming clearer day by day'.[18] He was ultimately heroic, the metaphysical warrior. As he declared defiantly in the forests of Noakhali when he had less than a year to live: 'The whole world may forsake me but I dare not leave what I hold is the truth for me. It may be a delusion and a snare. If so, I must realise it myself. I have risked perdition before now. Let this be reality if it has to be.'[19]

Notes

ABBREVIATIONS

Autobiography M.K. Gandhi *An Autobiography or The Story of My Experiments with Truth*

CW *Collected Works of Mahatma Gandhi*; references list volume number followed by page, e.g. CW 80 p. 209

Satyagraha M.K. Gandhi *Satyagraha in South Africa*

INTRODUCTION

1 *Collected Works of Mahatma Gandhi* (New Delhi: Publications Division, Ministry of Information and Broadcasting, Government of India, vols 1–100) 1958–97. CW 80 p. 209 c. 30 May 1945

2 Gandhi said of the title often given to him: 'The word "Mahatma" has been invoked in order to get drunk with it and commit many a wicked crime. That word "Mahatma" stinks in my nostrils and when, in addition, somebody insists that everybody should call me "Mahatma", I get sick to the saturation point and life becomes unbearable.' Mahadev Desai *Day to Day with Gandhi: Secretary's Diary* vol. 4 1968–9 (Varanasi: Sarva Seva Sangh Prakashan) p. 152 31 August 1924. The 'mahatma' title is avoided in this biography as a matter of course, along with other honorifics such as pandit, maulana, sardar and so on.

3 Thomas Weber *On the Salt March* (New Delhi: HarperCollins) 1997 recounts the historiography of the event.

4 *CW* 90 Foreword

5   M.K. Gandhi *An Autobiography or The Story of My Experiments with Truth* (London: Penguin) 1982 p. 16.

6   *CW* 8 8 February 1908

7   Sushila Nayar *Mahatma Gandhi* vol. 7 *Preparing for Swaraj* (Ahmedabad: Navajivan) 1996 p. 19

8   *CW* 21 p. 61 6 October 1921

9   *CW* 51 p. 343 4 November 1932

10   *CW* 80 p. 77 6 May 1945

11   Pyarelal, *Mahatma Gandhi* vol. 9 *The Last Phase* part 1 (Ahmedabad: Navajivan) 1997 p. 60

12   *CW* 55 p. 61 29 April 1933

13   *CW* 70 p. 203 25 September 1939

14   *CW* 70 p. 181 18 September 1939

15   M.K. Gandhi *Hind Swaraj or Indian Home Rule* (Ahmedabad: Navajivan) 1938 p. 53

16   *CW* 9 p. 446 1 October 1909

17   *Autobiography* p. 14

18   *CW* 23 p. 349 3 April 1924

1 CHILDHOOD AND MARRIAGE

1   *CW* 1 p. 40 4 April 1991

2   *Autobiography* p. 19

3   *Autobiography* p. 15

4   V.G. Desai *The Diary of Mahadev Desai* (Ahmedabad: Navajivan) 1953 vol. 1 p. 51

5   *Autobiography* p. 20 and passim

6   Pyarelal *Mahatma Gandhi* vol. 1 *The Early Phase* (Ahmedabad: Navajivan) 1965 quoting *Young India* 27 April 1921

7   Pyarelal *Early Phase* p. 215

8   *Autobiography* p. 23 and passim

9   Arun Gandhi *Daughter of Midnight: The Child Bride of Gandhi* (London: Blake) 1998 p. 12

10   *Autobiography* p. 26; other intimate details of the marriage, passim.

11   *Autobiography* p. 35

12   *CW* 72 p. 127 after 3 June 1940

13   Ibid.

14   *Autobiography* p. 37

15   *Autobiography* p. 41

16 Pyarelal *Early Phase* p. 44 and passim
17 *CW* 1 p. 54 13 June 1891
18 *Autobiography* p. 51
19 *CW* 1 p. 57 13 June 1891
20 *CW* 1 p. 4 (digital version, not in *CW* first edition) 12 November 1888
21 *Autobiography* p. 51 and passim
22 *CW* 1 p. 58 13 June 1891
23 *Autobiography* p. 53
24 *CW* 1 p. 59 13 June 1891
25 *Autobiography* p. 54
26 *CW* 1 p. 10 (digital version) 4 September 1888

2 LONDON LESSONS

1 *Autobiography* p. 58
2 *Autobiography* p. 87
3 *Autobiography* p. 59
4 James D. Hunt *Gandhi in London* (New Delhi: Promilla & Co.) 1978 p. 27
5 Pyarelal *Early Phase* p. 262
6 *CW* 1 p. 32 28 February 1891
7 *Autobiography* p. 67
8 *Autobiography* p. 63
9 Guy A. Aldred 'Gandhi, Pacifism and India' in *Gandhi Murder Trial: The Word Quarterly* spring 1950 p. 6
10 *Autobiography* p. 63
11 Pyarelal *Early Phase* p. 252
12 Hunt *Gandhi* p. 7
13 Pyarelal *Mahatma Gandhi* vol. 3 *The Birth of Satyagraha: From Petitioning to Passive Resistance* (Ahmedabad: Navajivan) 1986 p. 114
14 Mahadev Desai *Day to Day with Gandhi* (Varanasi: Sarva Seva Sangh Prakashan) 1968-9 vol. 4 p. 243
15 Munni Rawal *Dadabhai Naoroji: A Prophet of Indian Nationalism* (New Delhi: Anmol Publications) 1989 p. 13
16 Rawal *Prophet* p. 14
17 *Autobiography* p. 69
18 *CW* 1 p. 29 21 February 1891,
19 A.F. Hills *Essays on Vegetarianism* (London: Ideal Publishing Union) 1894 p. 247
20 Hills *Vegetarianism* p. 79

21   Hills *Vegetarianism* p. 81
22   *Autobiography* p. 70
23   *Autobiography* p. 80
24   *Autobiography* p. 75
25   *CW* 16 p. 201 1 October 1919
26   Hunt *Gandhi* p. 34
27   *CW* 93 p. 228 3 January 1947
28   *Autobiography* p. 93
29   *CW* 1 p. 52 13 June 1891
30   *CW* 1 87 28 April 1894
31   *CW* 1 p. 64 9 April 1892

3 ADVENTURES IN NATAL

1   Arun Gandhi *Daughter of Midnight: The Child Bride of Gandhi* (London: Blake)1998 p. 46 and *Autobiography* p. 92
2   *Autobiography* p. 95
3   *Autobiography* p. 98
4   *Autobiography* p. 101 and passim
5   Pyarelal *Early Phase* p. 298
6   *Autobiography* p. 115
7   *Autobiography* p. 120
8   *Autobiography* p. 133
9   Pyarelal *Early Phase* p. 303
10   *Autobiography* p. 126
11   *Autobiography* p. 126
12   *Autobiography* p. 137
13   Maureen Swan *Gandhi: The South African Experience* (Johannesburg: Raven Press) 1985 p. 49
14   *Autobiography* p. 138
15   *CW* 2 p. 74 Address in Bombay 26 September 1896. One month later he used the same notion, referring to 'the policy of degrading the Indian to the level of a raw kaffir'. *CW* 2 p. 100
16   *CW* 1 p. 202 Petition to Lord Ripon May 1895
17   M.K. Gandhi *Satyagraha in South Africa* (Ahmedabad: Navajivan) 1950 p. 9
18   *Autobiography* p. 200
19   *Autobiography* p. 151
20   Swan *Experience* p. 47
21   *CW* 2 p. 317 before 21 May 1897

22   *Autobiography* p. 153

23   *Autobiography* p. 159

24   *CW* 72 p. 127 after 3 June 1940

25   *Autobiography* p. 157

26   Pyarelal *Mahatma Gandhi* vol. 2 *The Discovery of Satyagraha – On the Threshold* (Ahmedabad: Navajivan) 1980 p. 6

27   Gandhi *Satyagraha* p. 47

28   *Autobiography* p. 181

29   Swan *Experience* p. 66

30   *Autobiography* p. 183

31   *Autobiography* p. 191

32   *Autobiography* pp. 255–6

33   *Autobiography* p. 202

34   *CW* 1 pp. 165–6 1 February 1895

35   *CW* 1 p. 139 3 December 1894

36   *CW* 1 p. 166 1 February 1895

37   *CW* 1 p. 90 June 1894

38   *Autobiography* p. 194

39   Vere Stent quoted in Appendix VII of C.F. Andrews *Mahatma Gandhi's Ideas* (London: Allen & Unwin) 1931 p. 364

40   *Autobiography* p. 209

4 CHALLENGE AND CHASTITY

1   M.K. Gandhi, *Gokhale, My Political Guru* (Ahmedabad: Navajivan) 1955 p. 47

2   *CW* 3 p. 214 27 December 1901

3   *Autobiography* p. 222

4   *Autobiography* p. 226

5   *Autobiography* p. 232

6   The eventual solution was a clumsy arrangement whereby South Africa became a dominion of the British Empire but each of the four colonies retained its own capital, legislature and administrators.

7   Gandhi *Satyagraha* p. 78

8   *Autobiography* p. 245

9   *CW* 6 p. 430 *c.*20 April 1907. In fact he says: 'My family comprises all living beings'.

10   Pyarelal *Mahatma Gandhi* vol. 3 *The Birth of Satyagraha: From Petitioning to Passive Resistance* (Ahmedabad: Navajivan) 1986 p. 370

11   *CW* 5 p. 334 27 May 1906
12   Pyarelal *Birth* p. 358
13   Pyarelal *Birth* p. 26
14   Pyarelal *Birth* p. 439
15   *CW* 6 p. 308 *Indian Opinion* 2 February 1907
16   *CW* 6 p. 270 5 January 1907
17   *Autobiography* p. 85
18   Swan *Experience* p. 112
19   *CW* 3 p. 453 24 September 1903
20   *Autobiography* p. 274
21   Pyarelal *Birth* p. 435
22   *CW* 96 p. 32 14 November 1909
23   *Autobiography* p. 289
24   Gandhi *Satyagraha* p. 91 and *Autobiography* p. 289
25   Desai *Day to Day* vol. 4 p. 249
26   *CW* 7 p. 457. *Indian Opinion* 28 December 1907
27   *Autobiography* p. 197
28   *Autobiography* p. 299
29   *Autobiography* p. 23
30   *CW* 6 p. 34 27 October 1906
31   Pyarelal *Mahatma Gandhi* vol. 1 *The Early Phase* (Ahmedabad: Navajivan)
     1965 p. 550
32   *CW* 9 p. 230 29 May 1909
33   *CW* 96 p. 13 3 July 1909

5 THE ARMY OF THE POOR

1   Louis Fischer *The Life of Mahatma Gandhi* (London: Jonathan Cape) 1951 p.
     72
2   Lionel Curtis *Civitas Dei* (London: Macmillan) 1934–7 vol. 1 p. 164
3   J.C. Smuts *Jan Christian Smuts* (London: Cassell) 1952 p. 106
4   *CW* 5 p. 417 9 September 1906
5   *CW* 5 p. 441 22 September 1906
6   Gandhi *Satyagraha* p. 97
7   *CW* 7 p. 72 6 July 1907
8   *CW* 4 p. 105 14 January 1904
9   Gandhi *Satyagraha* p. 101
10   Sushila Nayar *Mahatma Gandhi* vol. 4: *Satyagraha at Work* (Ahmedabad:
     Navajivan) 1989 p. 122

11 *CW* 96 pp. 9, 25 21 June 1909 and 30 August 1909

12 Nayar *Satyagraha at Work* p. 463

13 *CW* 96 pp. 25, 26 30 August 1909 and 10 September 1909

14 Gandhi *Satyagraha* p. 165

15 *CW* 8 p. 24 note to 10 January 1908

16 *CW* 84 p. 295 6 June 1946

17 George Paxton *Sonja Schlesin: Gandhi's South African Secretary* (Glasgow: Pax Books) 2006 p. 10. Schlesin's speech was in fact read by Gandhi.

18 *CW* 6 p. 30 26 October 1906

19 *CW* 6 p. 336 23 February 1907

20 *CW* 7 p. 230 14 September 1907

21 *CW* 8 pp. 3–4 4 January 1908

22 *CW* 8 p. 99 22 February 1908

23 Gandhi *Satyagraha* p. 141

24 Reproduced in *CW* 7 opposite p. 441

25 *CW* 7 p. 443 21 December 1907

26 Swan *Experience* p. 162

27 Sarah Gertrude Millin *General Smuts* vol. 1 (London: Faber & Faber) 1936 p. 238

28 Gandhi *Satyagraha* p. 147

29 Ibid.

30 Gandhi *Satyagraha* p. 157

31 *CW* 9 p. 149 16 January 1909

32 *CW* 8 p. 120 7 March 1908

33 *CW* 8 p. 135 7 March 1908

34 *CW* 9 p. 161 23 January 1909

35 Arun Gandhi *Daughter of Midnight: The Child Bride of Gandhi* (London: Blake) 1998 p. 158

36 *CW* 10 p. 447 letter to Maganlal 9 March 1911

37 *CW* 96 pp. 182–3 to Kallenbach 12 April 1914

38 Gandhi *Satyagraha* p. 214

39 Henri Troyat *Tolstoy* (London: Penguin) 1970 p. 874. Gandhi had a long letter from Tolstoy printed and distributed as 'Letter to a Hindu'; it criticised Indians for their compliance in accepting British rule.

40 Gandhi *Satyagraha* p. 222

41 Gandhi *Satyagraha* p. 217

42 *CW* 10 p. 282 2 July 1910

43 *Autobiography* p. 309

44 Narendra Singh Sarila *Once a Prince of Sarila* (London: I.B. Tauris) 2008 p. 30; Gandhi *Satyagraha* p. 242

45   Gandhi *Satyagraha* p. 223

46   *CW* 9 p. 495 22 October 1909

47   *CW* 12 p. 190 18 September 1913

48   *CW* 10 p. 429 5 March 1911

49   Arun Gandhi *Daughter of Midnight* p. 175

50   *CW* 11 p. 78 18 May 1911

51   Sushila Nayar *Mahatma Gandhi* vol. 5 *India Awakened* (Ahmedabad: Navajivan) 1994 p. 243

52   *Autobiography* p. 313. Recalling the fasts thirty years later, he wrote: 'Manilal was guilty of a grave error, for which I fasted for seven days and missed a meal every day for a year. I fasted for fourteen days on account of Jeki.' *CW* 72 p. 143 c.6 June 1940

53   Nayar *Satyagraha at Work* p. 599

54   *CW* 12 p. 410 22 April 1914

55   *CW* 96 p. 189 13 May 1914

56   Kathryn Tidrick *Gandhi: A Political and Spiritual Life* (London: I.B. Tauris) 2006 p. 97

57   *CW* 6 p. 431 c.20 April 1907

58   Yogesh Chadha *Rediscovering Gandhi* (London: Century) 1997 p. 145

59   Arun Gandhi *Daughter of Midnight* p. 167

60   Gandhi *Satyagraha* p. 227

61   Arun Gandhi *Daughter of Midnight* p. 176

62   Gandhi *Satyagraha* p. 244

63   Gandhi *Satyagraha* p. 257

64   Gandhi *Satyagraha* p. 259

65   *CW* 96 p. 150 23 October 1913

66   Chadha *Rediscovering* p. 183

67   Gandhi *Satyagraha* p. 271

68   C.F. Andrews *Mahatma Gandhi's Ideas* (London: Allen & Unwin) 1931 p. 194

69   Chadha *Rediscovering* p. 191

6 VILLAGE ACTIVIST

1   Gandhi *Hind Swaraj* p. ix

2   Chadha *Rediscovering* p. 146

3   *CW* 9 p. 508 30 October 1909

4   *CW* 10 p. 245 11 December 1909

5   Erik H. Erikson *Gandhi's Truth: On the Origins of Militant Nonviolence* (London: Faber & Faber) 1970 p. 217

6   Gandhi, *Hind Swaraj* p. ix
7   Gandhi *Hind Swaraj* p. xii
8   Gandhi *Hind Swaraj* pp. xii, 183
9   Gandhi *Hind Swaraj* p. 59
10 Gandhi *Hind Swaraj* p. 88
11 Nayar *Satyagraha at Work* p. 497
12 Gandhi *Hind Swaraj* pp. 131, 142 & 143
13 *CW* 37 p. 380 21 October 1928
14 *CW* 43 p. 40 on or before 11 March 1930
15 Shyamji Krishnavarma *Indian Sociologist* October 1913 p. 3
16 Sushila Nayar *Mahatma Gandhi* vol. 6 *Salt Satyagraha: The Watershed* (Ahmedabad: Navajivan) 1995 p. 402
17 *CW* 10 p. 245 7 May 1910
18 Sushila Nayar *Mahatma Gandhi* vol. 5 *India Awakened* (Ahmedabad: Navajivan) 1994 p. 7
19 *CW* 12 p. 524 8 August 1914
20 *CW* 12 p. 39 19 April 1913
21 Stanley Wolpert *Jinnah of Pakistan* (New Delhi: OUP) 2005 p. 37
22 Ved Mehta *Mahatma Gandhi and His Apostles* (London: Penguin) 1977 p. 211
23 *Autobiography* p. 340
24 Gandhi *Hind Swaraj* p. v
25 *CW* 96 p. 203 2 March 1915
26 *CW* 12 p. 410 22 April 1914
27 *Autobiography* p. 352
28 *Autobiography* p. 353
29 *CW* 13 p. 54 22 April 1915
30 *CW* 13 p. 38 after 14 March 1915
31 *Autobiography* p. 358
32 C.F. Andrews *Mahatma Gandhi's Ideas* (London: Allen & Unwin) 1931 pp. 101, 105. Gandhi's response is from the more refined version: *CW* 13 p. 229 'Speech on Ashram Vows'.
33 *CW* 12 pp. 46, 50, 51 26 April 1913
34 'Celibacy undermines coupling when presented as a higher state than sexual intimacy. This, in effect, gets people in couples to surrender to the guru rather than to each other. Gurus can exercise control over their followers in the most basic areas by decreeing whether coupling is allowed, who marries whom, how often and in what circumstances sex is permitted, whether couples can cohabit, and even whether they reproduce and how to raise the children.' Joel Kramer and Diana Alstad *The Guru Papers: Masks of Authoritarian Power* (Berkeley: Frog Ltd) 1993 p. 92

35 Pyarelal *Early Phase* p. 15
36 *CW* 13 p. 232 'Speech on Ashram Vows' 16 February 1916
37 *Autobiography* p. 359
38 *CW* 13 p. 127 3 September 1915
39 *CW* 50 p. 222 11 July 1932
40 Erikson *Gandhi's Truth* p. 311
41 *CW* 96 p. 237 24 June 1916
42 Arun Gandhi *Daughter of Midnight* p. 212
43 *CW* 96 p. 240 10 September 1916
44 Nathuram Godse *Why I Assassinated Mahatma Gandhi* (New Delhi: Surya Bharti Parkashan) 1993 p. 63
45 *CW* 13 p. 214 6 February 1916
46 Raojibhai Patel *Hind Ke Sardar* (Ahmedabad: Navajivan) 1972 p. 33
47 Nayar *India Awakened* p. 147. It is said that Tagore was the first to use the term; it doubtless occurred to many people at the same time.
48 *Autobiography* p. 373
49 Erikson *Gandhi's Truth* p. 299 from his interview with Ambalal Sarabhai
50 *CW* 14 p. 256 15 March 1918
51 *CW* 14 p. 263 17 March 1918
52 Erikson *Gandhi's Truth* p. 352
53 Erikson *Gandhi's Truth* p. 356
54 Anthony Read and David Fisher *The Proudest Day: India's Long Road to Independence* (London: Jonathan Cape) 1997 p. 134
55 Rajmohan Gandhi *Gandhi: The Man, His People and the Empire* (London: Haus) 2007 p. 194
56 *Autobiography* p. 403
57 *CW* 14 p. 438 21 June 1918
58 *CW* 14 p. 440 22 June 1918
59 *CW* 13 p. 483 14 July 1918
60 *CW* 14 p. 171 24 January 1918
61 *Autobiography* p. 405
62 Nayar *India Awakened* p. 235
63 *CW* 15 p. 70 10 January 1919
64 *CW* 15 p. 65 26 November 1918

7 AROUSING INDIA

1   *CW* 15 p. 87 9 February 1919
2   *Autobiography* p. 413
3   Nayar *India Awakened* p. 262
4   *CW* 15 p. 195 7 April 1919
5   *Autobiography* p. 425
6   Jawaharlal Nehru *An Autobiography* (London: Bodley Head) 1953 p. 35
7   Jad Adams and Phillip Whitehead *The Dynasty: The Nehru–Gandhi Story* (London: Penguin) 1997 p. 55
8   Vijaya Lakshmi Pandit *The Scope of Happiness* (London: Weidenfeld & Nicolson) 1979 p. 63
9   Pandit *Happiness* p. 73
10 Nehru *Autobiography* pp. 45, 46
11 Nehru *Autobiography* p. 54
12 *CW* 31 p. 369 8 September 1926
13 *CW* 96 p. 274 17 June 1920
14 Desai *Day to Day* vol. 2 1968 p. 154
15 Desai, *Day to Day* vol. 2 p. 163
16 C.F. Andrews *Mahatma Gandhi's Ideas* (London: Allen & Unwin) 1931 p. 360
17 *CW* 18 p. 104 1 August 1920
18 *CW* 19 p. 30 26 November 1920
19 Stanley Wolpert *Jinnah of Pakistan* (New Delhi: OUP) 2005 p. 70
20 Rabindranath Tagore 'The Cult of the Chakra' *Modern Review* September 1925
21 *CW* 18 p. 130 10 August 1920
22 *CW* 16 p. 497 23 January 1920
23 *CW* 17 p. 375 2 May 1920
24 *CW* 17 p. 366 1 May 1920
25 Margaret Sanger 'A Summit Meeting on Birth Control' in Norman Cousins (ed.) *Profiles of Gandhi: America Remembers a World Leader* (New Delhi: Indian Book Company) 1969 p. 39
26 *CW* 19 p. 138 17 December 1920
27 Millie Polak in Chandrashanker Shukla (ed.) *Gandhiji As We Know Him* (Bombay: Vora & Co.) 1945 p. 47
28 Pyarelal, *Mahatma Gandhi* vol. 1 *The Early Phase* (Ahmedabad: Navajivan) 1965 p. 8
29 Pyarelal, *Early Phase* p. 7
30 Pyarelal, *Early Phase* p. 10
31 Pyarelal, *Early Phase* p. 12

32 Ibid.

33 Ibid.

34 Hugh Tinker *Viceroy: Curzon to Mountbatten* (Karachi: OUP) 1997 p. 94

35 Nayar *India Awakened* p. 354

36 *CW* 20 pp. 381–2 17 July 1921

37 Nayar *India Awakened* p. 355

38 *CW* 47 p. 307 18 August 1931

39 *CW* 21 p. 183 22 September 1921

40 *CW* 18 p. 235 8 September 1920

41 B.R. Nanda *Mahatma Gandhi: A Biography* (New Delhi: OUP) 1996 p. 234

42 *CW* 22 p. vii 8 February 1922

43 Nehru *Autobiography* pp. 81–2

44 Nehru *Autobiography* p. 85

45 *CW* 23 pp. 118–19 18 March 1922

8 THE SALT MARCH

1   Sushila Nayar *Mahatma Gandhi* vol. 5 *India Awakened* (Ahmedabad: Navajivan) 1994 p. 411

2   *CW* 23 p. 93 13 March 1922

3   Nayar *Salt Satyagraha* p. 413

4   *CW* 25 p. 200 22 September 1924

5   *CW* 35 p. 229 3 April 1926

6   *CW* 33 p. 55 8 February 1927

7   *CW* 13 p. 277 5 June 1916

8   *CW* 13 p. 301 before October 1916

9   *CW* 21 p. 188 23 September 1921

10 Mehta *Mahatma Gandhi* p. 48

11 Mehta *Mahatma Gandhi* p. 51

12 Romain Rolland *Mahatma Gandhi* (New York: Century Co.) 1924 p. 3

13 Rolland *Mahatma Gandhi* p. 239

14 M.K. Gandhi *Bapu's Letters to Mira* (Ahmedabad: Navajivan) 1949 p. 5

15 *CW* 29 p. 298 4 December 1925

16 *CW* 41 p. 78 24 June 1929

17 *CW* 47 p. 49 24 June 1931

18 *CW* 49 p. 157 25 February 1932

19 Sushila Nayar *Mahatma Gandhi* vol. 5 *India Awakened* (Ahmedabad: Navajivan) 1994 p. 243

20 Mehta *Mahatma Gandhi* p. 7

21 Mehta *Mahatma Gandhi* p. 213. There were not so many European girls close to Gandhi in South Africa; there has to be a suspicion that this was Sonja Schlesin.

22 Mehta *Mahatma Gandhi* p. 50

23 *CW* 36 p. 261 26 April 1928

24 *CW* 40 p. 210 8 April 1929

25 Nayar *Salt Satyagraha* p. 201

26 *CW* 26 p. 244 7 March 1925

27 Mehta *Mahatma Gandhi* p. 216

28 Adams and Whitehead *Dynasty* p. 79

29 Tinker *Viceroy* p. 116

30 *CW* 1 p. 25 7 February 1891

31 *CW* 11 p. 169 22 October 1911

32 *CW* 43 p. 5 2 March 1930

33 Ibid.

34 Nayar *Salt Satyagraha* p. 236

35 Thomas Weber *On the Salt March: The Historiography of Gandhi's March to Dandi* (New Delhi: HarperCollins) 1997 p. 224

36 Nayar *Salt Satyagraha* p. 257

37 *CW* 43 p. 420 25 May 1930

38 Chadha *Rediscovering* p. 296

39 Chadha *Rediscovering* p. 297

40 *CW* 51 p. 71 26 January 1931

41 Adams and Whitehead *Dynasty* p. 89

42 Martin Gilbert *Winston S. Churchill* vol. 5 *1922–1939* (London: Heinemann) 1976 p. 390

43 Gilbert *Churchill* pp. 356–7

44 Earl Birkenhead *Halifax* (London: Hamish Hamilton) 1965 p. 299

45 Birkenhead *Halifax* p. 299

46 Andrew Roberts *The Holy Fox: A Life of Lord Halifax* (London: Papermac) 1991 p. 39

47 Tinker *Viceroy* p. 122

48 Nehru *Autobiography* p. 258

9 WORLD ICON

1 *CW* 47 p. 384 29 August 1931

2 *CW* 47 p. 133 before 15 July 1931

3 John Haynes Holmes in Chandrashanker Shukla (ed.) *Gandhiji As We Know*

Him (Bombay: Vora & Co.) 1945 p. 99

4   *CW* 47 pp. 119–20 9 July 1931

5   Muriel Lester *Entertaining Gandhi* (London: Ivor Nicholson & Watson) 1932 p. 241

6   James D. Hunt *Gandhi in London* (New Delhi Promilla & Co.) 1978 p. 200

7   Lester *Entertaining* p. 69

8   Hunt *Gandhi* p. 213

9   *The Times* obituary 31 January 1948 p. 6

10   *CW* 48 pp. 272–3 6 November 1931

11   *CW* 48 pp. 297–8 13 November 1931

12   Louis Fischer *The Life of Mahatma Gandhi* (London: Jonathan Cape) 1951 p. 319

13   Tinker *Viceroy* p. 130

14   V.G. Desai *The Diary of Mahadev Desai* vol. 1 (Ahmedabad: Navajivan) 1953 p. 130

15   *CW* 50 p. 383 18 August 1932

16   B.R. Ambedkar *What Congress and Gandhi Have Done to the Untouchables* (Bombay: Thacker & Co.) 1945 p. 85

17   Nehru *Autobiography* p. 370

18   Ambedkar *Untouchables* p. 313

19   *CW* 50 p. 102 20 September 1932

20   Pyarelal *The Epic Fast* (Ahmedabad: Mohanlal Maganlal Bhatt) 1932 p. 49

21   Ambedkar *Untouchables* p. 88

22   Ambedkar *Untouchables* p. 260

23   *CW* 52 p. 312 31 December 1932

24   *CW* 53 p. 3 11 January 1933

25   *CW* 62 p. 121 16 November 1935

26   Sushila Nayar *Mahatma Gandhi* vol. 7 *Preparing for Swaraj* (Ahmedabad: Navajivan) 1996 p. 5

27   Mehta *Mahatma Gandhi* p. 7

28   Mehta *Mahatma Gandhi* p. 11

29   *CW* 61 p. 36 21 September 1935

30   Mehta *Mahatma Gandhi* p. 13

31   Mehta *Mahatma Gandhi* p. 203

32   Mehta *Mahatma Gandhi* p. 200

33   Mehta *Mahatma Gandhi* p. 14

34   *CW* 13 p. 301 before October 1916

35   Desai in Shukla (ed.) *Gandhiji* p. 123

36   Margaret Sanger *An Autobiography* (London: Victor Gollancz) 1939 p. 458

37   Mehta *Mahatma Gandhi* p. 54

38 Nehru *Autobiography* p. 513
39 *CW* 62 p. 159 3/4 December 1935
40 Sanger *Autobiography* p. 460
41 *CW* 62 p. 212 29 February 1936
42 *CW* 62 p. 372 6 May 1936
43 *CW* 62 pp. 428–9 21 May 1936
44 *CW* 59 p. 111 3 October 1934
45 *CW* 61 p. 37 5 May 1935
46 *CW* 63 p. 7 6 June 1936
47 *CW* 64 p. 253 16 January 1937
48 *CW* 64 p. 37 13/14 November 1936
49 *CW* 57 p. 44 24 January 1934
50 *CW* 57 p. 51 26 January 1934
51 *CW* 57 p. 87 2 February 1934
52 *CW* 57 p. 392 15 April 1934
53 *CW* 59 p. 4 17 September 1934
54 *CW* 59 pp. 214, 218 23 October 1934
55 *CW* 65 p. 231 22 May 1937

10 QUIT INDIA

1   *CW* 68 pp. 203–4 12 December 1938
2   *CW* 68 pp. 137–8 20 November 1938
3   *CW* 68 pp. 138–9 20 November 1938
4   *CW* 72 p. 70 15 May 1940 'He [Hitler] has no vices. He has not married. His character is said to be clean.' *CW* 75 p. 177 17 December 1941
5   *CW* 73 p. 255 24 December 1940
6   *CW* 76 p. 187 6 June 1942
7   *CW* 73 p. 254 24 December 1940
8   Earl Avon of *The Eden Memoirs: Facing the Dictators* (London: Cassell) 1962 p. 516
9   *CW* 66 p. 436 27 March 1938
10 *CW* 66 p. 82 28 August 1937
11 Jinnah's speech at Lucknow 15 October 1937 reprinted in *CW* 66 p. 468
12 *CW* 70 p. 288 22 October 1939
13 *CW* 67 p. 61 3 May 1938
14 *CW* 67 p. 117 11 June 1938. Prabhavati was the wife of Jayaprakash Narayan, a socialist member of Congress. After Prabhavati came under the influence of Gandhi, she imposed celibacy on their marriage.

15 *CW* 67 p. 37 22 April 1938
16 Stanley Wolpert *Jinnah of Pakistan* (New Delhi: OUP) 2005 p. 166
17 *CW* 67 p. 117 11 June 1938
18 *CW* 67 p. 60 3 May 1938
19 *CW* 67 p. 104 2 June 1938
20 *CW* 67 p. 118 11 June 1938
21 *CW* 93 p. 175 after 2 June 1938
22 *CW* 93 p. 204 12 September 1938
23 *CW* 67 pp. 194–8 23 July 1938
24 *CW* 93 p. 237 3 February 1939
25 Mehta *Mahatma Gandhi* p. 203
26 *CW* 70 p. 175 15 September 1939
27 *CW* 70 p. 411 14 September 1939
28 Wolpert *Jinnah* p. 175
29 Wolpert *Jinnah* p. 176
30 Read and Fisher *Proudest Day* p. 295
31 Wolpert *Jinnah* p. 181
32 *CW* 71 p. 412 9 April 1940
33 *CW* 72 pp. 229–30 6 July 1940
34 *CW* 72 p. 232 10 July 1940
35 *CW* 69 p. 390 4 July 1939
36 Peter Clarke *The Cripps Version: The Life of Sir Stafford Cripps* (London: Allen Lane) 2002 p. 305; Nicholas Mansergh *The Transfer of Power* vol. 1 (London: HMSO) 1970 p. 498 27 March 1942
37 Kenneth Harris *Attlee* (London: Weidenfeld & Nicolson) 1982 p. 203
38 *CW* 76 p. 67 26 April 1942
39 *CW* 76 p. 106 14 May 1942
40 *CW* 76 p. 186 6 June 1942
41 *CW* 76 p. 334 26 July 1942
42 Clarke *Cripps Version* p. 306
43 *CW* 76 p. 197 14 June 1942
44 *CW* 76 p. 105 14 May 1942
45 *CW* 75 p. 205 8 January 1942
46 *CW* 75 p. 64 before 24 April 1942
47 *CW* 76 p. 392 8 August 1942
48 Chadha *Rediscovering* p. 383
49 Sushila Nayar *Kasturba: Wife of Gandhi* (Wallingford, Pennsylvania: Pendle Hill) 1948 p. 36
50 Nayar *Kasturba* p. 43
51 Chadha *Rediscovering* p. 391

52 Nayar *Kasturba* p. 44
53 Nayar *Kasturba* p. 70
54 Read and Fisher *Proudest Day* p. 346
55 *CW* 79 p. 84 1 February 1945
55 Read and Fisher *Proudest Day* p. 346
56 Arun Gandhi *Daughter of Midnight* p. 265
57 Ibid.
58 Nayar *Kasturba* p. 40
59 Sushila Nayar *Mahatma Gandhi* vol. 8 *Final Fight for Freedom* (Ahmedabad: Navajivan) 1997 p. 527

11 PARTITION AND DEATH

1 Victoria Schofield *Wavell: Soldier and Statesman* (London: John Murray) 2006 p. 316
2 Wolpert *Jinnah* p. 230
3 *CW* 76 p. 120 18 May 1942
4 Nicholas Mansergh *The Transfer of Power 1942–7* vol. 4 (London: HMSO) 1973 p. 1123
5 *CW* 78 pp. 87–8 9 September 1944
6 Schofield *Wavell* p. 91
7 Schofield *Wavell* p. 321
8 Hector Bolitho *Jinnah: Creator of Pakistan* (Lahore: OUP) 1969 p. 152
9 *CW* 80 p. 367 25 June 1945
10 Archibald Wavell *The Viceroy's Journal* ed. Penderel Moon (London: OUP) 1973 p. 147
11 *CW* 81 p. 310 3 October 1945
12 Pyarelal *Mahatma Gandhi* vol. 9 *The Last Phase* part 1 (Ahmedabad: Navajivan) 1997 p. 138
13 *CW* 81 p. 420 26 October 1945
14 *CW* 87 p. 70 11 March 1947
15 *CW* 79 p. 193 1 March 1945
16 *CW* 79 p. 192 1 March 1945
17 *CW* 67 p. 81 14 May 1938; *CW* 70 p. 220 30 September 1939
18 *CW* 79 p. 212 6 March 1945
19 *CW* 79 p. 222 7 March 1945
20 Arun Gandhi *Daughter of Midnight* p. 305
21 Fischer *Life* pp. 230–1
22 *CW* 83 p. 276 17 March 1946

23 Wavell *Viceroy Journal* p. 236

24 *Viceroy Journal* p. 314

25 *Viceroy Journal* p. 260

26 Read and Fisher *Proudest Day* p. 388

27 Pyarelal *Last Phase* part 1 p. 228

28 Wolpert *Jinnah* p. 282

29 Nehru had said they would go into the assembly 'completely unfettered by agreements and free to meet all situations as they arise'. *CW* 85 p. 5 17 July 1946

30 Wavell *Viceroy Journal* p. 341. Another version went: 'Gandhi said that if a blood-bath was necessary, it would come about in spite of non-violence.' Nicholas Mansergh *The Transfer of Power 1942–7* vol. 8 1979 p. 313

31 Pyarelal *Last Phase* part 1 p. 201

32 Alex von Tunzelmann *Indian Summer: The Secret History of the End of an Empire* (London: Simon & Schuster) 2007 p. 142

33 *CW* 74 pp. 14–15 25 April 1941

34 *CW* 75 p. 349 before 9 December 1941

35 *CW* 74 p. 132 30 June 1941 and p. 113 15 June 1941

36 Pyarelal *Last Phase* part 1 p. 6

37 Chadha *Rediscovering* p. 419

38 *CW* 86 pp. 451–2 6 November 1946

39 *CW* 92 pp. 345–6 18 October 1946

40 Mehta *Mahatma Gandhi* p. 187

41 Ibid.

42 Pyarelal *Last Phase* part 1 p. 575

43 *CW* 92 p. 310 11 October 1946

44 N.K. Bose *My Days with Gandhi* (Calcutta: Nishana) 1953 p. 117

45 Mehta *Mahatma Gandhi* p. 203

46 *CW* 94 p. 333 30 December 1946

47 *CW* 87 p. 108. To Rajkumari Amrit Kaur 18 March 1947

48 Pyarelal *Last Phase* part 1 p. 600

49 Pyarelal *Mahatma Gandhi* vol. 10 *The Last Phase* part 2 pp. 215–16

50 Pyarelal *Last Phase* part 2 p. 219

51 Erikson *Gandhi's Truth* p. 404

52 *CW* 86 p. 415 1 February 1947

53 *CW* 86 p. 453 10 February 1947

54 *CW* 86 p. 302 2 January 1947.

55 Bose *My Days* p. 160

56 Girja Kumar *Brahmacharya: Gandhi and his Women Associates* (New Delhi: Vitasta Publishing) 2006 pp. 223–4

57 *CW* 94 pp. 334, 335, 337 30 December 1946 and 6 January 1947
58 Wavell *Viceroy Journal* p. 428
59 *CW* 87 p. 126 20 March 1947
60 *CW* 87 p. 118 19 March 1947
61 Alan Campbell-Johnson *Mission with Mountbatten* (London: Hamish Hamilton) 1985 p. 52
62 *CW* 88 p. 13 26 May 1947
63 Campbell-Johnson *Mountbatten* p. 110
64 Pyarelal *Last Phase* part 2 p. 210
65 *CW* 89 p. 116 Mountbatten to Gandhi 26 August 1947
66 *CW* 87 p. 384 29 April 1947
67 Mehta *Mahatma Gandhi* p. 201
68 Manu Gandhi *The End of an Epoch* (Ahmedabad: Navajivan) 1962 p. 15
69 Adams and Whitehead *Dynasty* p. 129
70 *CW* 89 p. 232 24 September 1947
71 Manu Gandhi, *Epoch* p. 16
72 *CW* 89 p. 126 1 September 1947
73 *CW* 89 p. 134 2 September 1947
74 *CW* 90 p. 61 18 November 1947
75 Adams and Whitehead *Dynasty* p. 132
76 Nayar *Preparing for Swaraj* p. 201
77 Manu Gandhi *Epoch* p. 29
78 Pyarelal *Last Phase* part 2 p. 861. Pyarelal believes the last words were not 'Hey Rama' but 'Rama Rama'.
79 Manu Gandhi *Epoch* p. 43
80 *CW* 87 p. 408 4 May 1947
81 *CW* 87 p. 462 13 May 1947
82 Pyarelal *Last Phase* part 2 p. 775
83 Jawaharlal Nehru *Speeches* vol. 1 *September 1946–May 1949* (Delhi: Publications Division, Government of India) 1949 p. 42
84 *CW* 86 p. 335 10 January 1947
85 Manu Gandhi *Last Glimpses of Bapu* (Delhi: Shiva Lal Agarwala & Co.) 1962 p. 334
86 Sarvepalli Gopal *Jawaharlal Nehru: A Biography* vol. 2 *1947–1956* (London: Jonathan Cape) 1979 p. 25

12 LEGACY

1 Nathuram Godse *Why I Assassinated Mahatma Gandhi* (New Delhi: Surya Bharti Parkashan) 1993 p. 26

2 Godse *Assassinated* pp. 39–40

3 Godse *Assassinated* pp. 49–50

4 *CW* 89 p. 16 7 August 1947

5 Rajmohan Gandhi *The Man* p. 286

6 *CW* 77 p. 351 4–6 July 1944

7 Martin Luther King Jr 'Pilgrimage to Nonviolence' in Norman Cousins (ed.) *Profiles of Gandhi: America Remembers a World Leader* (New Delhi: Indian Book Company) 1969 p. 206

8 King 'Pilgrimage' in Cousins (ed.) *Profiles* p. 209

9 Nelson Mandela 'The Sacred Warrior' *Time* 3 January 2000

10 *CW* 90 p. 511 27–28 January 1948

11 *CW* 90 p. 522 29 January 1948

12 *CW* 74 p. 13 25 April 1941

13 Mountbatten, *Lord Mountbatten's Report on the Last Viceroyalty* (New Delhi: Manohar) 2003 p. 227 Knowledge of Gandhi's antics stimulated much contemporary ribaldry, such as 'He wore a dirty dhoti and he slept between two maids'; reference to Gandhi's 'virgin sandwich' can be found on the internet.

14 Pyarelal *Last Phase* part 1 p. xxiii. Pyarelal remarked of his chapter on brahmacharya: 'The key importance of this chapter for a full understanding of Gandhiji's philosophy of life cannot be overstated.' *Last Phase* part 1 p. ix

15 *CW* 30 p. 16 14 February 1926

16 *CW* 48 p. 403 8 December 1931

17 Campbell-Johnson *Mountbatten* p. 145, and widely reported elsewhere.

18 *CW* 80 p. 222 31 May 1945

19 *CW* 87 24 February 1947

Bibliography

Adams, Jad and Whitehead, Phillip *The Dynasty: The Nehru–Gandhi Story* (London: Penguin) 1997

Ambedkar, B.R. *What Congress and Gandhi Have Done to the Untouchables* (Bombay: Thacker & Co.) 1945

Andrews, C.F. *Mahatma Gandhi's Ideas* (London: Allen & Unwin) 1931

Avon, Earl of *The Eden Memoirs: Facing the Dictators* (London: Cassell) 1962

Birkenhead, Earl *Halifax* (London: Hamish Hamilton) 1965

Bolitho, Hector *Jinnah: Creator of Pakistan* (Lahore: Oxford University Press) 1969

Bose, N.K. *My Days with Gandhi* (Calcutta: Nishana) 1953

Brown, Judith *Gandhi: Prisoner of Hope* (New Haven: Yale University Press) 1989

Campbell-Johnson, Alan *Mission with Mountbatten* (London: Hamish Hamilton) 1985

Chadha, Yogesh *Rediscovering Gandhi* (London: Century) 1997

Clarke, Peter *The Cripps Version: The Life of Sir Stafford Cripps* (London: Allen Lane) 2002

Clarke, Ronald O. 'The Narcissistic Guru: A Profile of Bhagwan Shree Rajneesh', in Aveling, Harry (ed.) *Osho Rajneesh and His Disciples* (New Delhi: Motilal Banarsidass) 1999

Cousins, Norman (ed.) *Profiles of Gandhi: America Remembers a World Leader* (New Delhi: Indian Book Company) 1969

Curtis, Lionel *Civitas Dei* (London: Macmillan) 3 vols 1934–7

Desai, Mahadev *The Diary of Mahadev Desai* (Ahmedabad: Navajivan) 1953

Desai, V.G. *Day to Day with Gandhi* 9 vols (Varanasi: Sarva Seva Sangh Prakashan) 1968–74

Erikson, Erik H. *Gandhi's Truth: On the Origins of Militant Nonviolence* (London: Faber & Faber) 1970

Fischer, Louis *The Life of Mahatma Gandhi* (London: Jonathan Cape) 1951

Gandhi, Arun *Daughter of Midnight: The Child Bride of Gandhi* (London: Blake Publishing) 1998

Gandhi, M.K. *Hind Swaraj or Indian Home Rule* (Ahmedabad: Navajivan) 1938

— *Bapu's Letters to Mira* (Ahmedabad: Navajivan) 1949

— *Satyagraha in South Africa* (Ahmedabad: Navajivan) 1950

— *Gokhale, My Political Guru* (Ahmedabad: Navajivan) 1955

— *Collected Works of Mahatma Gandhi* (New Delhi: Publications Division, Ministry of Information and Broadcasting, Government of India) 1958–97. Vols 1–90 are chronological (though vol. 1 later reformatted and reissued). Vols 91–7 are papers collected after the initial publication; 98–100 are indexes. A new edition of collected works published in 2000 with a CD ROM led to controversy when its accuracy was challenged by Gandhi scholars. A digitised version was put online by the GandhiServe Foundation in 2002.

— *An Autobiography or The Story of My Experiments with Truth* (London: Penguin) 1982

Gandhi, Manu *Last Glimpses of Bapu* (Delhi: Shiva Lal Agarwala & Co.) 1962

— *The End of an Epoch* (Ahmedabad: Navajivan) 1962

Gandhi, Rajmohan *Gandhi: The Man, His People and the Empire* (London: Haus) 2007

Gilbert, Martin *Winston S. Churchill* vol. 5 *1922–1939* (London: Heinemann) 1976

Godse, Nathuram *Why I Assassinated Mahatma Gandhi* (New Delhi: Surya Bharti Parkashan) 1993

Gopal, Sarvepalli *Jawaharlal Nehru: A Biography* vol. 2 *1947–1956* (London: Jonathan Cape) 1979

Harris, Kenneth *Attlee* (London: Weidenfeld & Nicolson) 1982

Hills, A.F. *Essays on Vegetarianism* (London: Ideal Publishing Union) 1894

Hunt, James D. *Gandhi in London* (New Delhi: Promilla & Co.) 1978

Kramer, Joel and Alstad, Diana *The Guru Papers: Masks of Authoritarian Power* (Berkeley: Frog. Ltd) 1993

Kumar, Girja *Brahmacharya: Gandhi and his Women Associates* (New Delhi: Vitasta Publishing) 2006

Lester, Muriel *Entertaining Gandhi* (London: Ivor Nicholson & Watson) 1932

Mansergh, Nicholas *The Transfer of Power 1942-7* 12 vols (London: HMSO) 1970-83

Mehta, Ved *Mahatma Gandhi and His Apostles* (London: Penguin) 1977

Millin, Sarah Gertrude *General Smuts* vol. 1 (London: Faber & Faber) 1936

Mountbatten, *Lord Mountbatten's Report on the Last Viceroyalty* (New Delhi: Manohar) 2003

Nanda, B.R. *Mahatma Gandhi: A Biography* (New Delhi: Oxford University Press) 1996

Nayar, Sushila *Kasturba: Wife of Gandhi* (Wallingford, Pennsylvania: Pendle Hill) 1948

— *Mahatma Gandhi* vol. 4 *Satyagraha at Work* (Ahmedabad: Navajivan) 1989

— *Mahatma Gandhi* vol. 5 *India Awakened* (Ahmedabad: Navajivan) 1994

— *Mahatma Gandhi* vol. 6 *Salt Satyagraha: The Watershed* (Ahmedabad: Navajivan) 1995

— *Mahatma Gandhi* vol. 7 *Preparing for Swaraj* (Ahmedabad: Navajivan) 1996

— *Mahatma Gandhi* vol. 8 *Final Fight for Freedom* (Ahmedabad: Navajivan) 1997

Nehru, Jawaharlal *Speeches* vol. 1 *September 1946-May 1949* (Delhi: Publications Division, Government of India) 1949

— *An Autobiography* (London: Bodley Head) 1953

Noorani, A.G. *Savarkar and Hindutva: The Godse Connection* (New Delhi: Leftword Books) 2002

Pandit, Vijaya Lakshmi, *The Scope of Happiness* (London: Weidenfeld & Nicolson) 1979

Patel, Raojibhai *Hind Ke Sardar* (Ahmedabad: Navajivan) 1972

Paxton, George *Sonja Schlesin: Gandhi's South African Secretary* (Glasgow: Pax Books) 2006

Pyarelal *The Epic Fast* (Ahmedabad: Mohanlal Maganlal Bhatt) 1932

— *Mahatma Gandhi* vol. 1 *The Early Phase* (Ahmedabad: Navajivan) 1965

— *Mahatma Gandhi* vol. 2 *The Discovery of Satyagraha – On the Threshold* (Ahmedabad: Navajivan) 1980

— *Mahatma Gandhi* vol. 3 *The Birth of Satyagraha: From Petitioning to Passive Resistance* (Ahmedabad: Navajivan) 1986

— *Mahatma Gandhi* vol. 9 *The Last Phase* part 1 (Ahmedabad: Navajivan) 1997

— *Mahatma Gandhi* vol. 10 *The Last Phase* part 2 (Ahmedabad: Navajivan) 1997

Rawal, Munni *Dadabhai Naoroji: A Prophet of Indian Nationalism* (New Delhi: Anmol Publications) 1989

Read, Anthony and Fisher, David *The Proudest Day: India's Long Road to Independence* (London: Jonathan Cape) 1997

Roberts, Andrew *The Holy Fox: A Life of Lord Halifax* (London: Papermac) 1991

Rolland, Romain *Mahatma Gandhi: The Man Who Became One with the Universal Being* (New York: Century Co.) 1924

Sanger, Margaret *An Autobiography* (London: Victor Gollancz) 1939

Sarila, Narendra Singh *Once a Prince of Sarila* (London: I.B. Tauris) 2008

Schofield, Victoria *Wavell: Soldier and Statesman* (London: John Murray) 2006

Shukla, Chandrashanker (ed.) *Gandhiji As We Know Him* (Bombay: Vora & Co.) 1945

Slade, Madeleine (Mirabehn) *The Spirit's Pilgrimage* (London: Longmans) 1960

Smuts, J.C. *Jan Christian Smuts* (London: Cassell) 1952

Swan, Maureen *Gandhi: The South African Experience* (Johannesburg: Raven Press) 1985

Tagore, Rabindranath 'The Cult of the Chakra' *Modern Review* September 1925

Tidrick, Kathryn *Gandhi: A Political and Spiritual Life* (London: I.B. Tauris) 2006

Tinker, Hugh *Viceroy: Curzon to Mountbatten* (Karachi: Oxford University Press) 1997 p. 94

Troyat, Henri *Tolstoy* (London: Penguin) 1970

Tunzelmann, Alex von *Indian Summer: The Secret History of the End of an Empire* (London: Simon & Schuster) 2007

Wavell, Archibald *The Viceroy's Journal* ed. Penderel Moon (London: Oxford University Press) 1973

Weber, Thomas *On the Salt March: The Historiography of Gandhi's March to Dandi* (New Delhi: HarperCollins) 1997

Wolpert, Stanley *Jinnah of Pakistan* (New Delhi: Oxford University Press) 2005

Glossary

ahimsa non-violence
ashram a religious community
ayurvedic pertaining to ancient Indian medicine
Ba Gujarati for 'mother', often used of Kasturba
Bania merchants and traders, a subsection of the Vaishya caste of commoners, the third-highest caste after Brahmins and Kshatriyas
Bapu Gujarati for 'father', often used of Gandhi
brahmachari a celibate
brahmacharya literally, living in the Brahman, the absolute; in ordinary usage, celibacy, which is considered essential for attainment of that state
Brahmin a member of the highest caste, a priest
charkha a wheel for hand-spinning yarn
darshan a sanctified vision (seekers after darshan gain spiritual merit by gazing on an exalted person)
dharma duty in life, particularly spiritual duty
dhoti a cloth worn by Indian men around the waist
guru a personal spiritual leader
Harijan 'children of God', a name given to untouchables by Gandhi
hartal a strike
karma the law of transcendental retribution; a person's actions determining his or her spiritual future
khadi hand-spun cloth
Khilafat the 'Caliphate', or sovereignty over the holy places of Islam, claimed by the Ottoman Empire

ki jai victory to, as in 'Mahatma Gandhi ki jai'

Kshatriya a member of the second-highest, or warrior, caste

lathi a long stick used by police to keep order

Mahatma great soul

malish an oil massage

moksha spiritual realisation, release from the cycle of life and death

Mussalman common Indian usage for 'Muslim'

raj rule

Ram, Rama the name of God

Ramanama the ritual repetition of the name of God

sabha an assembly

sadhu a wandering holy man

sangh an association, a society

satyagraha firmness in the truth, sometimes translated as 'soul-force'

satyagrahi someone who practises satyagraha

Sudra a member of the lowest caste, a labourer

swadeshi home produce (cloth etc.)

swaraj self-government, home rule

vakil pleader in court

yajna sacrifice

Index

313